The Heart of Marriage

Also by Cathleen Rountree

Coming into Our Fullness:
On Women Turning 40

On Women Turning 50:
Celebrating Midlife Discoveries

50 Ways to Meet Your Lover:
Following Cupid's Arrow

The
Heart of
Marriage

Discovering the Secrets
of Enduring Love

Text and Photographs

Cathleen Rountree

HarperSanFrancisco
An Imprint of HarperCollins*Publishers*

Grateful acknowledgment is made to the following for permission to reprint material copyrighted or controlled by them:

Last four paragraphs in "A Poetic Love" by Tess Gallagher, by permission of Tess Gallagher.

"Ruminations" by Deena Metzger and Michael Oritz Hill, by permission of Deena Metzger and Michael Oritz Hill.

"Change of Life" by Judith Collas, by permission of Judith Collas.

HarperSanFrancisco and the author, in association with The Basic Foundation, a not-for-profit organization whose primary mission is reforestation, will facilitate the planting of two trees for every one tree used in the manufacture of this book.

◆ A TREE CLAUSE BOOK

HarperCollins Web Site: http://www.harpercollins.com
HarperCollins,® ◼®, HarperSanFrancisco,™ and A TREE CLAUSE BOOK®
are trademarks of HarperCollins Publishers Inc.

FIRST EDITION

Library of Congress Cataloging-in-Publication Data
Rountree, Cathleen.
The heart of marriage : discovering the secrets of enduring love / Cathleen Rountree. — 1st ed.
ISBN 0–06–250842–3 (cloth)
ISBN 0–06–250843–1 (pbk.)
1. Marriage.   2. Love.   3. Married people—Case studies.   4. Single people—Case studies.   I. Title.
HQ734.R775   1996   96–6367
306.81—dc20

96 97 98 99 00 ❖RRDH 10 9 8 7 6 5 4 3 2 1

With deep appreciation and affection
this book is dedicated:

To my mother and father,
who once loved;

To Michael,
who gave me my greatest gift;

To Christian,
who teaches me many lessons of love;

To the divine mystery of
the inner journey
that continues to
stir my soul.

Marriage:

I wonder what Adam and Eve

think of it now?

MARIANNE MOORE

Marriage is the new religion.

JONI MITCHELL

Several friends read sections of this manuscript throughout various stages of its development. Many thanks to Maurine, Claire, Linda, Christiane, Gay, and Craig. I especially thank those friends who patiently *listened* while I read certain chapters. Your responses always offered me new insights.

Loving gratitude to Maurine Doerken, whose special skill as an editor is surpassed only by her loyalty as a friend; Linda Leonard, who is such an uncommon blend of friend and mentor and who often pushes me to go beyond my known capabilities; Christiane Corbat, who always knows when I need her; Vicki Noble, whose friendship after fifteen years continues to deepen in my heart; Gay Schy, who, during the latter stages of writing this book, was often my only link to the "outside" world and whose sustenance means so much to me; Deena Metzger, whose great emotional depth and intellectual range remain models for me; and Hal and Sidra Stone, who remain a presence in both my waking and dream worlds. As the first couple to be interviewed for *The Heart of Marriage*, they so generously helped launch me into the profound world of process relationship and marriage as a spiritual path.

I wish to thank my literary agent, Ellen Levine, who continues to astonish me with her professionalism and to move me with her personal warmth. I also wish to mention the staff at Ellen's agency: Anne, Diana, Siobhan, et al. Amy Hertz was in many ways a midwife for this project. It was Amy who first helped me to believe I was ready to push my thinking and writing further than they had ever been pushed before. She was the catalyst for a major piece of work done on the emotional, intellectual, and spiritual planes. My editors at Harper San Francisco, Barbara Moulton and Lisa Bach, have been beyond supportive and patient with a sometime prima donna. The work on my behalf by the staff at Harper, especially Deanna Quinones, is also greatly appreciated. I thank Gloria Steinem for her continued positive influence and goodwill.

Affectionate thanks are also due these friends: Michael Wright, Michael Park, Kevin Connolly, Pat Zimmerman, Susanne Short, Jerry Prohaska, Deanne Burke, Patty Flowers, Ronnie Georges, the Gomes family, Marie and Randy Kramer, Linda Charman, Claire Braz-Valentine, Gigi and Albert for their hospitality during my stay in France, and Erica and Harold Ramis for their emotional support and financial assistance.

The services of Dennis St. Peter and Janet Medenwald have been greatly appreciated; as have those of Connie Rogers, Amy Hewitt, and Susan Drake.

There were many, many wonderful couples, as well as individuals, with whom I met and engaged in discourse. The kindness, joy, and humor they showed me and with which they live in their relationships have been deeply inspiring and influential. I wish to thank all who gave of their time, energy, considerations, and experience. Special thanks are due to Alex Kerr, Bodhi Fishman, Bob Walter, and Jean Erdman Campbell, who so graciously gave of her memories and feelings.

To the spirit of place and the staff at Esalen, Green Gulch, and Tassajara, which have provided such nurturing and reclusive environments for me and my work over the years, all Blessings.

My son knows of his paramount significance in my life. I love you, Christian. And you, too, Sienna.

Finally, my appreciation goes to Wendell Berry, whose evocative poem "The Country of Marriage" launched me on my journey into the Heart of Marriage.

Les mariages se font au ciel

et se consomonent sur la terre.

AN OLD FRENCH PROVERB

Seldom or never does a marriage

develop into an individual relationship

smoothly and without crisis. There is no

birth of consciousness without pain.

C. G. JUNG, "MARRIAGE AS A
PSYCHOLOGICAL RELATIONSHIP"

The amazement of man

and woman—only that

made me human.

FROM *Wings of Desire,*
A FILM BY WIM WENDERS

My initiation into the Heart of Marriage came when I was much too young: driven from an unhappy home, where I'd lived with my mother who was divorced and suffered from severe depression, I married my high-school sweetheart when we were both only nineteen. Our son was born one year later. I now look back on those early years during my pregnancy until my son was two years old as my personal experience of the Garden of Eden. Not that I saw myself as Eve or my husband as Adam, but my life, my family (which *was* my life) was like an idyllic, self-contained womb.

I still don't know "what went wrong"—if it was fate or youth or if somehow it was actually in my genes (since my mother and father had each been married and divorced three times), as if I'd been programmed from birth, perhaps from before birth, to matrimonially destruct like a time bomb set to explode in a certain predictable way, at a certain time. Over twenty-five years later I still think of those days as the happiest of my life—certainly not *conscious*, but happy in my innocence and incognizance.

I had a child I adored and a husband who loved me. My days were filled with caring for and playing with my son, organic gardening, baking bread, making yogurt, grinding almonds and cashews for nut butters (it was the '60s, after all). We lived in a charming hilltop cottage in San Francisco with a terraced bay view, and I spent as much time as I could painting and making pieces of art to sell at the local weekend arts and crafts festivals. But the sum total of the activities that made up my simple life somehow still resulted in a deficit. Like a recipe for bread: no matter what wonderful ingredients are in the dough, without yeast you still have only unleavened bread. There was an ingredient missing in my marriage, but I didn't recognize what it was for many years, until I came to accept the fact that there was actually something missing in myself: the ability to receive love and accept happiness.

Through a rosary of disappointing relationships, I began to realize that everything I'd ever thought was love wasn't love at all, but some misconstrued, predigested amalgam of the lyrics from 1950s pop music and 1960s rock and roll, consumer-oriented advertising, and celluloid images of perfect love.

By my early forties, I had chosen to remain single and celibate for several years. Although my hormones were impelling me toward physical union, my heart was prompting me toward emotional contact, my mind was calling for its intellectual equal, and my soul was crying for its mate. The AIDS epidemic has sobered a generation raised in the '60s and '70s on the philosophy of "free love." What we have since learned, some of us rather painfully, is that love is never free. It can only return to us what we are willing to give.

Finally, well into my forties, I clearly understood what romantic love had always represented to me: being in love with love rather than with another person. Another person may have been the vehicle for "love," but ultimately he remained inconsequential or subordinate to an all-consuming passion—an obsessive/compulsive addiction—that is so often associated with love, especially in its early or dying stages. Roland Barthes, the contemporary French thinker and essayist, in *A Lover's Discourse*, describes this state as, "To Love Love—It is my desire I desire, and the beloved being is no more than its tool." With embarrassment and guilt I've had to face my puerile predilection for romantic and erotic love and admit I don't have a clue as to what mature adult love is composed of. Expecting to traverse both blueprinted and uncharted territory alike, even as a single woman, I decided to undertake a journey to explore the Country of Marriage. Like an early explorer investigating the waterways and terra firma of the globe, I set out, often with only my intuition and instincts to serve as my compass and lodestar.

What is this "Country of Marriage"? What is its psychic cartography? Are there physical maps that uncover hidden regions, that gauge the distances in married life between periods of ecstasy and boredom? The Country of Marriage is vast and varied and spans the range of experiences of married couples from those who have just taken their wedding vows to those who, like the parents of a close friend, recently celebrated their *sixty-fifth* anniversary. Its topography is prodigious and endlessly fascinating. Why do some married couples divorce after only a few months of "wedded bliss" while others, perhaps weathering the severe storms of emotional or physical illness, infidelity, death in the family, or extended periods of living apart, continue to resolutely honor their vow "till death do us part"? I eagerly entered the Heart of Marriage.

I have learned that deepening love and commitment yield fecundity; broken trust and derision result in a fallow environment. Two souls plant their lives together in the ground of marriage whence new life flowers. Marriage involves more than just the bodies and minds of two people. As Wendell Berry writes in *Home Economics*:

It involves locality, human circumstances, and duration . . . plus their history together, their kin and descendants, their place in the world with its economy and history, their natural neighborhood, their human community with its memories, satisfactions, expectations, and hopes.

But these same conditions of marriage can fill us with fears as well as solace, for they can also be seen as forms of imprisonment, from which it is a human characteristic to wish to escape. The ultimate form of escape from marriage is, of course, divorce. D. H. Lawrence expresses this innate paradox in his poem "The Mess of Love":

The moment I swear to love a woman, a certain woman,
all my life
that moment I begin to hate her.
The moment I even say to a woman: I love you!—
my love dies down considerably.
The moment love is an understood thing between us,
we are sure of it,
it's a cold egg, it isn't love anymore.

Detractors may reproach Lawrence for his seemingly misogynist writings, but who among us can honestly say we have not had a similar experience, at least once, in our erotic lives? The truth is, love and hate are cut from the same cloth.

What happens? Where does love go? Is there a way to get it back or to circumvent the loss in the first place? Why, in addition to the world's countless species on the verge of extinction in the final decade of the twentieth century, plant, animal, and microbial, does the institution of marriage teeter on precious and precarious terrain? We live in a time and place in which nothing, it would seem, is held sacred, not land, love, or life. Relationships between men and women are now too often extremely tentative and temporary, even though we long for them to be sound and permanent.

In fact, the overall divorce rate in the United States has risen steeply in the last twenty years to 50 percent; in California the price paid by married couples living in the fast lane is frequently an astonishing and frightful divorce rate of *75 percent*. Still, weddings are on the rise, testament to the fact that hope indeed does spring eternal. And, in an atmosphere of profound concern for physical health and emotional well-being, people are forming a wide diversity of commitments.

Some time ago while changing clothes in the locker room of my local spa in a small town in northern California, I overheard this fragment of conversation: "Hi, Martha. I haven't seen you in ages. Are you still married?" To me, it forcefully exposed the insidious acceptance of divorce in our society. (When I heard it I felt like I was part of a living cartoon, perhaps William Hamilton's "The Now Society"—his characters would have been perfectly at home in this scene.) While the question seemed to be asked in complete sincerity, the questioning woman clearly expected her friend's answer to be "No."

Why is this so? And can anything be done about it?

One of the benefits that flows within relationship and from it is what Aristotle held to be most central: the ability of the other to mirror the beloved, to become a "second self" who is a means to one's own self-awareness. Relationship with an intimate partner can be viewed as a metaphor for relationship with ourselves. The partner becomes the mirror that indiscriminately and microscopically reflects our personality and character back to us—for better and for worse.

In my interview with Sidra Stone, psychologist and author, she revealed how this process works in her own life:

When you look in a single mirror, you see only yourself from one angle. My relationship has put mirrors above, beside, behind, and underneath me, forcing me to see myself differently and therefore to live differently.

The crucible of marriage is the cauldron of commitment. And, on a metaphysical level, the male/female composite of which Aristophanes speaks is also a metaphor for the dual nature that exists within each of us (and the "divine, or soul, wedding," of which Rainer Maria Rilke writes so eloquently in his poetry) and that we work toward. Jungian analyst Linda Leonard recounts in her book *On the Way to the Wedding*:

The man or woman searching for a soul mate is seeking the divine. . . . The divine mating, the mystical marriage, is, according to Jung, an a priori image, an archetype at the very heart of our human existence. It is that vision which inspires the soul's sacred journey to the divine. And while we most often first project the divine wedding as a mystery to be found outside us, ultimately we come to find that the dance of the divine wedding is a wedding within.

Once the transformational process for the "divine wedding within" has occurred, a cooperative, interdependent relationship between two people has a better chance of surviving. This mutual support or coupling, which is symbolized by the wedding ring, can be likened to the Greek concept *temenos*, a sacred circle paradoxically providing a support system in the world at large as well as functioning as a sanctuary from it. This sacred circle is part of the Country of Marriage.

The core of this *temenos* is the couple. According to Robert Nozich in *The Examined Life:*

The term couple *used in reference to people who have formed a* we *is not accidental. The two people also view themselves as a new and continuous unit, and they present that face to the world. They want to be perceived publicly as a couple, to express and assert their identity as a couple in public.*

"Why marriage?" I asked, time and again. "To express and assert [our] identity as a couple in public," was often an answer I received.

And, as the personal stories in *The Heart of Marriage* illustrate, if marriage is to grow, the superficialities must yield to a true perception of the other. In the Greek myth of Psyche and Eros, Eros forbids his bride, Psyche, to look upon him and comes to her only during the night, when it is dark. At the prompting of her sisters, Psyche eventually shines an oil-burning lamp upon Eros to see who he is. As a drop of oil falls upon him, awakening him, Eros becomes furious with Psyche, who now can no longer remain only a projection of who he wants her to be.

Myths are relevant only when we can relate them to our own lives. The point of the Psyche/Eros myth, for me, is that absolute intimacy cannot happen until you really know the person you are married to. If you are to truly see a relationship, you need to shine the light of consciousness on it in order to have the ability to look deeply and incisively. Otherwise, in darkness, the relationship remains totally unconscious. Acts of scrutiny and dissection can be jeopardizing to the relationship and painful to the individuals, but is there any reassurance in being loved by someone who is ignorant of our deepest and most private reserve of qualities?

Men carry images of who they think women *should* be, just as women hold images of who they *want* men to be. In Jungian terms these projected images can be referred to as the "anima" and the "animus," respectively, which are aspects of the masculine and feminine soul. Since the images are just that—lacking the blood, flesh, and bones to make them genuine—both men and women become disappointed when their partners fail to live up to their expectations.

In Western culture we seem programmed to fall in love with the *image* of someone, even before we are able to discover and delight in the person's essential self. The primary interest lies in the packaging rather than with the substance and content. This pathology is typified by a character in Milan Kundera's novel *Immortality*, who coins the word "imagology" to describe how the worship of the veneer, of the perfected image, has itself become a new ideology.

But this "new ideology" seems not far removed from the characters in Evan Connell's novel *Mr. and Mrs. Bridge*, written in the 1950s (and recently made into a film starring a Hollywood couple who have become icons themselves, Joanne Woodward and Paul Newman). Mr. and Mrs. Bridge inhabit a period of time when, even though clearly delineated, male and female roles were, in fact, vacuous, and often there was little enjoyment to be found in a marriage.

Is there something beyond the purposes of procreation, raising a family, and companionship that impels us to marry? What is this deep human yearning to belong and to seek relief, security, and sustenance from another? I think marriage signifies an attempt to satisfy this yearning.

As part of my research to find answers to this and other questions, I avidly sought films that portrayed positive relationships. During a one-year period, I hosted a cinema studies group in my home called "Scenes from a Marriage," in which five married women friends of mine met regularly to view and discuss films on the topic of marriage and relationship. What we found were mostly examples of the opposite: a litany of films practically celebrating disappointment, heartbreak, divorce, infidelity, and sometimes even murder. If this is what one artistic branch of our culture is reflecting back to us, what models do we have for joyous relationships in real life?

This deep human yearning to belong is the motivating force in *Wings of Desire*, a dazzling yet poignant film by German director Wim Wenders. In this modern-day fable, we are introduced to two disembodied seraphs, Damiel and Cassiel, who hover over the bleak city of Berlin listening to the innermost fears and desires of the city's inhabitants. Damiel, despite his ability to whisper consoling messages of spirit and strength into the ears of the despondent, feels lonely and hollow and longs to be human, to enjoy the sensory gratification of drinking a cup of hot coffee and the simple pleasure of holding an apple, to blacken his fingers with newspaper ink or to "come home alone and feed the cat like Philip Marlowe"—in a word, to *belong*.

The initial three-quarters of the movie is filmed in exquisite black and white, denoting the cool, detached, monochromatic beauty of the angels' world. But when Damiel first lays eyes on Marion (a French trapeze artist, a muscular, electric-haired beauty who swings dangerously and compellingly between heaven and earth), the world and his emotions (and ours as the viewers) come vibrantly alive with color. The message is that love not only makes life worth living, it infuses life with flavor, flushes it with warmth, intensifies it with chromatics. Damiel turns in his wings, so to speak, and falls to earth. In love, men, women, and angels move from heavenly sobriety to earthly intoxication. This is a love story that pays tribute to the best of Frank Capra (*It's a Wonderful Life*) and nods in agreement to Jean-Paul Sartre's existentialist theory that the nature of erotic desire and love lie at the very heart of ethics.

This film celebrates the marriage of spirit and matter, the innocence of childhood regained, and the everyday world and its magnificent offerings, and it affirms the possibility of lasting love between man and woman. In the final scene, Damiel, his sleeves rolled up and ready for work (on the relationship?), is steadying Marion's aerial rope, offering the male strength and support of which so many women dream. He has become one with the earth, with matter, with woman. An angel may have "fallen," but paradise was not lost.

The story of man and woman may be, as Marion muses, "the greatest story ever told," but, unfortunately, the story between Marion and Damiel is only the beginning. We don't get a glimpse of *their* Country of Marriage or see how *their* love has fared after living together for ten or twenty years. Did they get married and have children? Did they like their in-laws? (Did Marion *have* in-laws?) Did either of them suffer a life-threatening illness? Or have an affair? Did they live happily ever after? Or did they move to California and become another statistic for the divorce courts? For "marriages—and fairy tales—[may be] made in heaven," but they seem destined to find their dissolution on earth.

In a later film, *Far Away, So Close*, Wenders takes us back to Marion and Damiel. We visit them at their pizza parlor (of all places) in Berlin. We stare in wonder as we see Damiel twirling pizza dough in the air and performing the quotidian task of sweeping the sidewalk in front of his pizzeria. "Is this what he traded in his wings for?" I ask myself. "Are they happy?" you ask. We are certainly led to believe so. But two parallel stories in the movie show us evil doings: Cassiel has literally "fallen" down to earth and become a contemporary version of a homeless man, and Willem DeFoe plays a character who is the personification of evil. It is as if the director is telling us: "Happiness and stability are boring. They are not enough to hold the interest of an audience hungry for sex and violence."

Wings of Desire feeds so many of my personal romantic desires: to have a guardian (or someone) to watch over me, to be magnetically, irresistibly alluring; to meet a partner who knows my most private thoughts and deepest vulnerabilities and who responds without undo horror or threats of extortion; and to find all of this in a man who, in addition, was an angel in his previous life!

Coming back down to earth, one of the questions I asked the participants in *The Heart of Marriage* is: "Do Americans have an obsession with romantic love?" And, "Does romance have a place in your marriage?" *Wings of Desire* is certainly one of the most romantic films I've ever seen. The nineteenth-century Romantic poets would have loved it, being the first to advocate couples marrying only for love instead of bartering their futures in marital arrangements designed to perpetuate property rights. They reinvented the medieval notion of romantic love and, like Wim Wenders, believed in love as a fundamental principle of life. So does every couple I interviewed.

The Heart of Marriage offers a kaleidoscopic view of couples: women and men in search of common ground. The variety of ever changing patterns is provided by several long-term married couples of diverse ages, cultures, geographic regions, professions, and lifestyles. Some are famous, some are unknown in the public light; but each couple presents a compelling story as the partners speak of marriage as a spiritual path, of relationship itself as a teacher, indeed of it as a healing force in their lives. They scrupulously probe the components that enhance or destroy the possibility of a lasting union with another human being.

One couple managed to keep marriage and family intact after the death of a fullterm child during a home delivery. Another couple, married for nearly twenty-five years, continues on after the husband sustained a paralyzing stroke eight years ago. A third couple spends only ten days a month actually living together, but finds ways to make the time together of high quality. They all inhabit the Country of Marriage.

These contemporary couples are pioneers forging a new frontier in the geography of marriage: conscious relationship. The term "conscious relationship" refers to the concept of engaging in a one-on-one intimate alliance in which two people clearly make it their intention to deal with all the challenges, expectations, projections, cultural myths, and habitual behavior inherently involved in a relationship of this nature. The commitment is to maintain the integrity of the individual while surrendering to the requirements of the partnership.

Many of the individuals interviewed spent much of the '60s, '70s and '80s immersed in self-exploration. Now they possess a deep sense of personal well-being and wholeness, which they bring to their partners. According to these couples, marriage is pervasive in one's life and touches every aspect, personal, social and professional. To be married means to consciously engage in life with another human being. It has been called the greatest test in the world, but I believe all the couples would agree with T. S. Eliot, who says, in a letter to Isabella Stewart Gardner in 1915, it is much more than that:

I now welcome the test instead of dreading it. It is much more than a test of sweetness of temper, as people sometimes think, it is a test of the whole character and affects every action.

Some of these marriages have endured several decades; others are second or even third marriages. All but one couple have been married for a minimum of ten years and bear witness to the fact that a marriage becomes a partnership and a profound bond is developed while working through life's challenges together. The polar explorer Apsley Cherry-Garrard defines this bond when he writes, "The mutual conquest of difficulties is the cement of friendship as it is the only lasting cement of marriage."

During the nearly five years I spent writing this book, I kept a journal of my journey as a single woman through the heart of this metaphoric land of marriage. I wanted to explore, to excavate my deep-seated beliefs, fears, hostilities, misunderstandings, and confusion about men, love, and marriage. I have received gift upon gift during my pilgrimage and encountered countless surprises. Often I have felt like a lost wanderer—at times nearly a sleepwalker—as the overwhelming extent and intensity of what I was trying to capture was brought home to me. Suddenly I would come across something in my readings or in a film, in an interview or conversation, through my travels in France, Japan, Mexico, America, and—*grâce à Dieu*—the dimensions of my seeking would fall within a less threatening perimeter.

Thus, my personal fears and longings, the questions noted in my journal entries, dreams, memories, and reflections are woven through the fabric of the interviews. In most of the conversations with the participating couples, mine is included as an active voice.

It is my premise in *The Heart of Marriage* that the foundation for a solid, workable, meaningful marriage is in each partner's conscious commitment to fully experience the relationship. It is characterized by the willingness and ability to commit oneself to the concerns of the dailiness of living a life together: the spectacular moments as well as the mundane or even tragic occurrences. This kind of complicity contributes to the conviction that there is a *purpose* for the union and that together the partners provide a stronger, more loving base from which to interact with the world than they would alone.

Through conversations with a variety of couples (and feeling much like a cultural anthropologist documenting married life at the end of the twentieth century—a friend has dubbed me the Boswell of the baby boom generation), I set out on a vision quest of sorts to unravel the mysteries, reveal the components, and perhaps decipher some secrets of the ever elusive, but eternal promise of love: how to recognize it, how to nurture it, how to sustain it. I went in search of the Country of Marriage.

From each of the couples I interviewed (in addition to the nearly one hundred, there were at least two dozen individuals), I seemed to receive a direct transmission, both spoken and unspoken, of hard-earned information and experience. I created an opportunity to engage in conversation on a deep and intimate level with people who are of interest to me and whose marriages are sustained and deeply satisfying (even though that definition may vary with each couple). What I learned is that marriage brings with it the possibility of merging two biographies into one, along with the challenge of preserving the integrity and independence of each individual. Through analyzing my own experience, researching the lives of others, and reviewing popular culture and scholarship about love, marriage, and relationship, increasingly it has seemed to me that, amidst the battle of the sexes, we need each other in order to truly know and understand ourselves.

In *The Heart of Marriage*, I have chosen to interview both heterosexual and homosexual couples. Many complex issues are common to all relationships, gay and straight alike, although there are concerns unique to male/female alliances, for, as Simone de Beauvoir writes in *The Second Sex*, "Men and women understand love quite differently. That's why they do not understand one another." "Do same-sex relationships have better luck than their heterosexual counterparts?" I wondered.

Women and men alike have been victims of psychological roles forced upon them by history and society, but through the influence of the women's liberation movement, and now the burgeoning men's movement, those roles are no longer taken for granted. Because the relationships in *The Heart of Marriage* are open to a new honesty and freshness of expression, the couples find unique and original solutions to common dilemmas.

The inevitable death and conclusive loss of the beloved is also a province in the Country of Marriage, one through which we must all pass. Tess Gallagher and Jean Erdman Campbell both speak eloquently about life with and after their husbands, poet and short-story writer Raymond Carver and mythologist Joseph Campbell. The generous spirit needed to help a loved one make this final transition is exemplified by Helen Nearing in her book *Loving and Leaving the Good Life*. From the beginning until the very end of Helen and Scott's life together, marriage was "a test of the whole character and affect[ed] every action." Here she describes the process of the death of her husband—"my comrade and love of fifty-three years"—through voluntary fasting, at the age of one hundred:

He himself inaugurated his own technique for dying; let the body itself give up its life. I acquiesced, realizing how animals often leave life—creeping away out of sight and denying themselves food. For a month I fed Scott just on juices. . . . Then he said: "I would like only water." A week more on water, and he was completely detached from life, ready to slip easily into that good night. His body had dried up and he could tranquilly and peacefully retire from it. I was with him on his couch and quietly urged him on, the morning of August 24, 1983.

Through her words, the complete sense of surrender and the ultimate act of selfless love, generosity, and respect displayed by Helen Nearing toward her husband is palpable.

It is easy to understand why, after thirteen years, she still believes that their love affair, which lasted half a century, still goes on. This, too, is a state in the Country of Marriage.

The couples participating in *The Heart of Marriage* agree that you marry someone because you share values and enjoy each other's minds and company and because, as Deena Metzger pragmatically explained, "you want to do the work of *living,* together." Through the telling of their personal struggles and shared satisfactions, they affirm the possibility of marriages without the trappings of society's prescribed arrangements and conditions. They are often unorthodox in their attempts to create authentic, vital relationships, and they all include the prospect of lasting love between two people.

The Heart of Marriage offers a positive message: it celebrates the best of both married life *and* single living. As a single woman, I welcome you to the Heart of Marriage.

Cathleen Rountree
Aptos, California
9 September 1995

Chapter 1

In the
Beginning

Often I have wondered if my life hasn't shaped itself around this single event: I was eighteen months old when my parents divorced—and my father left. The idea of Man as Deserter is foremost in my thinking (and fears) about heterosexual relationship. The wound of abandonment never heals. It is the filter through which all of life presents itself to me, my twenty-four-hour home movie. It is as deliberate as a scar, as pervasive as breath. It is much of what has made me who I am: fearful of loving fully, fearful of fully accepting love.

"Sometimes it seems," writes Elizabeth Bishop in her journal, "as though only intelligent people are stupid enough to fall in love, and only stupid people are intelligent enough to let themselves be loved."

As previously mentioned, both my mother and father were married and divorced three times, only once to each other. That's five marriages between two people or fifteen marriages among six people if you include those of each of my parent's spouses. It becomes so abstract, a little like a geometry problem: if two people are each married three times and each of their partners is married two or three times, how many . . .

I admit it: the thought of marriage terrifies me! Not that I have a pack (a gaggle? a school? a den? a flock? a team? a swarm?) of prospective husbands beating down my door or, from a more feminist perspective, assuaging my defenses. But personal dreams, cultural myths, and Hollywood's romantic fantasies of "happily ever after" die hard. And the tenacious desire to do the work of living, to meet life, with the humor, support, and affection of a deeply loved and loving companion faithfully insinuates itself somewhere in my daily routine.

My father died five years ago. According to his sister, my aunt Gloria, despite two successive marriages, he never really loved again after my mother. "She broke him," my aunt bitterly told me after his "wake." "Drinks for everyone!" he'd stipulated in an alcoholic's will—at the local Elks Club in Merced, California, where he'd spent (if not wasted) his last thirty-one years. A deceptively romantic notion, that, and one that, in retrospect, interpreting faded (fated) photos of my parents handsomely posed on the fender of their sparkling 1947 Ford coup convertible—brighter days, hopeful hearts, innocent smiles—seems cruelly possible.

It's all right there in the photograph: the DNA, the sperm and the egg, the biological concept, the psychic imprint.

The Bible says something about the sins of the fathers [mothers] being visited on the sons [daughters]—"unto the third and fourth generation" is the uncanny exact phrase. There is no way to account for the fact that in my family, on the maternal side, four generations of women—from my great-grandmother down through my grandmother, my mother, and me—were deserted by their fathers. How does one justify such a precise repetition of fate? One doesn't. It is a mystery of life, a cross to bear. Was there an original sin somewhere in the family that caused this litany of losses? This collusion of genealogy and legacy of being left? Or was it *the* Original Sin? But my Catholic upbringing bleeds into sensible assessment here.

The Jungians say that in bed there are at least four people: the woman and her hidden inner man (animus) and the man and his hidden inner woman (anima). To my bed I know I bring my parents, who loved each other so much they spent all their adult lives tormenting themselves, each other, and me for their weakness, their "stupidity." I also bring my grandmother and ("the only man I ever loved") grandfather, a wealthy, spoiled man who died wrapped around a telephone pole, taking two passengers and very nearly my grandmother with him. It was a senseless, drunken car crash that left his wife a widow in her late twenties with two young daughters to raise on her own, penniless, after her mother-in-law disinherited them. Also, there's my great-grandmother, Mabel, whose husband, a prominent Welsh-bred graduate of Eton, left her, with three daughters under the age of ten, to make his elusive fortune in Nevada's Silver Rush at the turn of the twentieth century.

That's only my side. Any man who comes to my bed brings his own inventory of family skeletons, personal myths, and psychic archives. The only thing that makes this awareness at all tolerable is that, along with all the familial struggles, suffering, and re-criminations two people bring to a union with each other, they also bring those exquisite moments of grace and ingenuousness. That image of my parents together by the Ford, their faces magically luminous and proud, as if unconsciously saying to posterity, "Remember, we once loved," is as indelible to me as if I myself had taken the photograph yesterday. I gladly bring it, too, to my bed.

Just now I realize that *this* is the healing—this writing—this is the therapy: the sorting out, reexamining, separating myself out from a cast of characters, a repertoire of unforgiven souls I've carted around with me all my life. It has less to do with finding *a* man, the *right* man, than it does with freeing my own soul, or at least making a truce with those figures from my past who have haunted me, who have hissed in my ear—raping my thoughts—with their threats, "We weren't happy and you'll never be happy either."

Perhaps life isn't about getting to that ostensibly safe but transitory state of "happiness," but more about making peace with those parts of our life and our personal and collective histories we can never fully comprehend. To echo a line from Primo Levi: "There is no why here."

There seems to be a spirit or a soul of a family, and that soul continues through the generations. The mistakes and questions of that soul are a conundrum without answers, a maze without exit, a mystery never to be understood or resolved—only accepted.

Giving birth to and loving my son has helped me in so many ways. Loving him has helped heal the wound that the absence of my father gouged so deeply in my heart. Loving him allowed me to simultaneously love my own abandoned child who still exists within me. He teaches me about space, boundaries, respect for the other's territory, independence, individuality—where I end and he begins. He forces me to be less "energetically sloppy." My son has taught me to understand and trust the male human animal and, yes, even to enjoy him.

An unexpected benefit that is beyond any plan or any conscious human effort is provided by the mere fact that he is male. I recently read a fascinating article on genetic testing and how through DNA research the remains of the Russian imperial family have been positively identified. The human body contains two types of DNA, nuclear DNA, which is inherited equally from the mother and father, and mitochondrial DNA, which is inherited exclusively from the mother. From mother to daughter, it is transmitted intact. It is described as "a time machine, going from generation to generation unchanging." In other words, the very same genetic code would be shared by mother, grandmother, great-grand-mother, great-great-grandmother, and so on. It all makes such sense. The means of trans-formation, of finally disengaging from the spiral of family psychic tyranny, could be held in the fact that, although sons possess mitochondrial DNA received from their mothers, they cannot pass it along to their daughters or sons. It cannot continue through the male line. It is my prayer that with my son the lineage of wounded, abandoned women stops with me, that he and his descendants will be free of it.

Chapter 2

On the Way to the Wedding

The man or woman searching for a soul mate
is seeking the divine and often looks for the divine in
a concrete person who has divinity within. But the
human loved one, like the lover, is also finite and lives
in the ordinary realm, thus ultimately disappointing
when compared with the vision of divine love.

LINDA LEONARD, *On the Way to the Wedding*

I was on the way to my wedding. Though we hadn't yet set a date and I didn't have a ring, I had received the most romantic proposal of marriage imaginable. It was sweepingly cinematic—a scene reminiscent of *Dr. Zhivago* or *An Affair to Remember*. Of course, I wouldn't have expected anything less from my love: a French filmmaker and the polished personification of romance itself.

"Cathleen," he'd asked, in his tantalizing French accent that melted my heart and intoxicated my senses, "would you do me the great honor of being my wife?" I surrendered to the majesty of the moment and location; it was a request I couldn't refuse. We were stretched out in a grassy meadow at Sea Ranch in northern California, overlooking the great body of water that curves so expansively with the shape of the earth that you seem to be seeing through a fish eye lens. The endlessness of the Pacific reflected the infinite and eternal happiness I foresaw for our union.

"With pleasure," I agreed.

My Prince Charming and I had met while I was living in Berkeley, where I had studied at the University of California and received degrees in fine art/painting and art history, owned and operated a restaurant, and raised my son who, by that time, was seventeen.

Nearing thirty-eight when we met at a workshop on Tantra (a path to union with the divine through sex—well, it sounded good at the time, anyway), I felt desperate to change my life. I was emotionally chained in a corrosive long-term relationship with a man, a relationship from which neither of us could permanently break free. My restaurant had been mismanaged and I was scraping together a living by catering dinner parties and weddings. My son had only one year of high school remaining before he would be off to college. And I myself was ready to graduate to the next level of my life.

Unaware that I was leaping from one pit of quicksand into another, I was easily persuaded to leave my half life in Berkeley and move to Santa Monica, where my new lover lived. The insistent pull of that dream of the rescuer, the savior, combined with the fantasy of belonging to one special person is profound. Like salmon heading upstream against the current of surging water, we are programmed to believe in and pursue our delusion of "together forever." He would make a life for me, I hoped, because I felt unable to make one for myself. The compulsion was so powerful that I was willing to be wrenched away from the one person I valued most in the world, my son. At his tender age, he was more discerning than I; he made the decision to complete his final year at Berkeley High and live with his father rather than relocate with me to Los Angeles.

It didn't take long—less than a month—for my illusion of rescue and deliverance to collapse. The first serious sign that I was in trouble was a dream in which I was pregnant and in labor:

My close friend, Vicki, is assisting me in the delivery. We are in a natural setting, somewhere in a beautiful canyon. I assume the primitive squatting position women have used since they began giving birth. As I push the baby out of my vaginal opening, I realize in horror that it is dead. I continue to have more labor pains, and another baby emerges, also dead. This continues until I have given birth to twenty-four dead fetuses.

This dream was so horrific that it induced me back into therapy within two days. It was clear to me that the dream was not about—or solely about—whether or not to have an actual child with my new partner, although that was part of our reverie together. Having followed my dreams, penetrated their mysteries, and studied their messages for more than twenty years, I felt certain that this dream had more to do with my inner life and my own potential as an artist.

Browsing in a bookstore one day, I came across a new book by a Jungian analyst named Linda Leonard. The book was called *On the Way to the Wedding*. When I opened it at random, I read the following:

If the inner wedding is not reached before the outer wedding takes place or during the course of a marriage, the marriage frequently breaks up because it lacks the depth of a soul relationship.

I rushed home with the book and consumed it. Every page held some statement or revelation that seemed to speak directly to me. *On the Way to the Wedding* became an umbilical cord of sustenance connecting me to nourishing information. A wise and perceptive teacher lived in that book and I consulted it daily.

I learned that the concept of the inner, or divine, marriage seems antithetical to everything we are taught about romance, love, and marriage. To belong to oneself before one can belong to another as Linda Leonard described was the opposite of unconscientiously colluding with a partner in a life of high drama, as I had done many times.

It took several years for me to gain the courage to step out of that relationship with my Frenchman and out on my own to find my ultimate soul mate: the one who lives inside me. I had believed that relationship was my "last chance" for marriage and happiness. But, bitterly, every expectation and illusion had been stripped away one by one, until I was left with someone who had sold her soul for a scruple of love one too many times.

I knew that the redemption would come, as it only could, through many years of living alone. Just as my French lover had been the apotheosis for me—the final glorification of man and marriage—he had also been the conclusive station of the cross of love. The complex addiction to the melodrama and the melancholy that I found in relationships had to be tranquilized, eventually nullified. For forty-one years my *bête noire* had been my penchant to live in the adolescent posture of the tragic romantic. I had perfected it. It was time, now, to imagine a new way of being human, to learn a transcendent, compassionate love—one that had to begin with myself. Certainly the internal marriage surpasses in importance the external wedding. We each must make the commitment to our soul's journey and, as Linda Leonard writes in *On the Way to the Wedding*, "the commitment to this journey forms an alchemical vessel for transforming love." I was ready and willing to choose "divine love," to embark on the *creation* of my life, to become my own Prince Charming. I was on my way through the labyrinth to the inner wedding.

Chapter 3

Marriage as a Calling

Janmarie Silvera and Marius Landauer

The minute I heard my first love story
I started looking for you, not knowing
how blind that was.
Lovers don't finally meet somewhere.
They're in each other all along.

RUMI, *Open Secret*

One of the commitments we have, beside telling the truth and truly being oneself, is to take care of ourselves separately. Somebody told me that a long time ago and I had no idea what they were talking about. If you truly love someone, the highest gift you can give them is to take care of yourself. I think that's a forgotten piece in marriage.

Janmarie Silvera

One of the beautiful parts about having this kind of partnership is learning how to expose your own feelings in a way in which you feel safe and taking care of each other's feelings. In order to do that, you have to be able to recognize when something has to do with feelings and when something has to do with opinions. I think we've learned to do that with each other, and that is a rare gift between any two people.

Marius Landauer

Named after a character, a sailor, from French author Marcel Pagnol's trilogy, *Marius, Fanny,* and *Cesar,* Marius Landauer was in a vulnerable position from birth. Songs have been sung, novels have been written, films have been made about the archetype of the sailor, the man who is married to the sea, the man who got away. Seeking adventure, solace, and independence with abandon, this archetypal figure sails from port to port, leaving countless women in his wake—they stand on coastal shorelines or sit before the dying embers of a hearth, more often than not, heartbroken. But in that sailor, hidden behind the compulsion for freedom and the wanderlust of travel, is often the yearning for an anchoring to a person, place, or community. If life mirrors art, Marius *was Marius* . . . until he met Janmarie.

When they met, Marius was on a course of traveling. He had accepted a job on a tall ship as a navigator. "It doesn't get any better than that," he told me, a faraway look in his eye, "going to sea and doing something really fun."

One month before their marriage and after three years of working through painful misunderstandings alternating with blissful reconciliations, I met with Janmarie and Marius to ask "why marriage," what they had learned about each other and their relationship during these three years, and what they thought might lie ahead for them after their wedding. Although in their mid to late thirties, this was to be the first ("and only," they claimed) marriage for both. They spoke with an impressive maturity that often eludes people twice their age, yet exuded a refreshing hopefulness that befits soon-to-be newlyweds.

"Why marriage?" I asked. "Why not just live together? How did you come to the decision to make this lifelong commitment?"

"Marriage isn't really a decision; it's more of a realization for us," began Marius. "I think we've always been married. The wedding is an announcement of that realization to our families and friends. Acknowledging it in a traditional way, I think we discovered what was between us even before we met. I've been in love with Janmarie from before I was born," he said. An exquisitely romantic notion. "It's something that was already there and we just happened to discover each other. That meeting basically interrupted the paths that we were on.

"The life I had before I met Janmarie is over; it's gone. It's a little like dying and having a new life. It was a good life for the person I was at that time, but I now consider myself to have been an incomplete person. There's more of me available now to deal with life's issues as a consequence of my connection with Janmarie. Now I'm adjusting to this new life. Ironically, I chose the lifestyle of sailing around the world because I wanted to find myself, and I figured I wasn't going to find myself here in California, but someplace out there."

"I've never considered marriage anything I would be interested in," Janmarie reflected. "As a child or adolescent, I didn't have those fantasies of getting married that a lot of my friends had. I thought of having a lifelong partner, but I didn't see any difference between living with somebody and being married—until I met Marius. The only way I've been able to describe this feeling is that it is like a calling—similar to the call to an artistic expression—being called to a certain way of living your life. It's more about creating another state that doesn't exist, or wouldn't exist in our situation, by just living together.

"I wanted to elope, but Marius said, 'If we're gonna do it, let's have a wedding.' I don't think we will have any more or less of a marriage because we had a wedding, but there is an invocation of spirit that is very nice to draw on. If you have a true marriage, a wedding can complement it, but if you don't have anything to build a marriage on, then a wedding is just an expensive party.

"Our wedding has nothing to do with our marriage, as far as I'm concerned; although I *do* feel married to Marius, that's true. But going through a certain ritual does change people, will change us. If it didn't, there would be no point to rituals, they wouldn't have lasted so long if there weren't actual change."

"What do you see changing?" I asked.

"It doesn't matter where the marriage goes or what it becomes; what matters is that we have this commitment to discover those things together. My commitment to myself for many years has been to be honest with myself and in my friendships. I've never met anyone in an intimate, romantic relationship who wanted that too and who could also give it. That's the bottom line for me. It doesn't matter what happens—of course we hope good things will happen—what matters is that integrity is maintained, separately and together."

During their first year of knowing each other, Marius was off delivering schooners to far away destinations, and they calculated that they spent a total of six weeks together—unconsecutively at that. During that year, they feel they were as honest as they could be, "but it certainly didn't add up to the honesty that a marriage would take." While on a layover in Canada, Marius had a one-night fling with another woman. Janmarie feels that incident brought "a screeching halt to our behavior." And, in a way, they started over using infidelity as a bridge to go deeper into their relationship.

Janmarie now recalls that "it was the best thing that ever happened to us as a couple. It was horribly difficult, but looking back at the road we were on, I think if it hadn't happened, we probably would not have lasted. It took something that big to get me in gear. I had been willing to allow him his freedom, but at my expense. I had never set any limits for him. That wasn't a very good position to put myself in. When Marius came back from

Canada and told me what had happened, I was absolutely devastated; and at the same time, I was aware of that higher calling. This may have been a momentary lapse, I felt, but this wasn't the embodiment of our relationship."

I wondered how that experience had changed Marius.

"It certainly opened the door for the change that came down the road from there," admitted Marius. "Janmarie caught me off guard because I basically thought she would say, 'See you later!' Instead she suggested that there were some issues that both of us had to look at if we were to have further contact. The way she said it made me feel safe— that's the only way I can put it. How she felt about me seemed to take precedence over how she felt about what had happened. That shocked me because most people are focused on what someone has done to them as opposed to what their feelings are.

"When I first met Janmarie, I knew something very important had passed between us, but I didn't know what to do with it. I didn't know if I was going to have a relationship with her or if I was going to have just a very intense, passionate tangency. I'd never felt that strongly about anyone before, and it was a bit scary. It had been important for me to make it very clear to her, and I think I did, that I was not interested in getting involved with anybody in a practical relationship."

When Janmarie suggested they go into therapy together and see where that led to, Marius, who had never had therapy before, agreed. "It was like a calling to come back and work on this relationship." After a few sessions, it became clear to them both that their individual issues would best be approached through individual rather than couples therapy. "I don't think I would have been able to make the leap I've made in our relationship without the help of therapy."

"There were very specific issues we each needed to deal with, and we made the commitment to be with each other while dealing with them," Janmarie said, "to be there for support."

"One of the beautiful parts about having that kind of partnership is learning how to expose your own feelings in a way in which you feel safe and taking care of each other's feelings. In order to do that, you have to be able to recognize when something has to do with feelings and when something has to do with opinions," Marius continued.

"I think we've learned to do that with each other, and that is a rare gift between any two people. It's not necessarily commensurate with having a romantic connection with another. What Janmarie and I felt when we first met was intense and wonderful and scary— all those things you expect when you fall in love. But it doesn't necessarily mean that you make good partners; that's something you have to work at and develop a technique for. What happened in Canada was like a wake-up call; you can't go on like this forever. You are going to have to face certain issues that will prevent you from building a relationship. So that's what we've been doing."

"You know, it's funny, there should be more words or levels for the term 'marriage,'" Janmarie smiled. "Like 'We have a business marriage' or 'We have a marriage of convenience.' Many people think if they have a wedding, they will be married. Just by completing that act, things will be different. I don't think that's true. Because you go through a wedding ceremony doesn't mean you live happily ever after.

"I assume we will run into the same problems most people run into after they're married: periods of boredom, lack of money, different schedules of sex—times when one person wants it more than the other. Certainly if we have kids, there will be a whole other experience I can't possibly imagine."

Until he met Janmarie, Marius had "a very cynical" view of the terms "marriage," "wedding," and "love." "They just seemed inflated. This is it for me. I've met who I want to be with, and I've certainly been down the road of relationships many times before. If it doesn't work out with Janmarie, I can't imagine it working out with anybody else."

Janmarie concurred, "I can't imagine ever finding someone who fits my quirks better than Marius. We're such a perfect match. In every relationship I've been in, there have been things about me that have driven the other person mad. And none of them bothers Marius. I get to be who I am. I think the same is somewhat true for him, too. He certainly doesn't have the kind of freedom to sail around the globe at his whim because there's no place for it, but I'm so comfortable with him having certain freedoms in who he is—and I don't think those constraints have ever been lifted before—that maybe his need for sailing isn't so strong."

"She never put any constraints on me at all," Marius agreed. "That's probably what kept me from panicking. Because it was a pretty frightening experience for me to have the intensity of those feelings." During the long periods of voyaging, Marius would write letters to her that he was unable to mail until they anchored at the next port. In a delirium of romance one day, he wrote a note, sealed it in a bottle, and threw the message in a bottle out to the seas. At least it was off the coast of California. Janmarie still has hope of finding it washed up on the shore during one of their walks at the beach.

"What about children?" I asked.

Janmarie said yes, but Marius's feelings were mixed. "I like kids, and the idea of having a family with Janmarie. But for the first time in my life, I'm jealous and I don't want to share her with anybody else. Having kids would be an infringement. I never even contemplated having kids with anyone else. When I met her she epitomized everything that I ever wanted in a woman or a partner. She's everything graceful and beautiful and loving and honest. I've never seen that in anyone before."

"What have you found to replace sailing, as far as earning a living?" I asked Marius. A man of many trades, he has put his training in physics on the shelf and has turned to the world of computer animation. Working freelance helps maintain the sense of independence so necessary to his well-being. He openly admits, "I'll never have a job as exciting as sailing was to me, but I definitely have a better life. The job is secondary now. It doesn't really matter to me what I do; it's more how I do it and who I'm doing it with. In a way, computer animation is a lot like sailing: a voyage with some unknowns involved. I take it as it comes."

One day early on in their relationship, while driving home from a wedding, Marius told Janmarie, "I don't know if I could get married, because I would never want having a wedding and being married to be something that I do. I would want it to be something that I am."

She immediately felt in accord with his statement. "That summed up my feelings about why I had never considered getting married. I don't want to *do* a wedding; I want to *be* married.

"Marriage is a really big deal," she said. "There is a merging that happens, hopefully for as long as we both live. There's not a point that you get to one day and the marriage is 'done.' 'Oh, whew! Now we can focus on life!' It's the whole path. I was telling Marius the way I feel about him is very much the way I feel about age. When I was sixteen I thought, 'God, when I was twelve, I thought I was so mature, but, thank God, I'm finally mature now,' and then I got to be twenty and I thought, 'Oh, God, I was such an imbecile when I was sixteen . . . so ridiculous, but now I'm really an adult.' It just goes on and on. That's how I feel that I love him. 'No, now, this is love; this is it. Now I finally know what love is. What I was feeling before? That was just puppy love; it was fun but this is the real thing.' Then we get into our stuff and go through whatever quick or long transitions and get through to the other side, and *then* I know I'm there. I hope that never ends.

"One of the commitments we have, beside telling the truth and truly being oneself, is to take care of ourselves separately. Somebody told me that a long time ago and I had no idea what they were talking about. It took ten years to figure out what she meant: if you truly love someone, the highest gift you can give them is to take care of yourself. I think that's a forgotten piece in marriage. People marry so that someone else will take care of them. That's dangerous. There's a me and there's a him and there's something higher, which is us, that is not maintained unless I stay as a me and he stays as a him. It's a wonderful adventure that we get to go on together wherever it goes.

"We've been writing our wedding vows. It's so interesting because aside from the specific things I want to say about how I love Marius, the traditional vows stand out. When you say, 'Are you willing to be with this person through sickness and in health; for richer and for poorer; for better and for worse?' that's it. What more can you say? I'm there for the long haul. Whatever comes our way, we're there."

After the completion of our interview, they were on their way to pick up Marius's wedding ring from the jeweler. Marius described the ring that he himself had designed, "The ring is a Turk's head knot; it's like a French braid with four strands. The Turk's head knot is used to mark the point on the wheel of a sailing ship. When the knot is at the top of the wheel, the rudder is in line with the keel. So now I tell Janmarie, 'I'm on my straight course.'"

Chapter 4

A Framework for Acceptance

Jacob Lawrence and Gwen Knight

I would say that you don't think of your marriage partner as another, separate person, but as a part of you. They become a member, like an arm or leg, and you can't imagine being without it. They become an extension of you. I don't know if that's a selfish way of putting it, but it feels like that to me.

Jacob Lawrence

In marriage it's important to remember, first of all, that we are all human beings and fallible. We have to give each other the space to be human, to have certain qualities that you do appreciate and other qualities that might not be so great. We're not always perfect or meet each other's standards.

Gwen Knight

I saw my first Jacob Lawrence exhibit at the Los Angeles County Museum. The same exhibit traveled to the San Francisco DeYoung Museum, where once again I viewed it and the accompanying video. The video showed a thoughtful, philosophical Jacob Lawrence, and, fortunately for the viewer, it also included Lawrence's wife, artist Gwen Knight, a spunky, quick-tongued, and clearly independent spirit. While watching the interview I learned that Gwen and Jacob had met in their early twenties in Harlem, where they both lived, and that they had been married for more than fifty years. I thought immediately that they'd make a great couple for the book. "I thought you'd be a wonderful addition," I told Jacob when we met.

"I hope you still think so," he teased, putting me at ease with his humor.

A year later I also saw Jacob's exhibit at the New York Museum of Modern Art, "The Great Migration." It is rewarding to see an artist receive his due—especially during his lifetime.

We met at their home in Seattle near the University of Washington, where Jacob taught painting in the Department of Fine Art for twenty years. Living in the same neighborhood in which he worked was a necessity, as neither Jacob nor Gwen had ever learned to drive. Both near eighty, they may be slowing down physically, but their interest in the world around them endures. Their travel schedule is enough to exhaust anyone half their age.

Gwen greeted me at the door. The slender elegance of Gwen's shape is repeated in her face and the expressiveness of her hands. Born and raised in the Caribbean—until the age of seven when she moved with her family to the United States—she remains a great beauty. A bronze head of Gwen done by her teacher of so many years ago, Augusta Savage, is a prized possession and contains the same aristocratic carriage I admired in the flesh-and-blood Gwen.

Jacob is barrel-chested and still a handsome match for Gwen's beauty. He seemed amused at my interest in their relationship, but within a few minutes jumped into the spirit of the moment and welcomed the opportunity to consider his marriage.

A genuine spirit of generosity exists between them as they tease each other (with a hint of black humor) about who will die first. As expected, a symbiosis has developed between them after living with each other for so long, and Jacob refers to Gwen as his right (painting) arm. The couple remained childless. "This is the way life was," Gwen explained softly. "It just didn't happen." This fact, however, may have increased their interdependence and made them even closer.

"Over a period of years you come to the realization of how fragile relationships really are. Young people starting out in relationships have a romantic concept of marriage and don't realize how fragile it can be. But through that fragility can grow a strength.

Gwen and I are very fortunate in realizing that. When did I realize it? Oh, I don't know, maybe I'm just *now* realizing it," Jacob grinned at Gwen.

"Jacob's parents were separated when we met," Gwen said, "but most of my family and the friends of my family were in lifelong commitments. Through those examples I saw and learned that you have to make compromises in relationships and that you don't break up a relationship on a whim."

The exchange went on. "In my day," Jacob said, "and when I say 'my day,' I'm thinking especially of the 1930s, when we became conscious of things—there was a relationship without marriage called 'common law,' but it was very binding."

"Yes, it was the same commitment as a marriage."

"The same commitment. You just didn't *live* with someone, but the community recognized this as a solid commitment to each other. We knew this as young people because it was talked about. If the relationship lasted for seven years, it was recognized by the judicial courts as legally binding. I don't think that exists now."

"They *felt* they were married," Gwen added, "regardless of whether they went down to the city hall or to a minister. They made a commitment to each other. And it was the commitment that held them together."

"There wasn't a problem with this arrangement when people had very little in material goods," Jacob explained. "Now people have to sign prenuptial agreements. You didn't think in those terms before, because there was nothing to agree on in the way of material possessions."

I contributed, "It seems that until the 1950s, when suburban communities began to surround large cities and sprout the nuclear family, multigenerational families lived together in a house, in the same apartment building, or at least in the same neighborhood. The community was a basis of support for marriages."

"That's right," Jacob remembered. "People weren't as mobile. You belonged to a community, the community belonged to you. I used to walk through the streets of Harlem, and I'm sure this happened throughout communities in general, and I knew everybody. Maybe not by name, but certainly by face. You'd see them on Sunday going to church or at the ice cream parlor, the same faces over and over. That's the kind of community I grew up in."

I asked: "Is society's instability causing instability in marriages? You've had the privilege of longevity, living then and now. Were people happier? Did relationships last longer before the longing for independence or personal freedom and the fragmentation of communities began so dramatically to change our culture?"

"I don't think it's regrettable that people separate or divorce; it might be good," Jacob reasoned. "Think of what our parents' and grandparents' generations lived through, where they literally killed each other because they hated each other's guts. There was no communication. People would sit at the same table and eat without any verbalization. That's worse than divorce. So we've made some gains in that couples can separate. Society accepts this now to a greater degree."

"Most people think only about themselves now. '*My* joy, *my* desire, *my* whatever,'" said Gwen. "'If this person doesn't do for me what I think they should do for me, then I'm outta here!' Everybody feels he has to look out for himself. They say in the black community that the reason we have all the disturbance with drugs and the tragedy of young black men killing each other is because our type of society fell apart. The structure of the black community fell apart. I don't know why it happened."

"Referring to how the colonists destroyed the African culture, a Nigerian poet said: 'Things fall apart when the center cannot hold.' And that's what's happened: the center of community couldn't hold," Jacob speculated.

Taking the conversation back to a more personal level, I asked Jacob and Gwen what interests they share beside art and culture.

Jacob said, "We're both curious. I don't know if there is anything we *don't* share. I'll put it that way. We talk about everything, certainly the arts. We're very interested in what's going on in our neighborhood, our city, our country, the world—and we discuss these things in philosophical terms."

"We both even like track," Gwen laughed. "We see it in terms of the aesthetics, the beauty of the body. But everything is always filtered through the fact that we are visual artists. Even with our friends, our shared interests are filtered through their interests, which are the arts. Artists are so interested in life that they absorb all sorts of things, and luckily it exposes you to such a wide range of people.

"Another thing I would add is that artists—or people in the arts—don't have to solve things. We're always questioning. That's the beauty of the creative process—there's always the next place to go, to discover. I often think of this: materialistically you might not have a thing, except your appreciation of a flower, leaf, tree, your relationship to another person or persons, and that's what makes you feel happy or content, not the material things."

"I would not want to look back one day in retrospect, say ten, twenty, thirty years from now, if I live that long," Jacob joked, "and say, 'Oh, I wish I could be back then. Look what I had and I took it all for granted. I didn't appreciate it.' I imagine myself dying and looking back and seeing what I didn't appreciate then, so I want to fully appreciate them now, the simple things.

"That's why the artist's way of life is undervalued in our society, because we don't buy all those commodities that you see advertised on television and in the newspapers. I think Gwen and I thought we'd never get credit cards. I said, 'I don't need a credit card!' Then I started to travel and I realized that the service people in hotels and restaurants had more respect for the credit card than for cash."

"We had one experience in a hotel," said Gwen, "where they wouldn't take cash. And they wanted a driver's license. Well, we also didn't drive a car. We didn't have any plastic! I said to Jake, 'Oh, God, we're going to have to get a credit card.'"

"Years ago, if you had cash you were respected," Jacob chimed in. "Now it's the credit card. It's just the opposite."

"Have you ever felt competitive with each other?" I asked.

Jacob had a puzzled look on his face and said, "So many people ask me that question. I guess I should ask how competitiveness would manifest itself. I feel that Gwen and I are supportive of each other. A lot of that has to do with the character of a person. Gwen is the kind of person who would not think in those terms of competition and jealousy. She accepts things the way they are, as far as I know. As for me, it's not in my vocabulary."

"If someone was going to be jealous it would be me," Gwen said, "because he's *had* everything. But I can honestly say I have not been jealous of Jacob's success. First of all, I've had great training. I'm a woman artist and it would have killed me to waste my energy on that. I learned very early on that what is important is that you do what you want to do, and if somebody appreciates it, lovely. If you get an exhibition, wonderful. If I were going to be jealous of Jacob, I'd have to go and be jealous of that one and that one and . . . It doesn't stop. Jealousy destroys you."

"Let's talk about love," I said. "How do you define love, Gwen?"

"At different times in your life, I suppose, you react differently. In the beginning, it may be chemistry—you have an attraction to a certain person, but it has to go beyond that. You have to be a friend. The best part is when you begin to feel you understand this person, and you forgive or forget those things you really don't like very much. I think it's really love when you can say, 'I don't like that aspect or characteristic in him, but he has all the other qualities I love or want.' And you accept them the way they are. Of course you will always be irritated by something! And you are very lucky if the person you love is a good human being, because so many people become attached to someone who is not a good human being."

"I would say," said Jacob, "that you don't think of your marriage partner as another, separate person, but as a part of you. They become a member, like an arm or leg, and you can't imagine being without it. They become an extension of you. I don't know if that's a selfish way of putting it, but it feels like that to me. I'll give you an example. I tell Gwen (we joke about it), I say, 'Well, I hope I go first. Don't play dirty and go first.'"

"He just doesn't want to do the paperwork," she laughs.

With a look of fondness Jacob said, "It's not the paperwork."

"I don't know if that's such a good idea, because I wouldn't want a desperate and destitute human being left behind."

"So you won't go then?"

"I would hope that if Jake dies first, I wouldn't feel that he deserted me. I would hope I could carry on. And I hope he would feel the same way. I'd hate to think that he'd feel like he lost an arm, especially if it was his painting arm. The left arm you don't mind, but the *right* arm! I might come back and haunt you. I wouldn't want to be responsible for the loss of your painting arm."

"We're making a joke, but in all seriousness, although I put our connection in a physical sense, I think of the stimulation of the mind, the thinking and philosophical thoughts that develop out of a relationship, and they would no longer be there.

"Years ago, I used to go places alone—meetings across the country—and it wasn't 'necessary' for Gwen to be with me because the meetings only pertained to me. I'd go and come back. Then I began to realize I was missing so much in the experience by not having Gwen with me. When we go together we can come back home and talk about the different people we met, what went on, what the city was like. When we share an experience, it becomes much broader and means so much more, which then, I think, manifests itself in my work. If I were sitting here with you and Gwen wasn't here, you could ask the same questions, but it surely wouldn't mean as much to me if she wasn't here to answer the questions in her own way.

"I've heard of situations where the fellow in a couple will get a Fullbright or a Prix di Roma for a year and the spouse stays here in America. I can't imagine a year like that, away from Gwen. But everyone has to solve these issues in their own way. Maybe if they were together, they'd kill each other! I've been fortunate to have come in contact with and met Gwen and formed this relationship."

"Did trust develop easily between you?" I asked.

Gwen's response was, "I think it takes a while to develop trust in another human being, because you have to see them in many different circumstances."

"In fact, it's a good idea to see a potential marriage partner in as many different situations as possible before you marry them," I agreed.

"You have to exorcise yourself of all the destructive thoughts or fears," advised Jacob. "If you value a relationship, then you must get to that place where you no longer think in terms of trust or jealousy. I'm not putting myself up as a paragon or a saint, but it's something you work toward."

"Have you had the typical marriage in that you have been the cook, the housekeeper, etc.?" I asked Gwen.

"Oh, yes, indeed," she said without hesitation. "The housewife and the artist and the papers keeper. But I take that responsibility myself. If I don't work in my studio as much as I would like to, it's nobody's fault but mine. You can always say, 'I won't do this; I'm going to my studio instead.' It's my temperament, and I don't know if I would do it any differently actually, even if I didn't have all the other things to do. I've never felt that being a housewife was a burden. I have only myself to blame if I'm not in the studio enough. Jake brings in the money, and I'm happy to be relieved of that responsibility, so I can do most anything I want with my art.

"Sometimes people say they get this wonderful feeling about our marriage. I wonder what they're talking about, you know? I wonder if it's just because we've been married so long. In marriage it's important to remember, first of all, that we are all human beings and fallible. We have to give each other the space to be human, to have certain qualities that you do appreciate and other qualities that might not be so great. We're not always perfect or meet each other's standards."

"That's right," Jake agreed. "When you are much younger and lack experience, it's easy to attribute so much to another person as if they were a god or goddess. Then in time, you begin to realize how vulnerable the person really is, that they are only human. You *allow* them to be human. And, in doing that, you become more human, too.

"Respecting the other person's needs, like solitude, is important in marriage. You can be in the same room where solitude exists; there doesn't necessarily need to be a physical separation. You get a feeling when a person needs certain things: solitude is one. They don't have to tell you, 'I want to be alone now.' Somehow you feel it. That's the advantage of having been together so long."

"I think every human being needs a time when you are alone, not necessarily physically alone, as Jake said, but alone in your brain and in your soul, a time when you don't have to think at all—a sort of mesmerized state. That's why I can't understand why people come home and turn on their radio as soon as they enter a house. Never, never a moment when there is nothing but quiet, only the wonderful feeling of nothingness. That is a very important part of marriage: to just be."

"Do you think being artists has contributed to the quality and longevity of your marriage?" I asked as my final question.

"I think so," Gwen said hopefully, "because artists are much more forgiving of the quirks in people."

"Maybe even *more* appreciative," I added.

"I *hope* that artists are more accepting than other people. Maybe I romanticize, but I like to think they are. To me being an artist and experiencing other people gives you a framework for acceptance of somebody else," added Gwen.

Suddenly Jacob turned the tables and said, "You've been asking the questions. Now I have one: Why do you *want* to get married again?"

"Good question!" I replied. "The last few months I have seriously been thinking maybe I really *don't* want to marry again. I love my life so much."

"That's your answer. You love it so much you want to disturb it!" he joked. "The question you have to ask yourself is: 'Am I applying the conventional standards of attitude toward a single woman?' When people wonder—or you wonder—why isn't she married, the implication is 'There must be something wrong with her.' "

"That's exactly right," I said. "I'm now beginning to realize that this is a cultural myth, a fiction, that I have internalized; I've made it my own standard for myself: 'What's wrong with me? I'm single.' It doesn't matter how enjoyable my lifestyle is. The bottom line is I'm not in a couple."

"In Western society," Jacob continued, "often the woman is somehow faulted for not being married. People accept men who have never been married—he's a *bachelor*—it's okay; he's just eccentric. But with an unmarried woman they think, 'What's wrong with her?' That old double standard. Fortunately there is greater acceptance of that state now than there was a few decades ago."

"That's true," I agree, "but each individual has to deal with it in her or his own life, in her or his own way. That's what I'm doing. Writing this book, *The Heart of Marriage*, is the thesis for my doctorate on marriage!" I laughed. "Perhaps the outcome of the book will be 'She thought *Why marriage?* but she realized she didn't want to be married after all. And she lived happily ever after—as a single woman, with many friends, engaging work, and her beloved springer spaniel, Sienna.' Not a bad ending.

"All the information I'm gathering during the process of writing this book has to do with living, not necessarily living with a man and marrying him. It has to do with being a richer human being. It deals with one of the key issues in life: how I deal with and treat other people. Everything you've said can be applied to my interactions with my son, my friends, everyone I meet. It doesn't have to be a lover. That understanding brings with it a liberation. I'm feeling and finding a real sense of personal freedom about this question. And you two have helped. Thank you."

Chapter 5

Paris: In the City of Love— Alone

And so I travel

solo

in a crowd

of lovers.

SUSAN SAMUELS DRAKE

Journal Entries: 12 December 1992–10 January 1993

What am I looking for? I ask myself. Will I know it, recognize it, if and when I find it? As I lay in the single bed under the twelve-foot ceilings in my friend Gigi's old girlhood room in her parents' apartment, which is situated in the elegant 16th Arrondisement, the light from the Eiffel Tower only blocks away makes my skin the color of saffron.

I have come, at her invitation, for a much needed rest. But during the twelve-hour flight from San Francisco International to de Gaulle, I compose a list of the "real" reasons I am going. It quickly becomes a list of questions—the questions I must ask myself while writing *The Heart of Marriage*.

What are my fears about men and relationship? They are many. Fear of abandonment; betrayal; boredom; failure; loss of self/autonomy; contact/being consumed; not being enough: interesting, beautiful, intelligent, sexy; distraction; loss of personal space; being immature; being a woman; being hurt; being trapped; and the ultimate fear of discovering

I'm unlovable and/or incapable of loving. That ought to be enough to keep me out of a relationship with a man for the next two or three lifetimes!

Perhaps by scrutinizing my own experience, my soul, I will discover something universal, express something valid. Perhaps by truly being myself I will be Everywoman. By delving into, digging through, excavating every scrap of my past I will sew the crazy quilt of my life. By being relentless in my self-analysis and reflection, I will mine some truths about myself, about women, about love and marriage. It is my hope.

What am I looking for in a man/relationship? is the question I most often ask myself. What are my fears? Because we live in a world of duality, we are always driven by the desire and need for separation and connection, stasis and movement, solitude and integration with another. Both exist concurrently, but we want to *settle* on one or the other. *The Heart of Marriage* is a skeptic's attempt to believe in the relevance (even the benefits) of relationship. I'm after a different kind of information. Rather than to uphold the traditional myths of "forever," I seek to be reassured by nontraditional alliances. My organizing principle will be my preconceptions about marriage—both positive and negative. What is the human compulsion to couple?

During a discussion about the nature of love and *The Heart of Marriage* with my friend Hugh at an Indian restaurant on Rue Daguerre in Montmartre, he helps me envision the book's narrative structure. His description reminds me of the Native American images of animals such as elk, deer, and bear swallowing their own hearts. My heart is in my mouth, I wear it on my sleeve, it is an open book.

Hugh, a writer and musician, says that love is the awareness that the other person's well-being is connected to your own—whatever each of you has to experience, you will do it together. I think of the Buddhist definition of love, which is that the happiness of the beloved is most important.

Appropriate to my generation of adolescents, Henry Miller erupted like an orgasm into my life during my twelfth summer when I first read *Tropic of Cancer*. I read, reread, and still reread every book he ever wrote. His later works like *The Colossus of Maroussi*, *Big Sur and the Oranges of Hieronymus Bosch*, and *The Books in My Life* became broader, more philosophic, more compassionate than the early work. His writings awakened my untutored passions and *joie de vivre*, my love for and interest in France, food, sex, *l'amour*, writing, art, conversation, friendship, adventure, travel, and the value of an inner life. That first reading of *Tropic of Cancer* was the beginning of my life as an artist, my Pandora's box. Now I am walking along the very same back alleys where Miller and his wife June and/or his mistress Anaïs Nin walked more than sixty years ago.

———————

Memory, 1971: When I was twenty-two and my son just two, I attempted to run away from home—from my husband, from our cottage on the hill, from our life together—taking our son with me. Life was waiting for me—somewhere out there—and I had to find it. The plan was to go to Paris and study art and French Literature at the Sorbonne. We made it as far as London, where I momentarily lost my son in Harrod's and caught a cold that developed into pneumonia. Overwhelmed, I disappointedly returned to San Francisco.

The fantasy of Paris has since remained a leitmotif throughout my life.

———————

Paris, 1988: I was taken by a man, my French lover. It was the experience of a lifetime—for me and my creativity. I exploded into an arena of limitless potential out of a canon of stifling creative blocks. Like being steeped in strong black tea, I was infused by the Muse with inspiration; my sensibilities and talents were permanently invigorated to perpetual expression—a psychic caffeine mania.

Here I am in Paris again, the city of lovers, the city *for* lovers; and I am alone, the largest, most elegant erection in all of Europe projecting outside my bedroom window. Almost close enough to stroke with my hand, to lick with my tongue. But, then, I digress. I've clearly been celibate too long.

"Being alone too long makes one brittle," the man I met last summer and fell in love with said, over a shot of whiskey. I knew he was talking about me. Am I so transparent? The lines around my lips are a novel about loneliness, those around my eyes are an essay about despair. It makes one brittle. Indeed. As if he were speaking about a pair of old kid gloves, once fine and supple, left to the elements to weather on their own, longing for the lubricating oils from a human hand, a touch. My forlorn love for him remained unrequited.

———————

In *The Individual and Society* George Sorel discusses how modern individuals have become so idiosyncratic in their living habits that they can no longer find anyone who matches, complements, or is willing to put up with their particular idiosyncrasies. They need something called assortative mating, or like finding like. A way of matching neuroses. Is this happening to me? I wonder.

In this week's issue of *Newsweek*, Robert Bly says, "The part of feminism that believed women could do everything alone is over." Perhaps not. I have become entirely self-reliant and inner-directed. The deeper issue for me is: Am I happier this way? I have become so serious without even knowing it. When did this happen? My mouth is tense and tight. I have forgotten how to laugh, how to enjoy. I need love, to make love, to be with a man. "Don't make a man the center of your life," I tell the women in my lectures and workshops. And, yet, I remain besotted.

Finished *Gertrude and Alice* by Diana Souhami. I'm glad I brought them along with me to France, where together they spent forty rich and fascinating years. A pair of spirited, sagacious mavericks. Thankfully, their story has convinced me to include gay and lesbian couples in *The Heart of Marriage*. I visited their shared grave at Pere Lachaise Cemetery. Gertrude's name is solely prominent on the front of the grave marker, but when I walked to the rear of it I found the name Alice B. Toklas. How fitting that in death, as in life, Alice (who lived another twenty-three years after Gertrude's death) would continue to subordinate herself to the great Miss Stein. "I am nothing but the memory of her," Alice said, shortly after Gertrude's passing.

Reading *Gertrude and Alice* on the heels of Irvin Yalom's clever novel, *When Nietzsche Wept*, about a fictional relationship between a brilliant psychoanalyst and the philosopher, I am sobered (yet oddly comforted) by the inevitability of their message: no matter how close we may feel to another human being, we are essentially alone and we will die alone. Yalom, an existential psychologist, offers the dual message: the concept of a "continuous present" and the existential notion that although we are utterly alone in our lives, we share the same fate, which is that we all die. Thus, the awareness of our process or the "continuous present" must take priority over our knowledge of mortality. More and more I see the parallels between existentialism and Buddhism. Both are equally concerned with the Now as all—the perennial now.

Like Simone de Beauvoir, I write in order to explain myself to myself. All my work has had that purpose as its source, at its very core, a means of examining what I want and do not want in my life. What I want to generate, to attract. Deirdre Bair's biography of de Beauvoir, which I've read while in France, is extremely influential to me in terms of both what to do—think, write, live tirelessly, passionately—and what not to do in my life—put a man's needs before my own. Her relationship is inconceivable to me (at least the longevity—yes, sadly, I've handed my life over to a man, too, but, thankfully, not for fifty years), but it obviously provided her with a certain emotional (read: painful) and intellectual stimulus. Would she have been Simone de Beauvoir without Jean-Paul Sartre? But what price art? The term "codependent" could have been coined for this couple. If de Beauvoir couldn't develop beyond a codependent relationship, how can we mere mortals expect to? I also visited their shared grave at Montparnasse Cemetery (there is equal billing), which I photographed and where I sat quietly with my thoughts and questions.

At my loneliest and most cynical I think that perhaps love is just a diversion, like religion, philosophy, and art on a higher level, and television, money, sex, and drugs on a more base level. A way of coping with the miseries of the world, the uncertainties of life. One more thing to occupy our minds, to help assuage our aloneness, to keep us from ourselves, to delay our awareness, our thoughts about death—even if briefly.

Rudolf Nureyev died today, my last day in Paris. Art, grace, beauty, intelligence, a fiery spirit. A true artist of life as well as aesthetics. None of it mattered in the end—he still died a lonely man. I must have walked right past his apartment today on Quai Voltaire overlooking the Seine on the Left Bank. January 6, the Day of Epiphany (a Christian festival commemorating the manifestation of Christ to the Gentiles in the persons of the Magi), an appropriate day for death. (A sudden intuitive perception of or insight into the reality or essential meaning of something, usually initiated by some simple or commonplace occurrence or experience—like death.) The ultimate transformation. The culminating epiphany: death.

Some questions for *The Heart of Marriage:*

How do we overcome the belief that happiness comes from an external source?

How do we learn we are lovable without seeing it reflected in someone else's eyes? Our parents were dealing with the same deficiency and deprivation—so how do we cope, heal?

The presence of unconditional love is palpable. Is it realistic to expect this type of love from a mate? Is unconditional love the ability to look at a person and see past his or her neuroses?

Are we meant to exist in relationships that last "forever"? Philip Larkin asks the lover's eternal question, "Is it for now or always?" but reminds us that "Always is always now."

We are looking for a resting place or a refuge in relationship, but no such place exists. The most we can hope for is momentary comfort, because situations are constantly changing. And when the rules change, people get deeply disappointed.

Where does love originate? In the mind, the heart, the memory, or in our genes?

————————

My month in France has been shrouded in thoughts about and metaphors for death. My time here has been about the death (healing) of the psychological orphan who lives inside me. I must make a home for myself before I can make a home with a man. What is necessary to make a relationship work is a mastery of solitude. I recognize and accept that my primary commitment (with or without a man) is to my life and my work.

Chapter 6

Keep 'em Laughing

Natalie Robins and Christopher Lehmann–Haupt

This idea about being bored in your marriage is a fallacy. You don't look for your intellectual stimulation from the other person. If you are bored, the other person won't be able to end that. But the other person *can* help you figure out *why* you are bored.

Christopher Lehmann-Haupt

A difficulty in a marriage could be a sign that it's time to start growing. People don't want to accept negatives. They think negatives mean "It's over; I have to leave," rather than try and work through the problem.

Natalie Robins

As young adults they were equally committed to marriage, but their backgrounds were different. For Natalie, there was never a question of divorce in her family as she was growing up; her parents were deeply committed to each other. Christopher, on the other hand, experienced the divorce of his parents at the vulnerable age of thirteen. I wanted to know how their dissimilar backgrounds had formed their idea of marriage in general and had affected their own marital relationship in particular.

"There are so many things we don't have in common," Natalie explained, "but we have the same core beliefs in people, in life, in goals and values." These differences and similarities were expressed throughout our interview, making for a few unexpected, if sometimes argumentative, replies. The two even surprised each other a few times, which illustrated Natalie's belief that "you can never truly know another person" and that surprise is a crucial element in keeping alive the spark between two people.

I had met Natalie and Christopher, who are both writers, through their daughter, Rachel. She had piqued my interest in her parents and convinced me to meet them by her near idealization of their marriage. Rachel insisted that after a thirty-year partnership they were "even more in love now."

"How do they do it?" I wondered.

"They laugh a lot," she smiled.

Christopher confirmed her notion when he said, "We became immediately very good friends, which was the important thing. When Rachel meets a new boyfriend and says, 'Dad, this one makes me laugh.' I say, 'Well, maybe he's the right man.' Because humor is most important."

"We've had our share of family crises," Natalie added, "but the moment Christopher makes a little comment or joke about it and I laugh, then we know we're over the worst of it."

As it turned out, Rachel was accurate in her appraisal of her parents' marriage, although perhaps for reasons different from those she'd thought. Rachel, in her early twenties, was definitely looking for love, looking for a partnership that could provide some of what she saw in her parents. And, like the caring and supportive parents they are, Natalie and Christopher had recently been giving a good deal of thought to many of the questions regarding love and relationship I had for them.

Physically Rachel may have been three thousand miles away, but emotionally she was as close as the telephone (indeed calling while I was there), and her spirit was very present in the sunny kitchen on this November afternoon.

When I asked the first question, "When did you stop trying to change each other?" there was a clash of answers as the independent streak in each emerged. Christopher leapt in with, "What makes you think we did? We haven't stopped!"

Natalie, simultaneously and equally emphatically, said, "We never started."

"We've never stopped," countered Christopher. "I don't think you have accepted the things you are critical of about me. You continue to criticize me for them, the implication being that I could possibly change. And I'm sure I do that to you."

"Right. I see what you're saying," Natalie conceded.

"I still want you to swing wide into the garage, but you never will and I don't give up trying. To put it another way we could say, 'When did we completely accept each other?' I'm saying we haven't yet."

"And I'm saying we always did. So you have two answers," Natalie shrugged good-naturedly.

Where does romance fit into their marriage? They claim they were both "over the stage of romantic illusions" by the time they met. Christopher was twenty-six. Natalie, at twenty-two, "wasn't looking for a romantic figure."

"I wasn't looking for anything," Christopher said. "I just suddenly found this person who made me laugh and I got along with. I didn't think when I met her 'Is this someone I could marry? Does she fit my idea of a wife?'"

Natalie said, "That's what I'm always telling Rachel: 'You've got to stop asking those questions; it just happens.' She's asking a lot of questions lately. Last week she said to me, 'Mommy, do you still love Daddy as much as you did when you first met him?' And I said, 'More.' And it's true. She got weepy on the phone."

"What is the most important quality in love?" Christopher said, repeating my question. "I think it's respect, which comes from the Latin *spectare*, 'to see.' It is the ability to see and accept the person as they are, to love them for what they are. That seems to me the most mature form of love."

"That goes along with my belief," Natalie added, "that you can never truly know another person. We really are alone in this world. So when you get a glimpse of someone else, you just cherish it. As close as I've been to Christopher these past thirty-odd years, every time I see a new side of him, it's not like 'Oh, I finally know him.' It's like I'm *beginning* to know him."

An ever present concern for me about marriage is boredom. In past relationships I was bored, yet, alone, I find I'm never bored. As Orianna Fallaci says, "I am my best company." According to Christopher, "This idea about being bored in your marriage is a fallacy. You don't look for your intellectual stimulation from the other person. If you are bored, the other person won't be able to end that. But the other person *can* help you figure out *why* you're bored. Boredom is stasis; people get bored because they get stuck. It's not that the other person becomes your therapist, but the interaction between two people who get along and care about each other will inevitably move you out of that stasis."

"I never get bored," Natalie added. "Maybe it's because we're so used to being together all the time, but when one of us goes into town for the day, when we return we find there are a hundred things to tell each other."

"That was always true, from the beginning," Christopher continued. "It was always a pleasure to finish a day and then tell Natalie about it. That was particularly satisfying with her as it was with no one else I'd ever met. I don't know why that is, either."

"So it sounds as if you are touching on another aspect of marriage, its cyclical nature," I said. "*Life* is cyclical, so it follows that the rhythms in marriage would be as well."

"You brought up passion and sex earlier," Natalie said. "It's the same way. A relationship goes through cycles. I don't think sex and passion have to die if you go with the flow and accept the other person: what they're feeling, what they're thinking, what they're doing."

"The danger is when we internalize and project the media's images of romantic love and the Perfect Other that we are continually bombarded with," I observed. "Every time you make love, it has to be fireworks, but life isn't like that. So people get disappointed, and disillusioned—which may be good."

"That fantasy can exist in youth or in art—think of *Romeo and Juliet*," Christopher said as way of illustration. "Romantic love does exist, but it wears out and there had better be something else once it's over. I don't think it's the basis for a long-term relationship. Do I continue to see her as the Perfect Other? No."

But does romance exist in their marriage? According to Natalie the most "romantic thing" Christopher did lately was to buy her the "filofax of her dreams." It was more the way he went about it that amazed her: "He called me from a stationery store downtown and I said, 'You're in a store and you *remembered* I wanted a filofax and you *called* me?'"

"There is such pleasure in being able to do something that you know the other person will *really* enjoy. But it can be hard because even though we know each other very well, it's difficult to know what's just right." Christopher went on to tell the story of the time they lost a child shortly after delivery and he went to Bloomingdales and bought all new bedclothes and bedspread to make a new bedroom for Natalie when she came home. "I remember the feeling very vividly. I felt terrible for her, I felt terrible for myself, too, but I felt worse for her."

"That was the best," Natalie said softly.

For Christopher the idea of bringing flowers to Natalie, in the romantic notion, is "slightly solipsistic, because it's more about *me* bringing the flowers to her. I'm trying to prove something or make a self-conscious gesture. The cliché of it has more to do with expressing *my* feelings and seeing *myself* rather than the other person; it's more self-referential."

"That's true. If he brought me flowers I'd say, 'What's wrong?!'"

I admitted to feelings of immaturity, because I've always fallen for the notion of romantic love. Christopher gallantly explained his perspective to me. "Nature tricks you into thinking a lot of things, purely for Nature's sake, not for yours. I think romantic love is an early stage of that. Nature wants you to meet someone and reproduce. She sometimes diverts the message and different messages come across, but there is a very strong drive that way. There is a lot of illusion involved in that. If you say still having those illusions is being immature, then fine, but it's not really. Maybe there is something you don't want to see yet about marriage."

"It's also that both my parents were married and divorced three times," I explained. "It's a tough heritage to come from; I have no models of longevity."

"Actually, you have a very *strong* model, only it's a negative one," Christopher pointed out. "You know, at a certain point in my own marriage, the idea of divorce popped into my head. Not because I in any way wanted one. It just suddenly occurred to me, 'Why aren't we thinking of divorce the way so many of our friends are?' Then I realized it was at the stage at which my father divorced my mother. The repetition compulsion is extremely powerful. There was something in my past that was telling me it was time now to get divorced."

"You never told me that!" Natalie said, surprised.

"Come to think of it, you were the one who figured it out!" he reminded her. "I was sitting here and you were standing there, exactly where we are now, and you said 'Ah-ha. How long was your father married to your mother?' and I said, 'Exactly this amount of time.' You've repressed that."

"I know you're right," I told him. "These models that we have are very powerful. Do you think your marriage has been a way to heal that breach in your original family?"

His voice cracked slightly when he said, "Yeah, I've been able to be in territory that my father never reached and look around and see the things that were threatening and the things he never got to enjoy."

How do we carry over our patterns of behavior from our earliest relationships in childhood into our adult relationships? Anger and its inevitability, origins, and resolution were brought up by Christopher when he discussed how he began to see similarities between the childhood dynamics involving himself, his parents, and younger brother and how he and Natalie handled disagreements. "I began to look at my own occasional irritation with Natalie. I realized that she would get in a mood and provoke me for reasons that had to do with her own childhood—probably the relationship with *her* mother and brother and so forth. Instead of going on with the irritant, I would say, 'You're provoking me. You're needling me.' "

Natalie responded, "Then I finally got to the point where I could say, 'Hey, I am,' or 'I'm in the mood to needle you!' "

They both agree the realization made a difference in their relationship and how they resolve bad tempers. "It was suddenly like the kaleidoscope shifted and the pieces fell into a different position," Christopher explained.

"Before, when we'd been irritated with each other, there had been the immature fights, stupid fights," Natalie remembered. "Very often I would laugh. I'd be mad, but also I'd laugh because they were so stupid. Nothing enrages the other person more than when you laugh. We haven't done that in a long time, have we?"

"No, I haven't seen the blue waves lately. There comes a point where I'm so mad that I see blue waves."

"Getting through anger is a very important part of marriage, of *any* relationship. Don't you agree?" asked Natalie.

"I couldn't agree more," he said. "And there's got to be a forgiver, which, in our case, tends to be Natalie. That generosity of spirit is very important. I was thinking about my temper and a time about twenty years ago when I took all our clothes out of the closet and threw them down the stairs."

"You did?" asked Natalie. "You see, I have this capacity to forget."

"I merged that with a fight I had with a roommate in college, where we threw all of each other's clothes into a full bathtub. That was the moment when we became friends, because we looked at each other and we both started laughing."

"You never told me this," Natalie said in astonishment.

"The humor is what saved us. I think a lot of marriages go sour from the fact that one partner cannot accept the rage of the other."

"What about honesty in marriage?" I asked. "How important is it and to what degree?"

Christopher began, "Bill Buckley says the most legitimate lie is 'Honey, you're the most beautiful woman in the world.' It's witty."

"I think honesty is essential," Natalie proceeded. "Christopher is *brutally* honest. Some people might think he's harsh. He doesn't say I'm beautiful, 'cause I'm not. But he says the *right* thing: how great I look for my age or something like that. Better than clichés. In terms of my work, I know when I give him something, that's it. I might not follow the advice per se, but he always zeros in on something important. And I think I'm the same way with his work."

"But the honesty is also constructive. I don't remind her daily that she's not going to become a major league baseball player. (In fact, I don't think I've ever told her the truth about that matter.) I hope everything that's said, even in anger, has some ultimately constructive purpose. Not always, I suppose. She's never going to park the car at the right angle in the garage," he dead-panned.

"This is the first time he's conceded that!" cheered Natalie. "Thank goodness."

"But I'm not going to give up trying!" he said, laughing.

As with each of the other interviews I had conducted, I was struck again by the decency and vulnerability of the male partner in the marriage. I saw over and over again how men have the same fears and needs and longings as women. When I commented on that realization, Christopher asked, "Does that surprise you?"

It did. My preconceived perceptions and my mother's training had warped my ability to see men as people. Giving birth to and raising my son has been a major step in the process of understanding and appreciating males. But that was always tempered with a mother's unconditional love and a tendency to overreach in the opposite direction: seeing him as perfect (though I knew that seeing in terms of perfection is another danger). Men, like women, are not demons or angels; they are human, and at various times, under different circumstances, they can be all three.

"If you think in terms of cultivating yourself, fostering your emotional life, your intellectual life, then the context of the marriage in that sense begins to form you. Would you agree?" I asked.

Natalie spoke first. "Yes. Marriage is the deepest relationship that a person has, a relationship that allows you to be totally yourself. You feel content."

"There's no question," Christopher interjected, "that what is interesting about life, what keeps you going is the wonder of it, the wonder of how we got here. Certainly being married and having a relationship helps me in the frustrations that stand in the way of growth. We help each other to break down or get over—depending on how you look at it—these impasses. The object is not to improve; it's just easier to deal with the world when you have that kind of support."

They turned the question "What can be learned from a lifetime of experience in partnership?" into a comedy routine.

"I haven't had a lifetime yet, so I don't know," Natalie replied.

"Well, thirty years is a pretty good start!" I reminded her.

"Come on; that's just the beginning," she scoffed, in the same poignant manner that several other happily married couples I know refuse to admit the inevitability that their relationship will some day end.

"We're counting on thirty more, huh?" Christopher said in a soothing way. " 'What have you learned from thirty years of marriage?' That's the kind of question you want to sit down and write an essay on."

"Give it one of your one-liners," she encouraged the stand-up comic in him.

"How to work the VCR?"

"We haven't done that yet!" she said straight-faced.

"How has your professional life affected your personal life?" I went on.

"We are very lucky to be writers, although maybe that's one of the reasons why we married and our marriage has lasted," Christopher speculated. "Both of us being home all day, in addition to being married, in a sense we are also each other's water cooler, if you know what I mean. I miss the water cooler at the office very much, the place where you gather and gossip. So we meet occasionally during the day.

"Our professional lives are completely integrated with our marriage. It's also been a great benefit for our children, because we've both been there for them, literally. Sometimes too much. In a way, that was planned. We haven't had to go to an office. It also meant if one of us did have to go away on a tour or something, the other one was at home; it never conflicted."

My next question: "Why have marriages become so impermanent, thus raising the rate of divorce in the United States to 50 percent?"

"People seem to want the answer here on earth," Christopher stated. "The loss of the Calvinist principle of putting off pleasure, the loss of a belief in God for many people has encouraged them to want paradise now. They're not willing to work at relationship. If something doesn't go in an expected way, they seem to think that means they shouldn't be together, so they split. Whereas if there is something wrong, that's the *beginning* of a place to work from."

"A difficulty in a marriage could be a sign that it's time to start growing," Natalie added. "People don't want to accept any negatives. They think negatives mean 'It's over; I have to leave,' rather than try and work through the problem. Granted, there are some people that you will never, ever get along with, but, that aside, I think there is nothing you can't work through with people."

Sitting at their kitchen table about two o'clock that afternoon, I nearly had a full-blown religious experience—all that was missing were the stigmata. As my eyes widened and glistened and I covered my chest with splayed fingers, Natalie asked with concern, "What's wrong?"

"I'm having an epiphany," I cried, in my usual understated fashion. The utterance may have been melodramatic, but the emotion was true. As often happens during the course of an interview, either a new piece of the puzzle of marriage fell into place for me or some information that I had long known in my bones, my DNA, say, had finally made the journey to my brain, to active cognition.

It was a thrilling moment to understand that the relationship between two people is similar in practice to one's relationship with oneself. You continue to go deeper or expand further in your relationship with another, just as you do with yourself. After a lifetime of searching for self-knowledge, I grasped the fact that the way of being with myself was transferable to another. Habits of introspection and self-reflection are part of what we bring to a relationship. In other words, I reasoned, if I can sort through the difficulties and problems in my own psyche, I have a good chance of being able to do that with another human being. Although obvious to those in-the-know, it seemed a miraculous revelation to me. I appreciated the time and work I had devoted to fifteen years of psychotherapy, and I now knew I could continue to apply what I'd learned in reference to a partnership. I felt hopeful.

Christopher applauded my discovery, "That's right! And the wonderful thing is it all makes such sense the deeper you go. The craziest things ultimately yield such a wonderfully rational answer. It's breathtaking when you understand the complexity of the human mind and how utterly rational the answer finally is to the most irrational behavior. We happen to be deeply Freudian, deeply oriented toward psychoanalysis, which the country is drifting away from toward the 'now-centered' therapy: if I don't feel good, it's not right. That's the simplest possible answer to your question of why the impermanence in sexual relationships and marriage."

"You have to accept the negative parts of relationship," Natalie stressed again; "there are a lot of unpleasant things you have to work through."

"So there is an element of work, you do have to 'work' on a relationship?" I asked.

"I wouldn't call it work; I don't like the sound of work—it implies labor," Natalie corrected me. "But marriage is a process that you have to move along."

"Yes, it *is* work," Christopher challenged. "It's also, as Cathleen said, work in relationship to yourself. Often the worst thing is the best thing. When you come up against feeling terrible, when everything has turned flat and stale, or something about the other person becomes violently objectionable, it's usually—if you are willing to stay with it—a very good sign that you're coming to a crossroads. The objection can melt away."

"That's right, if you're willing to look inside yourself and be patient," said Natalie.

"This is really good news!" I grinned at both of them. "If we have the capacity to look within ourselves, to recognize our own projections, then we surely should be able to extend that kind of observation to a relationship. This is big."

"Remember though," Christopher qualified, "you have to find somebody, for better or worse, who is willing to do it too, to see it that way."

"Do you think there is a 'right person' for each of us, or is that nonsense?" I asked.

"Absolute nonsense," Natalie counseled. "My major advice to Rachel is: There's no Mr. Right; there are lots of them out there. So much has to do with luck and timing."

"The right person is often the one you think is the wrong person," Christopher concurred.

"Any advice for couples just starting out?" I finished up.

"Laugh. Keep laughing," recommended Christopher. "I should say, keep finding things to laugh about—don't just laugh—that could get you a sock in the jaw."

"Surprises, ecstasy, process. Ecstasy is making the impossible possible," Natalie said wistfully. "I have a friend who is working on a book on why marriage *can't* work. We can't really discuss this major issue because we disagree. My goal is to make her change her mind, so to me true ecstasy would be if she could break through and see what I see."

"True ecstasy for me would be if I could get you to park the car . . ." Christopher said, laughing.

Chapter 7

Finding a New Way Together

Love grows in different ways. After thirty years, our love is different—deeper in some areas, not as deep in others. You shouldn't look for it to stay the same, because it won't. Love *is* a constant change.

Joe Feury

Lee Grant and Joe Feury

I found a friend in Joey. I had nothing to prove to him; he accepts me the way I am. He has such staying power, and through that a friendship was formed. There was a healthiness we were finding together, whatever it was (and you couldn't put a label on it), but we were finding a new way together.

Lee Grant

L ee Grant hit the Hollywood scene like a comet when she won an Academy Award for Best Supporting Actress in *The Detective* in the 1950s. Shortly thereafter she was blacklisted by the House Un-American Activities Committee for twelve long, bitter, and bewildering years, because she would not name her husband (a New York intellectual and a Marxist) before the committee. She virtually started her career over again with a passion for political and feminist concerns that has remained unwavering for more than thirty years. The longevity of her career is truly remarkable when one realizes that it was short-circuited for twelve years.

It takes a certain kind of man to hold his own in a relationship with an independent woman. Joe Feury is that kind of man. He has not only held his own, he has developed his own niche as a successful Hollywood producer. Together Lee and Joey (as he is called by all who know him—"Joe" seems much too impersonal to describe the exuberantly warm, welcoming, and street-smart Joey) produce and direct award-winning feature films and made-for-television movies.

When I entered their vast, elegant apartment on the Upper West Side in Manhattan, I entered the same world Joey later spoke about having been enchanted by thirty years ago: art hung on the walls, the lights were plentiful but dimmed, delicious aromas wafted through the oversized rooms filling one sense, while Maria Callas's voice filled another. I walked past a dining room table that must seat twenty—comfortably. There is a sense of culture, of refinement, yes, but also a definite feeling of home.

Joey greeted me with a broad smile and—what else?—open arms. "Are you hungry? Dinner's almost ready," he said in his East Coast accent. Following close on his heels was Dude, the action-packed apricot toy poodle Lee had given to Joey as a present after Belinda, their daughter, moved away to college. Lee later explained, "Joey has a lot of energy, a high metabolism, a lot of 'Look at me,' 'Watch me, I'm doing this now,' and he focuses it on Dude. I can't give him what Dude gives him, that undivided attention and unconditional love."

They make an outlandish couple—not Joey and Lee, but Joey and Dude—the striking ex–ballet dancer with the clean-shaven head who, though perhaps heavier than in his dancing days, remains agile and with the impeccable posture that keeps his feet in a permanent V, hotly pursued by the dainty, five-pound fluffball of devotion with the incongruous name of Dude.

Joey took me into their bedroom to meet Lee. It was January and they'd just finished working on a film in Canada starring Carol Burnett. Lee was down with the flu, but flu or no—and without makeup—she embodied a Hollywood aura. She was also quite generous, as she accommodated this interview during my stay in New York even while she was ill.

Joey's dinner was delicious—pasta, salad, and steak; I'd brought pastries from Dean and DeLucca. There were six of us including Susan Strasberg (a longtime friend since the Actor's Studio days), who was temporarily staying in their apartment, and another couple who are close friends of Lee and Joey's. Clearly, their door is always open to friends.

Because Lee was under the weather we held our discussion in their bedroom. All four of us (including Dude, who panted into the microphone and flew off the bed yelping at a high pitch whenever he heard a sound—which was often) lounged on the king-sized bed. It was instant intimacy, no holds barred.

What a relief to be with a couple who, although they have been together for thirty years, *do not* complete each other's sentences. I noticed no hidden innuendos, no belligerent jibes. They have a playful sense of humor between them. There is a respect for the artistry, the uniqueness of the other, the space that separates them and keeps them individuals, keeps them interesting and interested, and that, as they both demonstrated during our several hours of conversation, keeps them "alive."

Lee began by describing how they started on an impossible basis. "Joey was in his mid-twenties when we met—he was *not* the man of my dreams. I'd been through the blacklist. I'd been through a marriage and divorce and had a four-year-old daughter. I was totally inaccessible to him. Consequently, because we thought it was only temporary, we formed a new type of relationship—one in which there were no preconceived ideas or images of what a relationship together would look like.

"I found a friend in him. He has such staying power, and through that a friendship was formed. Also, I had nothing to prove to him, because I knew it was 'temporary.' I could be myself in a way that had never happened before with a man. I'd learned to flirt, to charm, to seduce, to hold back, but with Joey I didn't put up any of that old female stuff.

"Joey had so much love to give. His was such a healing kind of obsession—I was always screaming at him, because whenever I had dates he acted like a little mafioso outside my window lighting cigarettes and trying to intimidate them. 'No' is just an interesting word to Joey. It has no more meaning than 'yes'; it's just a new hurdle."

"When I first walked into Lee's house—it was this style of house," Joey said as he motioned expansively to the art-filled walls and comfortable grandeur of their apartment, "which was filled with paintings and music and culture—I walked into something I'd never seen before and knew I wasn't going to walk out of so easily. I came from a working-class family. I was a neighborhood Italian boy from Delaware who worked with his father in plumbing construction and then decided to become a ballet dancer, which is about as far away from plumbing construction as you can get!"

But that desire for improvement was part of his character. "Joey had a deep, lyrical longing for something else, another window to express his soul. He brought a fresher approach to whatever he touched. His painting has a bolder viewpoint, and as time went on, I came to respect his thinking. He is an original person. He was so *solid* and basic, as was his family. They were interested in food, in *pasta*. In those days, I'd just gotten off the blacklist and I was very shaky and vulnerable about going back into the world of Hollywood, which I'd been shut out from for so many years. There I was—this fragile little

Jew—who got adopted by this family of Italian Catholics. The security I found there became a haven for me."

They didn't actually get around to marriage for another ten years. As a couple they wanted to adopt a child from Thailand, and adoption required marriage. Lee clearly loved telling the story about the night they wrote their wedding vows: "I'd had marriage already and I was afraid to break what was fresh between Joey and me—we had been doing fine, but I know what happens when those marriage rules start coming in.

"We had a few people to dinner and to play poker that night. I told them we had to go to the market, but instead we ran to a little church and I wrote these vows that we then read to each other. They weren't 'I do' or 'yes' or 'I take this man to love, honor, and cherish' and all those expectations that are impossible to live up to, but 'I will try to help you achieve your potential in this life,' which is all anyone can ask of a great friend. We said we would try and that's what we did. We *have* tried. But it's always a question mark as far as I'm concerned."

"I've always insisted that Lee do the things that frighten her or that she doesn't want to do," Joey said.

"Sometimes the only reason I was able to do something is because he said I could. Now I look back and I think, 'Why did he have so much faith? Where did it come from?' He just held a mirror up to me and said, 'You can do anything!'"

"I insisted she work all the time. I always had and have a respect for Lee's talents. Once you see that in a person, it's hard to let them get away with anything less."

———————

For several years while living in Malibu, Lee was off the map with her successful acting career and Joey produced lucrative commercials. "One day I just stopped doing commercials like that," he said with a rhythmic snap of his fingers. "I couldn't handle it anymore. For the next three or four years all I did was concentrate on designing and building an estate in Malibu. It was a great piece of work. I started out with a vacant piece of land, not a blade of grass on it. By the time it was finished, it looked like it had been there fifteen years."

"It was the kind of house from *Meet Me in St. Louis*, you know, the movie with Judy Garland," Lee remembered. "A huge veranda wrapped around it, turn-of-the-century stained glass windows we'd bought in Chicago. The kind of place that we were supposed to be happy in forever. But I felt imprisoned by it."

"I think we both did," Joey continued. "And once again my instincts said it was time for me to change my life. So we sold the house, made a great profit, and moved back to New York. It's a different life here; you're out on the street. New York is *alive*—whether you like it or not—but it's not those sun-drenched streets with empty houses and manicured lawns and nobody in sight.

"One of the reasons that has probably helped Lee and I stay together all these years is that we are apart a lot. I feel sorry for people whose circumstances don't give them space from one another. Lee and I hang out well together, so it's not a drag. In fact, I'd rather be sitting in this bedroom watching TV with her than out in a bar someplace or even at a friend's house. We don't know many people who have been together this long and still *enjoy* each other. I'm sorry for guys who are bachelors in their fifties, and for women in their fifties and sixties without men. We have many women friends—who are wonderful and beautiful—who don't have a man, but they've carved out interesting lives for themselves anyway."

"What about fidelity?" I asked.

"When we were first together," Lee said, "I expected that if I was away for any period of time and Joey had a flirtation that he would act on it. He just would. He's a very sexual guy; it's one of the reasons we're together. No matter what kind of good friends we were, if he didn't turn me on, what good is it? I just didn't want to know about it. I hate people who have to tell the other person—that whole confessional attitude. I think you act on it, you do what you have to do, and you come home. We were always free to leave if we wanted to. And we're free to leave today. Unless you are willing to let someone go, you can't have any honesty."

"From my side," returned Joey, "I'd also have to be really stupid to think that Lee, who all the men wanted, wouldn't act on an impulse if she was away on location and lonely. She never has, and I'd break her arm if she did, but . . ."

"It's nice to know my arm would be broken if he knew about it!" Lee said, laughing. "My being attracted to Joey—and I've *always* been attracted to him—didn't weaken me or diminish me. I didn't want to repeat my old patterns in relationship. I wanted to create a place where work became absolutely crucial to me—I wanted to make up for those twelve years on the blacklist—and I wanted the support to do that.

"When I left New York after the blacklist was over and I hit that beach in California, I started to run. My lungs just filled with air and I thought, 'I'm free. I'm free! I've got nobody to apologize to, to be terrorized by. Nobody can tell me I can't live with Joey. Nobody can tell me what to do anymore. Not society or the government. Not my parents. Not my husband. Nobody.' I felt a freedom but also an awareness that I had to protect that freedom, because it had been taken away from me by the government and I'd also given it away to my husband. I'm still very susceptible in those areas. When I'm told I can't do something, there is a feeling that rises up in me that I can't control and it can become very dangerous—out of proportion."

"Lee has a hard time seeing her place within the film industry. I look at her as one of the most important women in this country. She is a political thinker, an activist, a feminist, a director, an actress. So when I step back and say, 'Wait a minute, why am I still married thirty years later?'—well, who would I find, truthfully, who would be better for me? Somebody younger who would give me a hard time? Maybe her tits would stick up a little bit higher, but she certainly couldn't match Lee in the things that matter."

"Joey goes to *his* gym. He won't *let* me go to that gym. That's his place to make his connections, to meet his friends."

"There's *gotta* be a place that's mine. When I first said 'no,' we had an argument about it. I've got to be able to go someplace that's not our office or our work or our home. I'm the *star* of the gym. I don't want to compete with my wife, who is also a star."

"Everybody has to be a star in their own place," Lee justified.

"So, I think, since you only go round once, you should eat all the fruit you can, because you won't go past that place again. Like the Big Book says (my big book is *Shogun*— every time I get confused I open it up at random and read): 'There's no yesterday and no tomorrow, there's only today.' If you go out to the living room and look at those pictures of our friends, how many of them are dead in the last three, four, five years, you *know* there's only today.

"So my philosophy is: go ahead and flirt, it's harmless; but I don't really go out, I mean, she knows where I am *all the time!*"

"And him, he follows me like the godfather. 'Where are you going now? Where will you be at 3:40? Where will you be at 3:50? Why weren't you home ten minutes ago?' I think it's funny. I like it.

"When something comes up that we can't resolve between us we go to a third person—we have a great therapist! We can't work through everything on our own. We both have very strong points of view and try to convince each other that we are right. A therapist helps us safely let out the anger, because it *has* to be let out. We can be guided by someone who has known us for a long time, who knows exactly where we come from, what our dynamic is. I would say three-quarters of the time, just getting it out of our systems is what most helps to start healing the rift.

"He's a natural boss; I'm a natural rebel. It's built into our DNA. Joey is also a producer and I'm a director, which often places us, when we are doing a production, on a collision course."

———————

Money is a big issue for most couples. It can be an area of contention that makes or breaks a marriage.

"In my first marriage I had been controlled by money," Lee offered. "I knew what it was like and I didn't want to do that to Joey. During the twelve years I was with my first husband, I never had any money except what he gave me. So I knew how destructive that element could be. For the first time in my life, when I met Joey thirty years ago, I was creating my own world: my own work, my own house, my own people in my house. I didn't have to worry or be scared about doing something wrong or laughing when I wasn't supposed to. Joey accepted me the way I was. There was a healthiness we were finding together, whatever it was (and you couldn't put a label on it), but we were finding a new way together. As money came in, we paid our expenses with what I earned. Money gave me the freedom to be myself and the work gave me that freedom. I was *very* resistant to entering another relationship where the guy had the money."

"I was young when we met and Lee gave me the opportunity to grow into my money-earning potential. When I look back at my life, if there was ever a downside to it, it was that I felt I'd missed my apprenticeship period, in terms of my growth. I tried to start at the top of my professional growth rather than starting at the bottom."

"He just couldn't stand to be anything but the boss."

"She kids when she says I started out to be the boss, because Lee was always very gracious in the area of money during those years when I was trying to be an actor or feeling my way in the industry while she was working and earning the money. There was never any, 'Why aren't you doing this or that?' with her. But she was understanding and had a generosity toward me that gave me the time to find my way and do what I had to do."

"At a certain point, Joey got the itch to make his own money. He's very talented with money. I'm not! If it were up to me, we would have nothing. Thanks to him we've done okay. When I first started working again after the blacklist, I'd call my agent's office and say, 'I'm out of money' and they'd say, 'Again? We sent all those checks.' Later I'd find them fallen to the back of my bureau. I never knew how to handle it. Joey comes from a family who can deal with numbers. They're like adding machines! Joey is the one who knows when we need to go to work because we have to bring in more money. *I* don't know that."

"When Lee said, 'It's time for you to start carrying some of the weight,' I did. I was raised in an atmosphere in which you worked. So not working was hard for me. I think people's whole identity is mirrored for them through their family and their work. The smartest thing we ever did was to build that house in Malibu. The first thing I did was plant baby eucalyptus trees down both sides of the driveway."

"I made so much fun of him, they were *this* big, like toothpicks. I would laugh, 'Look what Joey planted.' "

"But when I broke ground in 1977, they were twenty-five feet high," Joey said.

"I was stunned. He'd known what he was doing. But I had a lot of resentment because I did not want to work to support a house."

"I insisted on it. I knew from the moment I started the project that it was going to be very, very big money, and I have great tenacity. I'm like a bulldog when I'm focused on something. It took me three years to do that job by the time it was finished and we were living in it. It was a phenomenal place.

"The only fear I've ever had in life was money. I kid a lot. I say, 'Save enough for a bullet. Don't run out of money in this country. Don't get old without money in this country.' If Lee and I have any big fights at all, it's over money. Because she doesn't have a sense of it and I do. I don't want us to be in our late sixties and find ourselves not having put away money or paid our bills. We are very fortunate: we have a beautiful home and we don't have any debt. Since we have business managers we never see any money. I bet Lee hasn't seen a paycheck in thirty years. That's why when we make a movie . . ."

". . . we go crazy," Lee jumped in, "'cause we get *per diems*—envelopes with *real money in them.* I go: *m-o-n-e-y!* We're like kids at Christmas."

"I think my biggest responsibility to Lee is to make sure that if anything should happen to me, she'd be okay. But I also believe in spending it while you're alive. There's a part of me that says when you die, you should be spending your last nickel. If you have anything left in life, you fucked up.

"No, I never get bored with Lee. Our life is alive! Our work lives are alive. Boredom is a killer."

"If you were bored, there'd be nothing to talk about," Lee said. "If there's no component of surprise in somebody, then what's the use of talking? All the rest you can throw out the window. I've already seen Joey in four or five incarnations. When we first met he was part man, part kid. He was somebody very different at thirty-four, and again at forty-four. This year he shaved his head. It's like I'm with a new person. His reaction to losing that great curly mop of hair he had was to say, 'Fuck you. I'm going to get there ahead of you,' and that was a bold stroke."

Summing up, Joey believes that, "Love grows in different ways. After thirty years, our love is different, deeper in some areas, not as deep in others. You shouldn't look for it to stay the same, because it won't. Love *is* a constant change. If you look for it to stay the same, it's over. Life is filled with things that are constantly changing. Life is a ship at sea."

"If you're lucky!" Lee observed. "To me it's a raft."

Chapter 8

The Periodic Desperation of the Single Woman

Journal Entry: 25 March 1993

The loneliness of the single woman.

I'm on the East Coast for conferences at the Omega Institute in Manhattan, Interface in Cambridge, and a lecture and workshop at the Open Center in Soho. Last night I saw Wendy Wasserstein's Chekhovian-like play *The Sisters Rosensweig* on Broadway. I related to the lead character, Sara, played by Jane Alexander, a fifty-four-year-old, Brooklyn-born divorcée who is a highly successful and assimilated expatriate banker with a teenage daughter. Sara meets Merv Kant (Robert Klein), a widower and fake-fur furrier, and in spite of herself begins a romance with him. It is fundamentally a play about possibilities for middle-aged women, about two adults connecting with each other, even if it's only for a night.

How I recognized Sara's sense of rightness—she's a "know-it-all," "can't tell-*her*-anything" kind of woman—as am I. After several years of being alone she realizes that romance still exists, that love is possible, although it may not be in a form that is easily recognizable to her. By the end of the play she has become less defensive and pessimistic about her life and more open to the possibility of falling in love again, even with a *faux* furrier. She is no longer a "bitchy, hard-bitten woman" who has been without a man for too many years. "Being alone too long makes you brittle," one man told me last year.

Of course, Sara fights her feelings for Merv to the end. She easily finds fault with him because he is "too Jewish," has the wrong career, doesn't play tennis, and any number of other excuses she can find to reject him. I left the theater thinking maybe it's not too late for me, either.

While waiting in the lobby to be seated I met Paul (coincidentally a look-alike for Paul Newman, with the same penetrating azure-blue eyes) and Joan, a lovely couple who have been married for nearly fifty-seven years. During the intermission we resumed our conversation. I was struck by the quality of attention and adoration they still convey to each other, how they look so lovingly into each other's eyes when speaking, and how she calls him "Pauley." I asked if they would be willing to talk with me about their marriage. We will meet next week on my return from Cambridge and Providence.

26 March 1993

Hope springs eternal.

Gave my first of two seminars at the Omega conference, "A Revolution of Hope." My book has arrived! I'm holding *On Women Turning 50: Celebrating Midlife Discoveries* in my hands. My second book and what a beauty. After my seminar at the New York Sheraton I went to celebrate by myself at a lovely vegetarian restaurant nearby called Zen Palate. Who should sit next to me at the counter but an interesting and attractive man named Stanley Young. We were immediately drawn to each other. He is a bright, quick-witted man who kept me in stitches throughout dinner.

I positively basked in his warm attention and shared the excitement of my new book with him. Later I invited him to accompany me to the theater to see *The Song of Jacob Zulu*. One of the benefits of being a single person is that I generally get the best (solitary) seat in the house at the opera, ballet, theater, etc. Today was no exception. I sat in the front row, while Stanley had an SRO ticket. During intermission I turned around and saw Gloria Steinem sitting two rows behind me. Exuberant to a fault, I again pulled out my book, which has Gloria's portrait among others on the cover, and luxuriated in the synchronicity of the moment. This was my night and I was savoring it.

The show was very moving and, with Ladysmith Black Mambazo as a Greek chorus-like narrator, seemed like a prayer in action. Later Stanley invited me out for a drink. We went to the top of a hotel that has an outside elevator and a revolving, glassed-in lounge on the forty-sixth floor. We spent an hour and a half nursing a bottle of Poland Springs carbonated water between us, while all the time wanting to nurse various parts of each other. I was aroused, tantalized—thank God—for the first time since last August and only the second time in three and a half years. "Please send me a lover," begins my nightly invocation to the stars, the moon, whoever in the cosmos might be listening, "someone to love me and accept my love." What a gift: to be wet again. How thrilling to look into a man's eyes and see desire. At last.

I love New York men. New York Jewish men. Being Jewish is a real bonus to me. Why am I so drawn to Jewish men? Is it because they feel like home to me? Part of my tribe? Because my family is descended from Morenos and they awaken my heritage? Is it their sensuality? Their neuroses? Or their ability to be intimate?

Finally a man for whom I'm not "too much"—too deep, too smart, too successful, too enthusiastic, too sexual, too *alive*. In fact, he seems attracted to the very quality that initially charms but soon overwhelms most men: my unadulterated ebullience. "Don't worry," he assures me, when I voice this concern, "I'm used to intense women. You have about 70 percent of my mother's energy level."

Okay, coming back down to earth. I do live three thousand miles away from this man! What's the term? Geographically undesirable, I believe. And I have no idea who he is, except that I like him and he makes me laugh. Still, we agree to see each other next week when I return from Rhode Island. We kiss lightly. We hug sweetly and wish for more.

Later that night I masturbate for the first time in several months. I'd stopped because masturbating became a stark and painful reminder to me of my aloneness, and I would end up crying myself to sleep. What's happening to me? Chemistry is beyond rational comprehension. This has been a magical day.

30 March 1993

Providence, Rhode Island.

What is a body?

The cartography of a life. A personal history, a visual diary of loves and fears. It takes courage to live a life—to run toward ourselves rather than run away. Reading from the novel *The English Patient* by Michael Ondaatje, I am mesmerized by this passage and read it over and over again:

We die containing a richness of lovers and tribes, tastes we have swallowed, bodies we have plunged into and swum up as if rivers of wisdom, characters we have climbed into as if trees, fears we have hidden in as if caves. I wish for all this to be marked on my body when I am dead. I believe in such cartography—to be marked by nature, not just to label ourselves on a map like the names of rich men and women on buildings. We are communal histories, communal books. We are not owned or monogamous in our taste or experience. All I desired was to walk upon such an earth that had no maps.

After my last two seminars in New York and Cambridge, three men came up to me and invited me out for coffee or gave me their telephone number asking me to please contact them. How lovely. I'm no longer invisible to American men. When I was a beautiful, healthy, sensual California teenager I had chocolate-brown skin during the summer and wore blossoms in my hair. I was a tropical flower. For these past three and a half years I've disowned my sexuality, my sensual aliveness and yearnings. But no longer. Aging—being middle-aged—is not a reason to deny my desire and my desirability. Thank God for Nature. The entirety of Nature has been my lover. My inherent sensuousness has been my salvation. People often don't differentiate between sensuousness, which has to do with being alive through the senses, and sensuality, which has to do with sex. Both are good and necessary for an integrated, healthy existence. I am opening.

Tonight my friend Christiane, who is such a skilled and perceptive artist, made a cast of my body from my neck to my knees. It brought up so many emotions for me, so many feelings of inadequacy. I'm too old to be attractive. I'm too fat, have sagging breasts, big thighs, and stretch marks on my belly. My hair is graying; my face is wrinkling. Poor women! We are merciless with ourselves. By whose standards are we trying to live? Certainly by those airbrushed faces and nipped-and-tucked figures of movie stars and other public personalities we see in the media—the perfected images of women *who don't even look like that themselves.*

Several years ago I was a personal chef in Los Angeles for a well-known film star, who, although in her mid-thirties, seemed more like a precocious twelve year old than an adult. One afternoon she came into the kitchen to show me her publicity shots. There I stood, photos in one hand, the actress less than a foot away from me. At that moment I received a gift, a real blessing, because I was hit full force by the fact that she looked *nothing* like the images in the photographs. I get it! I said to myself. Millions of women spend countless hours and fortunes trying to reach the perfection of these images, *but the women in the images don't even look like what they're trying to sell us.*

For the first time in my life I recognized the scam for what it is: a lie for the purpose of keeping women hostages to their own vanity. We allow ourselves to be tyrannized by films, fashion magazines, and advertising. In the documentary on Noam Chomsky, *Manufacturing Consent*, Chomsky brilliantly expounds on how the media create "necessary illusions" and reveals it as a "system of propaganda," a form of mind control at war for "men's [and women's] minds."

Why do we allow movies, newspapers, national sports events, television, and magazines to reduce our capacity to think, at least to think about anything that has any value or importance in our lives? Chomsky prescribes "a course of intellectual defense." This would entail arming ourselves by researching information sources beyond the mainstream media, thinking about issues that affect ourselves either directly or indirectly, and, not least important, talking with others in our community as if these issues matter. It's our life and well-being at stake.

According to Stuart Ewen in his book *Captains of Consciousness: Advertising and the Social Roots of Consumer Culture*, when advertising entered its first golden age, in the 1920s, it employed the psychology of self-criticism: "Did your bad breath, underarm odor, imperfect figure drive him away? Our product will remedy your defects." Women have carried this self-criticism to ruinous levels. Why do we yearn to look unreal, to look like anyone else but ourselves? On my last visit to Portland, Oregon, I visited the Museum of American Advertising, a fascinating place that illustrates just how insidious the "art" of advertising really is.

Christiane molded the shape of me in a semifetal position. Once it was finished and lying on the floor, I marveled at how full the breasts were and at how much smaller the body seemed than the way I perceive myself to be from the inside. I had such compassion for this body and all that it's been through in forty-four years: having given birth to another human being and certainly to itself many times over, having given and received pleasure from men who mostly appreciated it. Perhaps, I thought, I would be willing to share this body again with a man. Perhaps.

Fortunately I had Christiane's interested and sympathetic ear to hear my misgivings and fantasies. "Why on earth," I began, in my most self-righteous voice, "would I have sex with someone who had to wear a condom because I hadn't known him long enough to be assured that he was free of the AIDS virus?" (I sounded more and more like Sara Rosensweig to myself.) Christiane shook her head in patient agreement—although she's been married to her husband for nearly twenty-five years and condoms are a moot point to her. "And, secondly," I waged on in my self-righteous tirade, "I promised myself when I broke up with François three and a half years ago that I wouldn't sleep with a man unless we both felt there was at least a possibility for a relationship between us. Otherwise, why bother? What's the possibility across three thousand miles!" Of course, I was desperate to convince *myself*, not her. All she would say, wise woman that she is, is, "If you're in conflict, you must not be ready."

I knew that this was exactly the kind of situation Gloria Steinem had been referring to (warning me against?) during my discussion with her last year when she'd said, "Aging brings freedom from romance; freedom from the ways in which your hormones distort your judgment and make you do things that aren't right for you." It's as if running into her last week (on the exact day I met Stanley!) was a caveat, or at least a reminder to beware my hormones.

After my discussion with Christiane I had a telephone conversation with Stanley. We were in accord about one urgent truth: we can't wait until Friday. We will see each other on Thursday (April Fool's Day), the day I return to Manhattan.

1 April 1993

I'm a fool for love.

"It's a long time since someone asked me about love."

What disparate states are found in the Country of Marriage. Spending five years in *The Heart of Marriage*—albeit even as a tourist—gives me license to explore, an entree into, the most intimate compartments and quandaries of couples' lives—as well as my own. What am I looking for in a man? I ask myself. What does a healthy, satisfying, long-term, *alive* marriage look like to me? Will I know the potential for it when I see it? Gifts often come in such unexpected packages. In conversation with Thomas Moore last week in Cambridge, he mentioned the issue of "recognition"—the ability to recognize a gift when it presents itself to you.

Ellen, my agent, had a cocktail party this evening to celebrate the publication of *You Don't Need a Hysterectomy*, by her husband, Ivan. A gynecologist, he exposes in his book the epidemic of unnecessary hysterectomies performed on unsuspecting women in the United States. The book provides a much-needed antidote to the thousands of male and (surprisingly) female doctors who prescribe this radical solution to a variety of "female problems" without an essential scrutiny for alternatives. An insider's view from the medical establishment.

Here for the first time I met Colette Dowling, author of *The Cinderella Complex*. This book was a crucial "piece of work" for me on my journey to myself and away from emotional and financial dependence on men thirteen years ago when I first read it. It was a delight to meet her and personally thank her. I told Colette, my voice tinged with regret and embarrassment, "Even after I knew the 'cure' for my dependency, it still took so many years to outgrow it." "It takes years for all of us," she said. And I knew she was speaking from personal experience.

The concept in her book that was perhaps the most important for me was that of the motivating element of fear in women's lives:

The first thing women have to recognize is the degree to which fear rules their lives. Such fears trace back to profound infantile loneliness. The need for love that goes unfulfilled in childhood can lead to a passive and potentially destructive wish to give oneself up to anyone.

This possibility, "to give oneself up to anyone," remains my greatest anxiety in relationship to men. Soon it will be challenged. Carolyn Heilbrun, the feminist scholar and biographer of Gloria Steinem, another of Ellen's clients, was also in attendance. I had met her briefly once before, so we were able to spend part of the evening together while I probed her thoughts on marriage and, in particular, on the possibility of middle-aged women finding a satisfying heterosexual relationship.

I remember how, on the cusp of forty I'd read Carolyn's book, *Writing a Woman's Life*, and found a mentor for both my spiritual and professional lives.

What is renounced is the old way of love, being the object of male desire and the male gaze, that acknowledgment of personhood that, in the conventional world, only a man can bestow.

How deeply this passage had affected my life then and was partially responsible for my choosing a period of celibacy more recently. Now as "the object of male desire" once again, I find myself grateful for it, and not a little guilty. Why? If desire is natural, does that make celibacy artificial? Am I throwing the baby out with the bathwater?

"Is it possible to redefine marriage, or is that institution already so close to extinction that we need not try?" I asked the woman who herself is an anomaly: a feminist who has been happily married for over forty years, thereby proving that marriage and feminism can indeed coexist.

"It's a long time since someone asked me about love," she began.

We agreed that Hollywood is largely responsible for creating the impossibly romantic images that have filled people's minds for the last seventy years. Both literature and movies are filled with women who fall for inappropriate men. Carolyn gives the example of a novel by Anne Brontë (one of the three sisters who knew more than their fair share about unrequited love), *The Tenant of Wildfell Hall*; I offer the example of the character Bathsheba in one of my favorite novels, Thomas Hardy's *Far from the Madding Crowd*.

"A marriage has to be continually remade, recreated," she tells me, "because the two people are always changing."

"Is companionship an important part of a marriage?" I ask.

"Yes, but it sounds so unsexy," she exclaims in her droll humor. "The idea of sex has become so vigorous and athletic." In *Writing a Woman's Life*, Carolyn gives the examples of Leonard and Virginia Woolf, and Vita Sackville-West and Harold Nicolson as couples who built their relationships on companionship. "I'm not condoning sexless marriages, but rather marriages based on a fundamental friendship. The fireworks of sex never lasts." Again, in *Writing a Woman's Life*, Carolyn states, "we accept sexual attractiveness as a clue to finding our way in the labyrinth of marriage. It almost never is."

What about women in their forties and fifties who are looking for love? "The woman must first ask herself: What do I want in a relationship? What's most important to me? That could be companionship, sex, an intellectual colleague, a dinner partner, someone with whom to enjoy the theater—usually it's all of the above. All of these needs might not be met by one man," Carolyn suggested. "Certainly a variety of men could serve different functions in our lives, just as do our women friends." This idea brought up another point: middle-aged women (and men) become less willing to relinquish their independent lifestyles and living arrangements. "Our personalities and points of view can no longer be molded as they once were when we were young women." "Exactly," I said, "I *like* living alone."

"This is something no one is talking about: the idea of women wanting their own space. The satisfaction women derive from doing their own work, at last. One more point," said Carolyn, "unless a woman has the ability to leave a relationship, she is trapped in it." By this she meant that if a woman stays in a relationship because she is emotionally afraid to be alone or financially unable to support herself, she is a slave to the relationship. "Of course, we are only talking about people who have some financial security and a means to earn a living, which excludes most of the women in the world!" she clarified.

We ended our conversation on the upswing when Carolyn pointed out, perhaps wanting to leave me with a thread of hope, "some men are by nature husbands and companions." It's a comforting thought.

2 April 1993

Stanley, the man from Harvard.

He was already waiting for me when I arrived at my friend's Greenwich Village townhouse last night after Ellen's party. In the cab from 95th and Park Avenue down to the

Village I found my projections were running wild. I've only seen this man once in my life, I tried to reason with myself. It didn't seem to matter. And it got even worse when we were face to face. He looked like a lumberjack in a red and black flannel shirt and Levis; my primal instincts were even more aroused. Both of our faces were eager and illuminated and our bodies were like magnets. We walked to a nearby cafe where we could be more private because we would be surrounded by strangers. We couldn't stop looking into each other's eyes; I couldn't stop giggling. There I was back in the world of adolescence. I was sixteen again—and it felt great. How could a man do this to me? I know I'm smarter than this. "What would Carolyn and Colette and Gloria say?" I tried to intimidate myself. "You make me feel like a natural woman," wailed Aretha on the jukebox. She was no help. He was selling; I was buying. "Love" hormones are an intoxicant, a natural opiate—I was sliding into the den.

"I made two agreements with myself when I broke up with my last boyfriend," I began. And we were immediately thrust into conversation about past sexual encounters, most recent blood tests, and safe sex. This isn't at all how I'd imagined it would be with the next man I'd sleep with. It's been nearly eight years since I last met a new lover; AIDS was just beginning to be discussed then and the public still thought of it as a gay disease. Now I know that the fastest rising segment of the population to contract the disease is heterosexual women. We have to proceed with coolness, thoughtfulness, I reminded my-self, knowing that these qualities are the complete antithesis of the passion I was feeling.

"I thought a year was a long time to be celibate, but three and a half years!" he de-clared incredulously. "That has to be a record." A record aching to be broken, I thought. I'd forgotten how much of sex is simply logistics, the old "your place or mine" routine. I was staying with friends in a room barely large enough to hold a single bed, and Stanley, having just moved, was also rooming with friends. The idea of a hotel was just too un-friendly and seedy. My concern no longer was *if* I would make love with this man sitting before me, it was a question of when and where. I resigned myself to the fact that it wouldn't be tonight and began to cool down.

Walking back I became aware of that familiar old feeling of "losing myself"—of wanting to be more than myself, to be what "he" wanted me to be, to be perfect. I remem-bered a poem I'd written some years before in response to just this situation:

The Benefit Performance

> *I have no smiles for you.*
> *Unmeant smiles hurt*
> *my face, blacken*

my heart.
(But you would never know.)
This mask sags in dissipation.
Its plastic form immobilized by excess
sorrow and pleasures.
My pantomime fails.

I won't go back to that place of pretense, I refuse to be a "female impersonator" again, I assured myself, no, *demanded* of myself. *I am* enough. We didn't hold hands on our walk back to my friends' home.

Chapter 9

The Prize Is the Relationship

Joan and Paul

We're really in love. It may sound silly to say at my ripe age of eighty, but we still have strong feelings for each other, both physically and emotionally.

Joan

It's important to let your kids go when they grow up. Some people still keep their children the center of their lives—it's bad for them, their spouse or second spouse, whatever, and the kids can't stand it.

Paul

After lunch at Joan and Paul's apartment, Joan began, "You know, your question about why our marriage has lasted so long got me to thinking. We never fought over money." Even when they first got married in 1936 and their furniture consisted mainly of orange crates, they shared "a common pot." Joan worked for a Yiddish newspaper, where she met Isaac Bashevis Singer, and Paul worked at his father's business, which he would eventually inherit.

True to their early training in socialist politics, they feel that money is one of the biggest causes of problems in the world. "People become avaricious and just want to accumulate more and more," said Paul. They have lived a socialist sensibility in a capitalist structure, but have remained faithful to their values.

Shared values, a regard for family, and an ever present sense of humor laid the foundation that has sustained this couple for nearly sixty years. There was a steady, gentle teasing by Paul when he said, "One of our secrets of a good marriage is that I did what I was told by Joan and shut up."

"I'm taking this because I've heard it before," Joan responded good-naturedly and grinned at Paul. She insists her husband was always very supportive. When the women's liberation movement began in the 1960s, Joan would irritate her friends by saying: "'I don't need women's lib; I've always had it with Paul.' Although I admire what women have done, I've seen so many women in the movement who are divorced or remained alone and unhappy. It wasn't for me."

Joan worked for a few years at the Yiddish newspaper and then remained at home for nearly fifteen years taking care of their three children, who were all born within six years. Two years after a hysterectomy at the young age of forty, she embarked upon a new career, that of student. She loved the courses in sociology and child development she took at Hunter College. In 1959, after her graduation, a position at their local grammar school opened up and Joan became a kindergarten teacher, a job she continued for twenty-five years.

What is the key to a happy marriage? "After the first few years of puppy love," Paul answered, "after the hormones have stopped raging and the intensity wears off, what's important is companionship." Unfortunately, many people haven't learned yet about companionship. Joan was nearly incredulous when she described how a couple in a restaurant might just be sitting and eating. "They're not even talking to each other," she said, truly mystified.

"Loneliness is a terrible thing," said Joan. "Flexibility is important in all areas of life—the small as well as the large matters—and it extends to your friends. We've noticed that neurosis grows with age. Whatever a person did or whoever they have been becomes even more ingrained—they become more of themselves."

Paul looked thoughtful for a moment and then said, "Many older people like ourselves find it difficult to make new friends. You have lots of acquaintances, people with whom you may play bridge and such, but to have a friend, there has to be a common background, goal, or interest. I find as we grow older and our friends die off it's harder to do that." Using a business analogy, Paul stated, "You invest in a friend, and if it turns out to be nothing, it's a poor investment." To illustrate his point, Joan told me about the people they'd met at the Jewish Center during their two months in Florida. Apparently, when the members learned that the couple would only be staying briefly, they withdrew their interest because they were seen as a "bad investment."

"It's only human," reasoned Joan. "If you don't mind my saying so, I found myself wondering if you are a bad investment. I mean, will we ever see you again?" she questioned me.

"On the other hand, we have many lifelong friends—even some people from the '30s with whom we're still friends," said Paul. Over fifty years ago, they bought a cottage in upstate New York. They spend several months a year there and enjoy physical and intellectual activities with several close friends.

"It's also important to let your kids go when they grow up," said Paul, adding to the list of necessary components for a lasting relationship. "Some people still keep their children the center of their lives—it's bad for them, their spouse or second spouse, whatever, and the kids can't stand it.

"I'll tell you another thing," he continued, "we're not contentious. Many people are—they argue for the sake of arguing. We don't act that way. We tell each other when we disagree, but we don't fight about our differences of opinion."

"You know, we're really in love," Joan said, almost apologetically. "It may sound silly to say this at my ripe age of eighty." And, having said that, I knew what it was that first attracted me to this elderly couple. It was so simple—they were genuinely in love with each other. You know when you are in the presence of true love.

"We have very strong feelings for each other, both physically and emotionally," affirmed Joan. "We've grown by what we've learned from each other and made it part of ourselves. I can't face anything that has to do with death or either one of us dying."

"She becomes an ostrich," Paul agreed, trying to give some levity to a painful subject.

Two years ago, Paul had open-heart surgery. Joan described her anguish to me. "The doctor had to talk to *me* more than to Paul! It turned out okay, but what if it hadn't?"

I turned the subject of conversation to something more life-affirming: sex. Joan recognized that "sex helps reseed your life together," but as time goes on, she admitted, it becomes less important and just being close is enough. They have kept their double bed and continue to enjoy sleeping together at night. When they hear of friends who are moving to a new apartment and trading their double in for separate twin beds, it "says something" to them.

With an obvious feeling of pride and what I interpreted as an element of innocence, Joan revealed to me that, over the sixty years they have been together, she and Paul have remained faithful to one another—"We were the first and only," she said, deservedly proud.

A pair of living, breathing anachronisms sat before me. "This must be a record," I said, touched by their revelation. "Is there a prize for this longevity?" I teased.

"The prize is the relationship," responded Joan without hesitation, "and the feeling we have for each other. That's not to say I don't enjoy seeing other handsome men or even beautiful women. I'll even point out a beautiful woman to Paul and say, 'Look at that woman, Pauley. Isn't she beautiful?' "

Chapter 10

Proceptivity:
Preparing
the Way

Journal Entry: 7 July 1993

Happy Birthday to me!

"... burning through the shit." That's what I told Deena when she called today. "I'm burning through the shit of relationship," I repeated, even convincing myself, "the projections (mine on him/his on me, my image of myself that I project to him/his image of himself that he projects to me) that assault each other like bumper cars, the intoxication of infatuation, the obsession/compulsion of lust, the addiction to romance, the codependency, the illusions, in short, all the lies we tell ourselves in order to fit into someone else's fantasy. It's over. Finished. If my reality doesn't fit his fantasy—screw the fantasy. I'd rather stay single than go back to the old ways of relating to a man, and I'm *not* staying single! I'm on an expedition to the Country of Marriage."

"So you've met someone," she coyly surmised.

"I may have, but unless I break through the behavioral fossil of adolescent love, I'll be stuck there for the rest of my life. I'm forty-five years old today and, after a lifetime of hard work and by the grace of God, I'm moving through it, burning through the shit. I can feel it. Hallelujah!"

"I don't know any other way to do it," she said, and I knew hers were words of experience.

———————

The process of an individual's integrating the male and the female within her or his own psyche begins at birth and continues until we take our last breath. But there are periods in one's life during which the process is accelerated to such an extent that we can actually track our progress as if it were a scientific experiment. For those pioneers who proudly wave banners that read "Enlightenment or Bust" as they explore the frontiers of their psychological and spiritual landscape, the recording of this process becomes fascinating and resonates with the signposts and signals from ordinary activities, synchronicities, neuroses, fantasies, and dreams.

In May 1991 I spent a few days with Hal Stone and his wife, Sidra, at their home in Mendocino, a charming northern California coastal town. I had interviewed them for this book and also taken the opportunity to have a long therapeutic session with Hal. The session focused on my writing *The Heart of Marriage* and why, after two years, I was still without a man. As with my previous written and visual artwork, I had chosen a subject about which I wanted to learn, one I wanted to grow into, to become. I wanted to explore, to excavate my deep-seated beliefs, hostilities, fears, misunderstandings, and confusion about men, relationship, and marriage. When one takes on this seemingly Sisyphean quest as a vocation, the unconscious begins to reciprocate, to test one's seriousness with outrageous, humorous, and sometimes terrifying and uncanny demands, as well as some rather astonishing gifts—all in the name of growth and transformation. "You asked for it," the unconscious amuses itself by reminding you during those moments of weakness when you beg for mercy. That night, after my meeting with Hal, I had the following dream:

In a sun-filled room there is a little girl, about three or four years old, who is naked and has the normal body of a child that age. She steps up onto a small wooden platform (something like a stage) and says, as if speaking to an audience, although I'm the only other person in the room, "I'm going to show you something that I didn't know I had—and no one else knows about . . ." She speaks with great poise and a lack of self-consciousness. An older woman in her sixties, also naked, comes onto the stage and stands beside the little girl.

The next thing I know I'm on the platform, naked, standing beside the older woman, who remains in the middle. I suddenly realize that I have a penis. It is very long (between eighteen and twenty-four inches) and narrow (perhaps one inch wide). It is flesh-colored, circumcised, and flaccid. My initial reaction is the fear that I'm no longer a woman. I immediately check and find my female genitals perfectly in place as usual.

The penis doesn't seem like a sexual object or tool, more like an umbilical cord. The other woman and the child then show me their penises, which are identical to mine in size and shape. It's like belonging to some secret club of hermaphrodites. The penis seems almost independent in its ability and willingness to cooperate with me through a telepathic means. It is "on my side," so to speak. I feel a sense of extraordinary power, independence, and well-being, as if I belong completely and totally to myself. I am fulfilled within myself. I wake up.

The next morning I wrote in my dream journal. It's an enticing, intriguing dream—a dream of initiation—and seems important in light of my beginning this new project on male/female relationships. However, it does present a conundrum, or a Zen koan, if you will: if I'm so complete and self-sufficient within myself, how can I make room in my life for a man . . . and why would I want to? I think this is one of the issues I will be researching and contemplating during the writing of this book. I faxed a copy of the dream to Hal for his edification and said, "Is this a potent illustration of integrating my animus or what?!"

8 July 1993

Yesterday was my birthday party. Last week, after a bout with the blues I associated both with turning forty-five and entering my fourth year as a single woman, I decided to change its course. Calling several of my closest women friends in northern California, I organized a birthday celebration for myself. My request to each woman was, first, that she hold in her mind the image of me as virginal or complete and whole unto myself and, second, that she carry a vision of me in relationship with the man best suited to be my friend and lover—whoever he may be. This is my way of conjuring my partner. Although I don't put a face on him—love comes in such unexpected packages—I know I'll recognize him by the "feel" of his energy.

Judy said, "I envision for you the ease of a good relationship. It will be smooth for you, no longer a struggle." Sumahsil held the vision of me and my partner comfortably alternating the roles of "the lover and the beloved." Curious. Having experienced both sides of the equation in different relationships, I never thought of these positions of sovereignty and surrender as satisfactorily alternating within *one* relationship. Claire wished for me "a spirit strong enough to bear up under the pressure of ecstasy." Amen! "Remember that just as you are thinking about and looking for him, he is thinking about and looking for you," Deanne reminded me. "And you will find each other."

Last night I felt so loved and loving. Romping and frolicking at my favorite beach. I cooked chicken breasts marinated in orange juice, garlic, and cumin, fresh white corn and sweet pepper salad, spicy black beans, handmade tortillas, mango and avocado salsa, gateau au chocolat and homemade caramel/Babcock peach ice cream for my friends. The elements: sand, wind, ocean and sun/open fire surrounded and soothed us. I realized once more that I can face my depression and break through it by my attitude. I wanted to *celebrate my midlife discoveries*. These are not just words; there's a strength behind them—the power of personal authority harvested from my life experience. I truly can change my life by changing my attitudes.

I recognized and appreciated how living these past several years almost exclusively in the company and comfort of women has healed me. Women are natural healers. I vowed to continue to honor the women in my life and my work with them.

9 July 1993

"I'm the shit you're burning through!" said Robert, the man in my living room sitting opposite me on the couch after I'd read my birthday prose to him. I'd only met him ten days earlier, but already I'd corrupted what little potential there was between us into a deranged fantasy of lust, true love, and "happily ever after." How had he known? As the calamity of projections, illusions, and obsessions (rendering me emotionally dysfunctional) started up once more, I made it my most critical task to break the stranglehold. Thus, my conversation with Deena.

He was right, of course, he (and so many like him) is "the shit I am burning through." And it is as painful and formidable as the labor of childbirth. It *is* a birth in a way: harsh, violent, smelly, bloody, but crucial for a healthy body and a healthy new life. This character flaw is like old chewing gum stuck to my persona. Heloise's Helpful Hints advises ice cubes to remove gum from your hair or clothes; it offers no suggestion for scouring the immaterial substance of one's soul. There is a purification at work here (the proceptivity of preparing my way for marriage), fueled by boredom with the repetiveness of the game—the broken record of romance—and determination.

A further message of the integration underway in my psyche came to me last week in the form of another dream:

I'm traveling alone in Mendocino. I stop at someone's house (it seems to be a gathering place for people of interest and onlookers) and find myself observing the cast of characters. The man I've just met in Berkeley walks in and we eye each other without speaking. After a short period of time, I decide to move on. I don't say anything to anyone, just leave. Sometime later I am at another home that is crowded with people. Again, I find myself people watching rather than becoming actively involved. I'm sitting on the couch where I have a full view of all the activity. Soon the front door opens and in walks the man from Berkeley. He glances at me, but walks into the next room without speaking to me or anyone else. About ten minutes later he walks to the doorway between the rooms and faces me directly for the first time. Without warning, my heart opens to him completely, and, as we stare at each other, I stretch out my arms and open my legs (although there is no sexual intention). He walks over to me and sits with his back to me as I fully encircle him with both my arms and legs. We are comfortable with and comforting for each other; known, recognized. I realize that all I have to do is relax, be calm, luxuriate in tenderness, and be fully myself. I awaken.

I've been slowly making sense of this dream. Each day a new interpretation has surfaced.

1. Originally, it seemed pretty straightforward: I'd met a new man. All I had to do was let it develop naturally between us.

2. Then I remembered that my last partner, François, had been practically haunted by a need to have his woman, me, protect his back. I thought it was a North African superstition or fetish. Because of the circumstances of our relationship and of who I was at the time, I was unable to uphold that part of our bargain. The dream signified to me that I am now prepared to protect a man's back, the back being the part of our body that is most vulnerable because, of course, we are blind there; we cannot see danger behind our own back.

3. The back could also symbolize the unconscious, in that we trust our partner to tell us when we become insensible, when we are blind to our own hubris and ego.

4. Finally, it occurred to me that the dream had nothing to do with the man from Berkeley, François, or any other human male for that matter; it simply had to do with recognizing, meeting, trusting, and embracing my animus, my own inner male. It is the fulfillment of the dream of the three females with penises I had more than two years ago. Much inner work and professional work in the world have been done during the interim and "The Three Graces" have evolved into a recognizable male image: solid, powerful, sensitive, protective, interdependent with the coexisting female, me.

5. The expressive encompassing of the male figure also conveys a willingness and a capacity to contain my animus within me, to assure him that even when a living man enters my life, I will not abandon him as I have done in the past.

This is what Hal had anticipated for me two years ago: "Only when you are complete and self-sufficient within yourself will you have a chance to build a lasting relationship with a man." To carry the theme of integration a step further, at my birthday celebration I wore my colorfully embroidered, white Mexican wedding dress as a reminder of my commitment to my spiritual strengthening and in honor of the inner marriage that is taking place. So be it.

Chapter 11

Love and Marriage in Japan— A Sense of Gratitude

I don't know which one of us will die first, but at that moment, to be able to say to the other one, "Thank you," that's the key. During the decades with each other, you fight, but you can say thank you as you are dying. That is love. That is marriage.

Yoshitaka Nishino

Yoshitaka and Naoe Nishino

Suppose we had never gotten married, we just remained friends; there would not have been any real spiritual advance. It is through the interactions of daily life, through the exchanges that we grow.

Naoe Nishino

I n 1993, I spent the month of September in Japan. A lifelong interest in Japanese culture, art, music, cinema, cuisine, gardens, architecture, and, as I saw it, a core spiritual and aesthetic sensibility had culminated in my being accepted to the Oomoto School for the Traditional Arts of Japan. An Oomoto maxim says, "Art is the mother of religion"; in other words, it is believed that the aesthetic and the spiritual are interconnected, bound by a mutual reciprocity. Every activity (making and drinking tea, writing a letter, practicing a martial art, making love, arranging a vase of flowers) is, at its most fundamental, an opportunity for both sacramental observance and artistic expression.

Oomoto in Japanese calligraphy literally means the Great Origin or the Great Source. And, indeed, one of the elements that drew me to Oomoto is their belief in animism—that animals and objects and nature have soul, that everything in existence comes from one God. This principle and many ritual functions are derived from the Shinto tradition, but a distinguishing characteristic of Oomoto doctrine is its extremely tolerant attitude toward other religions. Therefore, among the other participants in my seminar were Christians, Buddhists, and Jews.

The followers of Oomoto pursue a particular way of life. Oomoto offers more than a religion, because many of its activities and doctrines are involved with secular concerns in politics and economics, culture and education, art and science. Both partners in one couple I met through Oomoto are each descended from families who have been devoted followers of Oomoto principles for generations. Yoshitaka and Naoe Nishino worked for many years in the Oomoto offices in Kameoka near Kyoto and live with their sixteen-year-old son, Shotaro. Yoshitaka was chief of external affairs, or public relations. Naoe had the task of ordering and classifying over one hundred years' worth of photographs and negatives belonging to the organization. In 1994, Yoshitaka left the administration of Oomoto and now works with Alex Kerr, a transplanted American scholar of Japanese art and culture. However, through Alex's work with the International Department of Oomoto, and as a volunteer, Yoshitaka continues to keep an active involvement in Oomoto. As we did not share a common language, Alex was generous enough to offer not only accurate translation, but a sensitive intelligence and humorous insight.

Oddly enough, our discussion of marriage began with the topic of divorce. Alex specified that the Nishinos were not the typical Japanese couple I might interview. Because they are Oomoto followers and their parents were Oomoto followers, a strong teaching about the sacredness of marriage has been instilled in them. The fact that they had spent five years getting to know each other *before* they married combined with the implied threat that Naoe's father would "murder" her if she even thought of divorce has added to their solidarity.

Although Yoshitaka admitted he would understand that people who were totally incompatible would want to get divorced, the thought of getting a divorce over something "silly like having an affair" wouldn't have occurred to him "in a million years." Only a few days earlier the couple had passed their nineteenth wedding anniversary; Yoshitaka, who had forgotten, mocked, "We could get divorced any minute now!"

They found it advantageous in the earlier years of their marriage that Yoshitaka worked at Oomoto. His position then was exactly like that of a salaried man in a big corporation: he worked very late at night and had little time with the family. But because Naoe was familiar with his work and responsibilities and *believed* in what he was doing, she actually appreciated the nature and importance of his job and did not begrudge his time away from home. However, nowadays Yoshitaka has more time at home, and he feels that the timing for this is good. "When he was younger, our son, Shotaro, needed Naoe more than me," he said, "but now, at the age of sixteen, he needs a father at home."

"Naoe said something, which I also think is true about him," Alex added. "It's the way he thinks. He gives advice to her based on Oomoto and its teachings, but he has a wide view and it's personally very helpful to her. It's actually a very good description. That's why everyone wants to talk to him." As if on cue, Yoshitaka was called to a meeting with the new director of the Kyoto newspaper.

During his absence, Naoe's answers became longer and more animated. It was as if a space opened up for her to be more expressive. "He gives me a sort of spiritual wealth; it's certainly not material," she laughed, "but it is very important."

"Has it made a difference being married?" I asked.

Naoe believed so. "Suppose we had never gotten married, we just remained friends; there would not have been any real spiritual advance. Because we are married means that we have a child and we live with Yoshitaka's parents and it is through the interactions of daily life, through the exchanges, that we grow."

"How has it been living with your in-laws?" I queried. "In America it would be perceived as a nightmare."

She felt the same way in the beginning. "The first few years were difficult, partly because both my mother-in-law and I tended to be reserved and we didn't know where the line should be drawn and what areas to stay out of in each other's lives. Over time, I became more and more comfortable, and I feel I gained a lot.

"I was never out in the world on my own. I went straight from school to Oomoto and from Oomoto to my marriage. So I never had much experience in the 'rough and tumble.' I've learned so much by watching Yoshitaka's parents: how they treat people or handle things, plus hearing them talk is useful. Through them I meet older people in Kameoka and I learn how to wait for them, how to be more patient. But in general, instead of making decisions on your own, having experiences on your own, I have learned to incorporate them into the larger picture of what I am doing. Living with them has made me a stronger person and I am better for it."

Naoe also stressed that living with her husband's parents has given her insight into him, to see how he was brought up and what his values were. At first, however, she didn't know "what in the world to do" and she cried a lot. "But he supported me very much. That was one of the points at which our relationship became stronger."

Alex explained to me that typically in Japanese households the son totally supports his parents, especially his mother. So what Naoe said about his supporting her as his wife was fairly important and somewhat exceptional. She feels that Yoshitaka is extremely fair and considerate of both sides. In fact, "I feel that he is probably the one who has been in the hardest position, actually," she said sympathetically.

"How do you resolve anger and disputes?" I inquired.

"It's changed over the years," Naoe explained. "In the old days I would get furious but was unable to express it. So then he would get frustrated and say, 'Whatever it is you are so angry about, let's talk about it,' but I couldn't, so he would then get angry, too. Usually after a day or two it would blow over. Eventually the one- or two-day periods got shorter and shorter as I became better able to cope with whatever was making me angry."

Alex described Naoe's position: "She feels these days that she's becoming a little 'larger,' as they say in Japanese, in the sense that she can give more and doesn't get angry. She has become more forgiving."

"Does that come naturally from the years you have been married?" I asked.

"It is the time," Naoe replied, "but, in order to live together, you have to make compromises and you must learn how to do that. I think we were both very spoiled. My husband was the older son, who, in Japan, is always the spoiled, special one. I was the last child in a large family, also the spoiled one. So, before marrying, both of us tended to have an easy way with everything. Through living together we became more adult, better human beings.

"There is a teaching at Oomoto that when you are worried or upset, your spirit shrinks, and when you are happy, your spirit is larger. We are able to literally sense that about each other and see when one of us is upset and then we try to talk about the issue together and advise each other."

The Oomoto community and teachings have been a thread through their entire married life. Naoe said that in the secular world outside their community, a couple may have ten components that bring them together, and if one goes wrong, that might be grounds for divorce. In Oomoto thought, if there are ten components and only one that is right, that is something to work on to keep the couple together. An Oomoto belief is that the whole point of a family is to bring two people of different personalities together to create children. From a larger perspective, that's what a religious community is: many different people with different ideas and views all aiming at the same goals.

Yoshitaka, who had returned from his interview with the Kyoto press, was quick to point out to me, however, that, as far as he is concerned, "To do something because Oomoto told you to do it, or *not* to do it, is nonsense, or to have a certain kind of marriage because Oomoto taught you to is nonsense. It's really the opposite. It's what you experience through your ten or twenty years of marriage that you then return to the Oomoto teachings and say, 'Ah-ha, that's what it's about, that's what it means!' But if you get too bound up in the religion and its teachings, then you shrink as a human being."

I was curious to know if romance played as large a role in Japanese marriages as couples in the West expect it to.

"First of all," Naoe revealed, "we knew each other a long time before we got married. We lived in dormitories, but we were together every night until we had to go back to our dorms. We did not sleep together until we announced our marriage before the gods. It was like the coming together of yin and yang, two different personalities and abilities. So when we finally got married, it was like a snap."

Yoshitaka laughed when he heard this and agreed.

"It started out as a romance but it became love. Now we are like water and air to each other," Naoe concluded.

That sounded pretty romantic to me. In America you might hear newlyweds describe themselves in a similar poetic fashion, but you would rarely hear a couple who has been married for nineteen years speak about being the basic elements for each other.

Those early years of constant togetherness seemed to root in them a trust and respect. Actually they probably spend less time together since being married, "so maybe that's kept it fresh," said Naoe.

From his point of view, Yoshitaka said, "You can't eat honey every day for every meal. If it's something you want to eat every time for all your life, you want a little lighter flavor, something more like water, something as pure as that.

"Traditionally the Japanese did not express their feelings of love for each other as freely as Westerners, but that is changing rapidly with TV and movies. So the members of the younger generation today are very different from their parents. In fact, the young generation of men is now looking back nostalgically to the older, more modest, generation of women.

"It's probably true everywhere, even in the West, that when you've been married a long time, and you ask for something, you don't even have to say what it is. You just say,

'Could you bring me that uh—' and the other person knows exactly what you mean. That's ideal."

Early in their marriage, Yoshitaka spent five years as an Oomoto missionary.* He came to be respected and sought out as a marriage counselor. When a couple wanted to get a divorce, he would always ask one question: "Why did you get married?" They would respond, "We loved each other at the time." If they continued to complain about each other he would say, "*you* are the one who made this choice irresponsibly, so before you start blaming the other person, you have to examine yourself. In all things there are beginnings and endings."

My next question: "Why has the institution of marriage become so impermanent?"

Yoshitaka thought it was due to a lack of religious feeling. "Not that you have to belong to one certain sect or another, but a basic lack of spiritual understanding. Although there are a lot of religions around, they are not necessarily spiritual. So people don't know what to do; they are at a loss.

"Japan has a very low divorce rate, compared to the West, because we are taught to be patient and endure. It's not that there are so many happy marriages, but there are a lot of patient people enduring unhappy marriages. Although that background in Japanese culture that teaches people to be patient and endure can actually be beneficial and is probably really necessary in love."

"What advice would you give to other couples?" I asked.

The answer given by Yoshitaka seemed to be somewhat in conflict. To the husband he might say, "The more you are dominated by your wife, the better for you."

"Is that on a business level, financial, in the home?" I asked.

"In Japan that is usually considered *not* a good thing; traditionally the man is not supposed to be under the thumb of his wife. But in fact when you see Japanese families that work well, the best ones are where the wife sort of does everything and the husband keeps quiet and stays out of the way."

Then came, what seemed to me, the contradiction. "If I would say anything to the wife, it would be, 'See if you can be a good secretary to your husband.' "

"Perhaps that explains why Naoe is the ultimate secretary—she is totally competent in everything," Alex added.

---

*The term *missionary* is somewhat of a misnomer here as it implies conversion. In Oomoto a missionary is one who attends to other followers who might live somewhat isolated from their Oomoto community and keeps them conversant with changes and new teachings.

"If you think of parents and children," said Yoshitaka poignantly, "there is a blood bond between them; whether they like each other or not, they are bound together. But a husband and wife, no matter how close, are actually *not* related. Even after decades they are still different people. That's why you should always think about the other one first. Also you should feel a sense of gratitude toward the other person. To feel gratitude toward your parents, that's natural, but to feel gratitude to the person who is not inherently bound to you in any way, except by the fact that they *are* with you, has to be learned.

"I don't know which one of us will die first, but at that moment, to be able to say to the other one, 'Thank you,' that's the key. During the decades with each other, you fight, but you can say thank you as you are dying. That is love. That is marriage. There's one more thing I'd like to say to Naoe. It is, 'Please don't die before me.'"

Chapter 12

What
We Talk
About
When
We Talk
About
Sex

There exist two
great modes of
life—the religious
and the sexual.

D. H. LAWRENCE

T his is what it means to be a woman, I thought to myself after seeing *The Seven-Year Itch.* I was only six years old at the time. From that movie I learned that sexiness brings attention (and possibly affection). Sex is alluring. Men are enticed by a sexy woman. And I never forgot it. The celluloid aphrodisiac of Marilyn Monroe not only captivated every male's fantasies, it captured the imagination of females of all ages. Although it took me years to figure out what the "itch" was, the liquid sensuousness of Marilyn's bodily movements, the radiance of her platinum hair, the breathy, little-girl quality of her voice could spell out only one thing: sex. Marilyn *was* the personification of sex, and she continued to haunt me as the role model for the expression of my libido through my adolescence, my twenties and thirties, and into my forties.

The news reached me on Sunday morning after eleven o'clock Mass on 5 August 1962: Marilyn Monroe is dead. I stood on the church steps of Our Lady of Mercy by the Sea as my grandfather rushed up to tell me. I was too stunned to even ask the circumstances. I had just turned fourteen the previous month, and I had already been in a woman's body for two years. I had quickly learned to encourage the attention it brought to the lonely little girl living inside. Marilyn had been a good teacher and I had graduated with honors from the School of Marilyn. All that was necessary for this course of study was repeated viewings of her films, especially *Some Like It Hot, Niagara, Bus Stop, River of No Return, The Asphalt Jungle, Let's Make Love,* and her final (completed) film, *The Misfits,* and hours in front of a mirror. This, of course, was pre-video days, so I had to be especially vigilant to catch the films when they returned to theaters and take advantage of the first runs when they came to my small town.

As it did for the rest of the world, my obsession with Marilyn continued and grew until I realized that it didn't serve me well and was actually detrimental. By the time I was forty, I had perfected my impersonation of the great female impersonator. And I had grown tired. Sex had developed into a performance art for me. It didn't have to do with orgasm. I wasn't satisfied until each new man I fell in love with told me I was "the best show in town," "the sexiest woman around." But I got fed up with sex as aerobics. Performing had dulled my sensuality. By the time I left my last relationship, I knew that a period of celibacy was the only course I wanted to follow. Gaining fifty pounds ensured that course and became my armor against men and my insulation against my own desire.

Being single and celibate during these past six years has taught me about what so often is missing from sex: true intimacy—emotional, spiritual, and physical intimacy. Intimacy has nothing to do with being multiorgasmic; it is a surrender to vulnerability. Intimacy is disquieting and challenging; it is the effect of being present and spontaneous with oneself and the beloved; it is the result of being known. By *not* having sex I've been able to understand just what sex means to me. It isn't a question of exchanging something *for* sex, because a genuine exchange of souls *can be* sexual. It isn't about the endless lists we read of what makes people good in bed, either, or the lists of activities we should explore and experiments we should do to get more sexy.

In order to move beyond my imprinted childhood notion of eroticism and the influence of Madison Avenue, I needed a vacation from it. I don't mean to idealize celibacy and pathologize sex—I often miss the lustful craving that quickens us to roll on our backs and fornicate—I just needed some relief from the tyranny of sex that I had created for myself. I wanted a respite from pulling it toward me, pushing it away, or numbing out to it. In Buddhism it's called passion, aggression, and ignorance. I still deeply believe in passion: passion for my work, the world, life, and, yes, passion in love. I have given aggression (or assertion) to other areas in my life, primarily professional ones. And ignorance, well, I'm still working on that one. But sex is no longer my vocation, no longer holds the promise of happiness and fulfillment that it once did.

We can bond with another through sex when we realize that there is an entire world open to us beyond copulation, when we see that, like creativity, it can be kindled by our every action. An act of kindness or consideration can be a turn-on. And I agree with Timothy Leary, who said that "intelligence is the greatest aphrodisiac." Sex is a way of resting into another, a way of understanding, accepting, forgiving our loved one. Anna Keck understood this when she said, "There's a bonding that happens through sexuality and spirituality, a complete downtime of letting go. It's not particularly about making love, it's that the lovership is part of the friendship and, if it is a healthy, vital part, *can* make one more forgiving."

One of the great questions for couples in long-term relationships is how to maintain sexual desire for each other. According to Leonard Rosenblum, it is "partly through the *continuous* redefinition of what you mean by sexuality. An evening of real intimacy may or may not include genital sex. For both of us, the intimacy of touching and contact is very important."

Leonard's wife, June Reinisch, added, "We have both made a conscious, verbal commitment to the sexuality of this relationship, and keeping it alive. In modern life, it's very easy for the spark to disappear when everything else—work, children, sickness—seems to take precedence and overwhelm the relationship. In a way, sexuality, which is much more ephemeral when you're not just getting to know each other, has to be fought for and defended by both members of the couple."

Perhaps the best sex or the most enduring sexual relationship is, as D. H. Lawrence, the primitive Priest of Love himself, describes it: a combination of the spiritual and the sexual. If this is true, then surely intimacy is their bridge and love is their anchor.

Chapter 13

A Mutual Commitment to Joy and Pleasure

Leonard Rosenblum and June Reinisch

Who has the right to demand that all their needs be met by a marriage partner? I feel it is my responsibility to meet my own needs and Len's responsibility to meet his needs. What we do for each other is enrich each other's lives and support each other in our searches, our development, and give each other pleasure—that's a big one—it's not all puritan work.

June Reinisch

I was very happy to get married; I continue to be happy we got married. It's hard to pin down, but for me, it's not so much the public statement; it's more the sense of connection with the historical precedent. I like feeling the continuity with the past, with my parents.

Leonard Rosenblum

Although June Reinisch has always aspired to be a pint-sized Katharine Hepburn, to me she seems to carry the looks, energy, and panache of a Shirley MacLaine. Of course her short reddish-blond hair, sparkling blue eyes, and pixie demeanor emphasize that comparison. Think of *The Apartment, Sweet Charity,* not the subject matter, but the star quality, and you get my point.

Leonard Rosenblum's tall, fluid carriage conveys his lineage; he comes from a long line of psychologists. The graying beard and suggestive pipe seem *de rigueur* to that image. But, in the last few years, he has added another hat (or beret)—that of *artiste!*

Scientist, psychologist, professor, administrator describe each of them, but you could accurately include comedian/comedienne and talk show host. You can almost march to the cadence of their speech as they speak simultaneously; they echo each other's sentences and finish each other's thoughts. Welcome to "The Len and June Show."

———————————

"June is an immensely competent person, in all kinds of ways," said Len. "She is very well organized. That is not to say that I always agree with that competency, but nonetheless, she's very competent and I am not threatened by that competency."

"In fact," June returned, "he'd like me to take over everything and then he would just lie there and smoke his pipe. His secret wish is to just be an artist and be taken care of."

"That's true," Len admitted, smiling as he reclined on the sofa, pipe dangling from the left corner of his mouth. "It's not that because I'm an artist I don't care about order . . ."

". . . he's against it on principle!"

"That's exactly right," he nodded. "As a scientist, that attitude is opposed to the whole first part of my life, which was very linear: go to school, get to a class, get a job, get tenure, get a professorship. Now, when I'm not doing that, my feeling is, pardon the phrase, 'fuck whatever.' I don't want to write down what I'm supposed to do tomorrow, because, frankly, if I forget it, good. That is something that drives June up the wall."

"It drives me nuts that he forgets things. I have enough trouble remembering the things in my multilayered life, but then somehow I think it's my responsibility to remember things for you in your life."

"Other than urging me to exercise, which I also put in the same ballpark."

"Everything he doesn't like he labels as work and work is bad. Very simple formula."

"Simple formula. Absolutely."

"It doesn't have to do with money or getting paid for an activity. For him it is literally whatever he doesn't like to do. It could be in an arena that has nothing to do with work, that other people would say, 'This is pleasure, to go exercise and get healthy.' Anything that has to do with health, in my husband's opinion, is work and therefore he hates it."

"I'll give you an example. I don't like to prepare canvases. I don't want *work*. I'm there to have fun. I don't want to spend two hours getting ready to have some fun. Doesn't that make sense?"

As a painter myself for thirty-five years, I had no quarrel there.

"I have to admit," Leonard continued, "I'm my favorite artist. If I have any jealousies, it's that I don't like giving wall space to other people."

Suddenly a red squirrel appeared on their deck carrying a dead mouse. "Oh, Lenny, our carnivorous friend has come to visit us," June squealed. "Aren't you glad I got the squirrel feeder?"

"Talk about nice neighbors!" was Leonard's comeback.

———————————

For ten years, although the couple lived together, they also maintained residences seven hundred and fifty miles apart. Living separately half the time came out of the complexities of the beginning of their relationship: June worked in Indiana as the director of the Kinsey Institute for Research in Human Sexuality and Len worked as the head of the primatology lab at the Medical Center of the State University of New York in Brooklyn. Their independent spaces turned out to be a fortuitous arrangement for Leonard, who had lived with a woman his entire life, going from his mother's house to his first wife and now to June.

"So in 1983 when we got an apartment together, I flew in and out of New York a couple times a month and Len would come and visit me. But for the first time in his life (which I think is extremely important) he lived alone. He found out in fact that he could do it and, actually, enjoy living alone."

"Self-sufficiency was something I had never examined in myself, at least in being alone. That definitely was a maturing time for me, in the sense that it enhanced my self-esteem. I think I'd always had pretty good self-esteem professionally, intellectually, socially, what not . . ."

"And friends, my God, the most popular boy in the United States!" teased June. "He has more friends than any human in the world. This man has more *best* friends, *men* best friends—he also has women best friends—than anyone I know. His men best friends are seated all over the globe, and they all love him, and he loves them."

Leonard was on his way to Siena, Italy, the very next day, it turned out, to spend two weeks with one of his multiple best friends.

In a manner akin to free association in psychology, the discussion led to my beloved springer spaniel, Sienna, and his importance to me in having someone to love and be loved by. June asked, "Do you know how many thousands of years people have worked to make those animals what they are? One of those purposes is for loving."

"I'm a believer," I confirmed.

"June and I share the conviction that while the sense of being loved is very important to human survival, something that is underplayed is that for many of us being in a position *to* love and being *able* to love is just as important as being loved."

"Maybe more important," June reasoned, "because it changes you. It grows you. The *act* of loving is great."

"I've known couples where men—and I've seen it in women, too—are frustrated in their wish to express love. The getting, the doing is either ignored or abused or rejected," explained Leonard. "In successful relationships, I think, this is something that couples know how to do: they know how to let their partner love them. It's very important."

"One of the ultimate values shared between Len and me is that love in friendship and family has to take precedence over work or anything else. When a decision has to be made, it's always made in the service of friends, family, and love. Len has helped me to define that in my own life.

"Maybe you disagree with me," she questioned Leonard, "but even though we're first for each other, we have great respect for each other's relationships outside our own. We think it's vital for each individual to have people outside their couple to love and care about and interact with. The point is to have a rich life, to grow as much as you can, learn as much as you can, and have lots of input."

"If you expect one other person to fill all your needs, you're headed for disappointment," I observed.

"Who has the right to demand that all their needs be met by a marriage partner?" asked June. "I feel it is my responsibility to meet my own needs and Len's responsibility to meet his needs. What we do for each other is enrich each other's lives and support each other in our searches, our development, and give each other pleasure—that's a big one— it's not all puritan work."

"The boundaries between trust and appreciation are important ones," Leonard continued. "So often you see married people who are terribly jealous of their partner's relationships with others. What is the nature of the jealousy? They feel left out, underappreciated, they feel in some sense abandoned."

"Their fear is that their partner will like their friend better."

" 'If you really loved me, why would you be with her instead of me?' "

" 'Why would you *need* anybody else?' "

"There's a big difference between a person reluctantly *accepting* their partner's other friendships and activities and *appreciating* them, feeling that they are important and enhancing to that person's well-being. June made this distinction from the start: she saw the fact that I had all these close friendships, and rather than see them as a threat to her, she saw them as a very positive statement about who I was.

"And we also realize that, although each person is the totality of themselves, the Me that exists in the space that June and I have together is unique to that space. In other words, if, God forbid, something were to happen to June, if she were to die, then not just in an emotional sense but in a very real sense, a part of me would cease to exist because of her death. There is a Me that exists in this relationship that does not exist elsewhere. That is true and that is how I felt also when one of my friends was ill for a while. I remember thinking about what it was I was grieving for. I realized, in a way that first embarrassed me and I later accepted, that to some degree I was grieving for myself. What was going to be lost was a part of Me that would cease to exist if he died. I understand that June can have a variety of experiences with me, but with her girlfriends she has a kind of merging quality that can't be duplicated."

"One of the things that allows this to happen is that I feel absolutely convinced that, bottom line, if Len had to make a choice between me and everybody else, anybody else, at anytime, I would be first. Therefore, whether it's true or not, I feel confident that there is no competition. He can go off and do what he needs to do with his friends.

"We are extremely committed to honesty and communication. The best indication of the fact we communicate a lot is that when we commuted for eleven years, we spoke every night on the phone, for an average of an hour. That's not an exaggeration. In fact, we often spoke a lot longer. Even overseas we would skip only a day because of the different time zones, but it always bothered us. When people asked us how we handled the commuting thing, we would say, 'Well, you know what the data are on how much time couples who live together talk to each other? It's twenty minutes a day.' Our phone bills were enormous, but we maintained the continuity, the day-to-dayness of the relationship."

"How do you fight?" I asked.

"Our fights are about who we are in this moment, if one of us being interfered with by the other," June began. "Fighting is one of the ways you learn to know each other. You really have to confront each other, I think."

"June was great! At the end of a battle she would say, 'That was terrific. Oh, boy, you really stuck up for yourself.' You have to remember that our training in psychology makes for a sort of self-analysis; the sense of self-observation is such that when we would get done having one of these battles, after we calmed down and made up, one or the other of us would say, 'I particularly liked the touch where you threw the glass.' "

"And the other would say, 'Yes, I had the feeling that was effective.' "

" 'I thought that was good. What'd you think of the time I did this?' 'No, that seemed false. It didn't move me.' "

"The interesting thing is that now, and I guess for the last five years or so, we don't get into that anymore. The real anger now lasts perhaps ten minutes or so. We have worked it out so that we don't get to that point."

"Yeah, it's too bad!" complained Leonard.

"That doesn't mean we don't yell, but it's rare and very short-lived and we usually re-solve it, apologize or whatever. So we believe that previous era was important. We gained more trust and knowledge of the other. We made this rule that, no matter what was going on, we weren't allowed to leave. We had to stay in the arena until it was over. Sometimes that might take six or seven hours of sometimes heated, sometimes calm discussion.

"One of the reasons we don't have those kinds of fights anymore, I'm convinced, is because we really know the other person loves us. It's difficult to sustain those feelings for long when you know the other person loves you and wants you to be happy. We call it the reservoir of goodwill. So it only takes us ten minutes to remember that this is the person who loves us and wants our happiness. Clearly, if there is a problem, we have to get to the root of that, figure it out and resolve it. It's either a misunderstanding, or the person has done something unconsciously or that they didn't mean to do."

"That need to 'figure it out' is part of our training, both culturally and profession-ally," Leonard acknowledged. "We have a sense of the unconscious motives that people have and of which they are unaware. I know when I counsel friends who are having bat-tles, I'm prone to say, 'You aren't fighting over the restaurant; neither of you gives a damn about the restaurant. You can spend two days arguing over who said what, when, but the real question will remain unaddressed.'"

My old issue of overfamiliarity in relationship was once again raised. June and Leonard seem entirely fascinated with one another. No boredom there.

"You know why most men are boring?" June asked me. "It's because they are unable to reveal themselves. They are not essentially boring. Over time, the surface is not inter-esting. When you get down to it, it's not Len's art that enthralls me, it's what he's think-ing about it, why he's doing what he's doing. People have to be courageous enough and safe enough to reveal themselves and they have to have *thought* about it so they can articu-late it.

"One of the things you look for in a long-term relationship is somebody—and you never know until it happens of course—who, when there is trouble, is going to be there by your side and help you to be stronger. So there's the teamwork aspect of relationship; we work very well as a team during all kinds of problems. We have each taken turns at being the support. Then you deal with the kind of support it's going to be. I'm a problem solver, so if Len tells me about a problem, my immediate response is, 'That's terrible; here's what we should do about it.' I know Len would like a little empathy, some response to the emotional aspects of the problem before it gets solved."

"That's right. I'd like her to say, 'Awww, Jeez, that must be terrible. That son-of-a-bitch.' Instead she goes, 'Okay, here's what we're gonna do: Write a letter to the president and tell him'. . . That's it! 'Next.'"

"Len is better at the emotional stuff, but sometimes doesn't provide me with the 'What would you do?' aspect. We sort of both straddle the currently popular stereotypes—each with one foot on Venus and one foot on Mars. We are a good match in that way. And you can't expect the person to be exactly what you want them to be at every particular moment; they provide you with their treasure, and that treasure is what it is. In his case, it's a great treasure but not exactly every piece I might need for every occasion."

———————————

I thought my next question a particularly good one for these two, with their training in psychology. "Can a good marriage heal childhood wounds?"

Rather than the word "heal," June chose "repair," which indeed does seem more accurate, because for many of us those early woundings never disappear. They are the warp and weft that constitute our character and personalities and, in many ways, the very fabric of our physical being. They saturate the texture of our lives.

"You have to be healthy enough to be able to take a risk with a person. And they have to be healthy enough to be able to respond appropriately to that risk that you take. If you at least have that much, you can repair each other tremendously, but sometimes you've been so damaged in childhood that you can't take your own risk or receive it from the other. You've got to find somebody healthy enough. Then you can do miraculous things with each other, because you can remake the parental relationship. A good marriage is *everything*: it's friendship, parent-ship, it's being each other's brother or sister, it's child-ship—it's every possible relationship rolled into one. I don't mean that it resolves all the wounds, but you can do all kinds of repair as well as growth.

"You get to be the child, the father or mother, the sister or brother, you get to be the friend and the lover. You get to play all those roles and receive all those roles in your partner."

"When does it not work?" Leonard invited. "When your injury and your partner's injury are in some sense similar, so that you don't want to hear about or deal with that particular injury, because it is touching—whether or not you are conscious of it—that unresolved place inside yourself."

"So, basically," I said, "you have to find someone who is curious, perhaps curious to the same degree you are, who wants to probe, to reveal, as much as you do."

"Yes," June concurred. "They have to be healthy enough, curious enough so that they won't disappear, they won't be unduly frightened, that they will catch your ball and not let it go bouncing off."

"Remember, however, that this is one model of marriage that June and I ascribe to rigorously, vigorously, emotionally. It's not the only model that works, but it works for us."

"One of the things a marriage needs in order to work long-term," June theorized, "is a mutual commitment to joy and pleasure. You have to both agree and work in your own ways to make sure there is fun. I consider fun to be very serious! You work toward that—whatever that means for each couple. Whether it's regularly going to the opera together or sharing wonderful wines or traveling or just spending time together. Len and I will say to each other, 'Now tomorrow, we're not going out of the house; we're going to watch three videos and eat all the bad food that we're not supposed to eat.' We'll take a twenty-four hour period off, and only do what we want. But it might be different for other couples. I love to travel and Len likes it, too, once he gets there."

"That's right. Being the woman in the relationship," he mocked, "I'm much more the homebody, the cook. I like to travel, but I need to have a nest."

"I want to put on our safari clothes and go out and ride elephants into the jungle," June laughed.

"Back to this idea of repair," Leonard said, "it's not just being tolerant of your partner's foibles. Obviously if they are serious and you can't live with them, you've got to work on them. But I think it's very important to get a kick out of your partner. I will watch June on television or at a party. It's not just that I'm judging, which I do because we want to be sure that she's doing it right . . ."

"If I make a mistake, he's going to tell me when I get home. I don't mind that, I trust his judgment."

"I find myself sitting there smiling saying, 'Good one. Good one. Yeah, right!' That element—and I can't think of a better way of describing it than getting a kick out of your partner—is so important, particularly those things about which your partner may not feel all that comfortable within themselves. So I talk too much, as you may have already gathered, and in certain situations, people (or June) will stop me, sometimes physically. I can just go on indefinitely. It's not uncommon at the end of an evening with other people for both of us to say, 'You didn't let me say a word.' "

"I'll say, 'That was after I struggled to get in there.' I'm the kind of person, in most social situations, who would rather hear what other people have to say. I get to listen to Len all the time, and I love it. He's fascinating, but during many hours of talking

I'd like to hear who the other people are and what they are thinking. Len is perfectly willing . . ."

". . . to hear myself; true, no question!"

―――――――――

"How are you able to maintain a sense of romance and sexual desire for each other after twenty years?" I posed.

"I think it's nice if you love each other," June cracked. "Things are different all the time for us. See, we're not into a routine, and I don't think we ever will be. I'm very unroutinized, in fact. The way he feels about work, I feel about routine. I don't want to wake up at the same hour any two mornings in a row. Len likes routine more than I."

"I've heard June say on the air, as part of the answer to how do you keep sexuality going, that it's partly through the *continuous* redefinition of what you mean by it. If you're talking about eighteen-year-olds sticking it in and taking it out, that changes. That changes through a compounding of time together, since all of us get older not younger. Those two things—redefinition and time—march in step with one another. An evening of real intimacy may or may not have genital sex. That balance of certain elements of intimacy gets defined, redefined, refined—whatever is the right word—at different times. There may be a period in which genital sex may be a prominent element of the intimacy, but for both of us, the intimacy of touching and contact is very important."

"Then, I think," continued June, "you have to have a conscious, outward commitment to your sexuality, which many couples don't. And as a couple, you need to become sort of an intimacy police, in that both of you are charged with a responsibility to make sure that it doesn't get lost. That's another shared value that is expressed in our relationship.

"It's also, 'Am I still sexy to you?' which seems to be very important, even when you are ninety. We have both made a conscious, verbal commitment to the sexuality of this relationship, and keeping it alive. In modern life, it's very hard because it's easy for the spark to disappear. It disappears because everything else—work, children, sickness—seems to take precedence and overwhelm the relationship. In a way, sexuality, which is much more ephemeral when you're not just getting to know each other, has to be fought for and defended by both members of the couple. You have to have a verbal commitment to do that."

"Sex is not just in bed. It's June coming over to me and saying, 'What am I, a piece of wood? You haven't kissed me in twenty minutes! What is this? I can live alone! I need this?' We do that with each other. One element to romance for me is the sense that I'm on June's mind when we're apart. So I love it when she comes home and says, 'I was doing this, but I kept thinking you would have just loved it. I kept wishing—it would have been so much better if—you were there.' "

"That's what flowers mean, and men don't understand that. They mean he thought of you when he was away and stopped for two minutes and said, 'I'll get pink ones' and brought them home. That's the meaning; it's not the *flowers*. So I'm very big on gifts. I love it when I get a present, but I always bring him presents, too. They can be little things; it doesn't matter. The fact is that it's a tangible proof of thought when the person wasn't there."

"I like the idea of us as a couple," Leonard said. "I like the idea that we are these two characters . . ."

". . . who are getting more eccentric. We like eccentricity and actually encourage it in each other."

"Sometimes I'll get an image of the two of us sort of floating through various scenes, and I'll have the sense that 'they couldn't do it with anybody else but each other.' That is a romantic feeling for me."

————————

It was my turn again. "Being in similar fields, do you find you are competitive with each other?"

"In general," June began, "we are both very competitive people, but not with each other. There's a commitment—although not at the expense of other people—to be the best ones."

"The key is whether an achievement of June's is experienced as a threat to me. You understand, in our culture, it's one thing for her to be Mrs. Rosenblum; it's another for me to be Mr. Reinisch. Now, when I go with June, as I often do, and I am the spouse who runs the slide projector for her or what-not, and she's the star, I'm often seen as Mr. Reinisch under those circumstances."

"Are you?" June asked in a concerned voice.

"Sure. The question becomes, and probably is a more defined question for a man, 'Do her achievements and recognition and accolades diminish me or enhance me?' I take the view they enhance me. I take the view of 'I got someone second rate here? No, I'm the one with the star.' Not only am I the one, I'm the only *possible* one. This woman is such a piece of work that I'm the only person in the world—and I absolutely, unequivocally believe this—who can fully appreciate June. I absolutely believe that!"

They both believe in the Jewish concept of Ba'shert, in which two people are destined for each other. It's the idea that your other half is walking around the globe somewhere in search of you. Leonard and June feel that they were fated to be together, and, at the same time, they are still very lucky to have found each other. One of the problems with that theory, however, as Leonard explained, is that people tend to seek a partner who is already a perfect match. "There has to be a certain amount of that, obviously, but the commitment to *evolve* together has to be there, too. Not the attitude of 'I'm perfect and all I have to do is find a woman who is perfect.'"

"In any long relationship," said June, "there are going to be days—or even longer periods—in which life intervenes in some way on your feelings for each other. But if you have that reservoir of goodwill, you can fall back on your commitment to *act* loving toward that person, and you'll get through those periods without the earthquakes that many people experience and lose each other in the process."

"One of June's characteristics that was an extremely important attractant for me is that she knew the difference between the things that matter and the things that don't matter. Not that we don't make mistakes and sometimes put one in the wrong category, but we have the general sense, first of all, that there *are* things out there that matter a lot, lot more than other things. I believe I certainly couldn't spend my life with someone who mixed those up."

"It's also essential that you are able to admit when you are wrong. That's the ultimate vulnerability. It sounds so simple, so stupid, but to be able to say to your partner, 'I was wrong. I did it wrong. I said it wrong. I acted wrong.'"

"Actually, I said that once to her."

"I'm very good at admitting when I'm wrong. He's not *quite* as good."

"You're more practiced; you're wrong more often!"

We had surveyed their similarities, but what about their differences? It was clear to see that Leonard was the worrier in the family and that June was more action oriented, again an indication of their traditional role reversals. "I'm *more* action oriented," June corrected me. "That doesn't mean I don't worry, but my response to worry and anxiety is to act. His is to worry some more."

"That's true."

"But we balance each other that way."

"We scientists say, you can't run life as a control group; it's not an experiment. You can't say, 'Okay, I lived my life this way, now I will try to do it the other way; we'll see which is better and that's the one I'll use.' Can't do that.

"Here's another difference," June continued. "I'm an optimist, he's a pessimist. So I'm the active optimist, which you have to be, I think, in order to be an actor. My philosophy is don't worry about it until it happens. Don't do a lot of worrying in advance. You have to put a little anxiety into it in advance or you might not do what you need to do to get it to happen. You can't just lie back, but don't get into a serious worry because often it doesn't happen and then you've wasted all that time, worrying about something that never came to be."

"As scientists you must have a distinct perspective on why marriages are so much harder to sustain today than they seem to have been in the past," I said. As usual, June responded first.

"People defined marriage much differently in the past. They were willing to put up with a great deal in order to have this relationship that permitted them to take part in adult society. As of even a few decades ago, you had to have a marriage in order to participate in your society. So people were willing to give up a great deal of joy and pleasure in order to have this form, this institution, this contract. Many people are now demanding love and emotional support within their marriage on an ongoing basis. That's a very big demand, and we can't expect it to work the same way anymore. If people are unhappy they don't stay, because now you *can* be a single person, or divorced or remarried, and still participate fully in the culture."

"All right, so playing devil's advocate," I interjected, "why marriage?"

"Len was not pushed to get married; he thought we should just live together. And I, the '60s wild one, felt it was important to be married. I do believe being married changes and enhances the quality of the relationship. There is a meaning in that public expression and statement."

"I was very happy to get married; I continue to be happy that we got married. It's hard to pin down, but for me, it's not so much the public statement; it's more the sense of connection with the historical precedent. I like feeling the continuity with the past, with my parents. I like being able to, even though she uses her own name, periodically say 'So, Mrs. Rosenblum, where do you want to go for dinner?'"

"Then, of course, being married gives Len and me permission at least to explore some interesting issues like economics, and we are still struggling with that. We have very different views—not diametrically opposed views, but different—about the economics of a relationship. Because we're married, it permits us to wrestle with that issue, to try and come up with what's best for us. We have both shared and separate finances. We're grown-ups. I feel we need to have our own money so we don't need to ask permission.

"And when it comes to buying gifts for the other person, it's important because you might want to buy them something they would never buy for themselves or even allow you to buy for them because they think it's too extravagant. I made the decision to buy Len a nine-hundred-dollar easel because I thought he deserved it and should have it. He would have never bought it for himself. He loves that easel!"

"That autonomy allows people to express their love," Leonard said fondly, reaching for June's hand.

"The other thing that marriage does that's also important is, should Len get sick or be unconscious, I need to have the right to go into that hospital and say, 'You can't do this' or 'You're going to do that!' In this culture, without marriage, you have to make all kinds of legal contracts. It gives me the security that I'm going to be able to protect my investment here."

I was curious about one other thing. "How did you deal with jealousy during those years you lived seven hundred and fifty miles apart?"

"Can I say something about that little part?" June implored, slightly raising her hand like a shy schoolgirl.

In all graciousness and thoroughly getting a kick out of his wife, Leonard smiled and replied, "Please." A mensch for all seasons, he.

"You have to trust. You can't have the kind of relationship we have without trust. Len can go off to Italy tomorrow and I don't worry about him on two levels. One, I don't really think he's going to fool around with somebody else. The other thing is even if he did, I know it wouldn't be meaningful."

"I don't take that to be an invitation," Leonard smiled ironically.

"I wouldn't give him up just because of that."

"Had someone said to me that two dynamic people like June and me could have gone through ten years of commuting, being apart 50 percent or more of the time and that either one of us would have remained faithful, I would have doubted them—let alone that we *both* would remain faithful. Yet it has never been an issue. It's simply never come up."

"We feel very confident with what we have. It couldn't be reproduced in some one night stand. It would take years. And we *like* where we are. He's my best friend! Why would you hurt your best friend just to get a little nooky?"

"There's that reservoir of goodwill," I pointed out.

"And this illustrates what we were discussing earlier about sexuality," Len added. "If your definition of sexuality has become less about where you put it, and more about the love and caring that has developed between you, passion is not even an issue—it's there."

Chapter 14

Does Love Have a Gender?

"Angelo? Angelo d'Amici?"

"Yes."

"You're a doctor, right?"

"Yeah?"

Okay, now what? I'm sitting in a hotel, packing away a jar of roasted, oversalted cashews, calling a man I met six years ago and haven't heard from since. Will he remember me?

"This is Cathleen Rountree; I met you at Michael Park's house in Topanga Canyon in 1989," I say, remembering the moment and feeling once again the rush I felt when I first laid eyes on him.

"Sure, I remember you," he said. But later when we met in person, I disappointedly realized he had confused me with Myrna, another woman who had also been at Michael's that spring evening.

"I'm here in Miami presenting a keynote lecture at the local college and doing a reading and book signing tonight at a bookstore. I'd love to see you if you're not busy," I baited.

He marched in wearing the recognizable brown leather hat he'd worn those years before. He had the same forward-tilting, long-strided gait, the purposeful tread of a hunter. His face was older, grayer, sadder, but still strikingly handsome—not so pretty.

"I never forgot you," I told him later at his home over a cup of mango tea. "I had a crush on you for an entire year after we met and wrote a poem about you called 'The Stranger.' I'll share it with you sometime."

We spent hours talking—mostly about him—his travels to Africa, China, and Spain; his subsequent breakdown from the stress of seeing with the eyes and heart of a visionary; his childhood; his medical practice; his love affair with another man. *Another man!?* I thought to myself, *O, my gawd, he's gay!*

With the impact of his words, everything fell into place like a home movie being played in reverse: no *wonder* he'd never called or written; *that's* why he'd been physically unresponsive to me; *this* explained the echo of mystery I'd felt when he answered no to my question "Are you married?"

Angelo d'Amici—a commanding name for a compelling, seemingly enigmatic, impervious man. In Kenya he was known as Indiana Jones, a testament to his daredevil tactics and sense of adventure. All he lacked was Indiana's bullwhip.

The danger of an image. Was Indiana Jones gay, too?

What is attraction? Love? Does love have a gender? Is it species specific? People laugh when I say that Sierra, my golden retriever, was with me longer than any man—thirteen years. Why is that funny? Other than my son, there is no one I've loved more than that dog. The day Sierra died in my arms my heart broke deeper and more lastingly than at any time I had ever left or been left by a man. I grieved in a way I'd never before known—real anguish, not neurotic suffering and self-indulgence over a lost boyfriend. Always in the past after a breakup I would gain weight, but this time I lost twenty pounds. My aching, fasting body commiserated with the sorrow and emptiness in my heart.

Some of the most romantic (in the true sense of the word) moments in my life were experienced with Sierra—walking for hours upon a deserted wild beach in Point Reyes, driving four hundred miles with his head on my lap, and every time I entered the front door he was beside himself with joy to see me. That was love. It's true he was male and I, female, but do dog and woman count? I think so. To put your mind at rest, our love did not spill over into the sexual, although he was jealous and passionately possessive of me—I liked that—and he disliked most men I was involved with (mostly with good cause). He also became particularly enamored of me during my monthly periods; I liked that, too.

The moment Angelo said, "I'm gay," my entire perspective on him changed. The image of him as a macho man dissolved; the fantasy of him as my future husband also shattered. In

Western culture there seem to be three main criteria for love: it has to be romantic, het-erosexual, and genital. His "coming out" had been a revelation to me, an epiphany, a free-ing from an inflexible pattern, a crystallized imprint of what Relationship must look like. Love took on a different message, too. Instead of the depreciating structures and restric-tive boundaries of a personal-ads mentality—"tall, dark, and handsome, forty- to fifty-year-old, professional, SWM, heterosexual only need apply"—I began to look at Angelo as a human being. A human being who is funny, fun to be with, intelligent, curious, cre-ative, adventuresome, and a raconteur par excellence—and, yes, even tall, dark, and hand-some. But I don't have to marry him or even sleep with him. And what have I lost? Not a thing. But I've gained a friend.

Interestingly enough, when he came to hear my lecture at the bookshop I had shared my "Program for Meeting Your Soul Mate" with the audience. Although it was in part meant to be humorous, they responded to the logic and good sense of "the program" as quickly as it rolled off my tongue.

Step 1: It's an inside job. Be yourself! Develop self-knowledge. Appreciate yourself for who you are and allow your self-knowledge to inform what you are looking for in another. Use the wisdom gained from your past experience as a guide through the process of elimination to lead you to the person who is best suited to be your friend and lover. Be well read, well informed, well intentioned.

Step 2: Find out what you most enjoy doing, what truly engages and excites you. Ask yourself the ques-tion: "When do I feel most alive?" and do those activities that come up for you. By following your interests, you will meet like-minded and -hearted people through your activities. Remember to nourish yourself, which often means a period of solitude. Welcome it! Sometimes it takes being alone for a period of time in order to fully understand what it is you are looking for in a relationship.

Step 3: Live your life passionately and to the fullest. Develop a passion for the world itself. Embrace life like a lover. Endorphins are contagious! Enjoy your independence—independence can be a turn-on. What would you want with another person who was dependent on you? Be willing to venture out on your own rather than sitting at home because you have "no one to go with." Enjoy your own company—if you don't who will? When you are independent, your life is truly your own.

Step 4: Be very clear about what real sexual appeal is and is not. Sex appeal is a mystery. It is related to beauty, but has nothing to do with perfect features or a perfect body. That's why you can be literally stunned by the beauty of an older woman, say, in her seventies or eighties. Sex appeal has much to do with pleasure and the promise of it. Only half of beauty is in the eye of the beholder; we carry the other half in our image of and attitude about ourselves. Feeling good about who you are and how you look is sustaining and real sex appeal!

Step 5: Make a written composite of who and what you want in a relationship. Then forget about meet-ing someone. No need to mail a letter twice. Better to have an open mind than too many expectations about the ideal mate.

Step 6: Think more along the lines of building long-term friendships, rather than finding your soul mate in every new person you meet. Nothing can suffocate a budding relationship quicker than a swarm of overbearing fantasies. Consider each new person you meet on his or her own merit as a unique and worthwhile individual. Regard the person in this moment rather than projecting onto him or her as a potential life partner.

Step 7: Remember, love is accessible and flourishes in many ways and forms. Look for a wide variety of ways to give and receive love. There is an entire repertoire of loving relationships available to us if we can but recognize and appreciate them. Unfortunately, Western tradition is fixated on one: the sexual. "If it's not romantic, heterosexual, and genital it can't be 'love.'" Family, friends, same-sex relationships, Nature, creative expression, work, are all possible means of engagement in a loving manner. The problem is that we have only one word (a four-letter one at that) to describe a plethora of human involvement and exchange. Since being single my creative work—art, writing, photography, teaching—has become my lover. It asks my devotion (love), often requires of me a similar kind of passion, an obsessive preoccupation, that many men in my past have exacted from me. My close association and empathic rapport with (love for) all animals, especially dogs and horses, is legend among my friends. And, since regaining my childhood appetite (love) for swimming in the ocean, my youthful passion has been rekindled and my womanly senses have been nourished in marvelously fresh and liberating ways.

Step 8: Don't get hung up on the packaging, the superficial. Go for the substance of character and shared values. Don't stereotype—you can't tell everything about a man by his profession or a woman by her dress size.

Step 9: Be yourself! Give the most credence to how you feel in the presence of another. Can you be yourself and be appreciated for that self? The emotional comfort and physical pleasure you feel with a particular person can't be contrived—it either exists or it doesn't. Be still within yourself; listen to your intuition and instincts, and follow them.

Step 10: Never tell yourself: "I'll be happy when I meet my soul mate." Be Happy! You'll have a much better chance of meeting another reasonably fulfilled and contented person. You can't postpone happiness. Court it, cultivate it, treasure it. Foster and exercise a sense of humor—everyone "loves" to laugh and to be around an upbeat person. Experience life as if you are already happily engaged in the relationship you seek.

Step 11: If all else fails, pray (that's ay, not ey!). Accept the fact that you might not have all the answers when it comes to your love life. My mantra to life is: "Please send me (and let me recognize) the person who is best suited to be my friend and lover." I acknowledge that I may have chosen poorly in the past and need a little guidance this time.

Step 12: Become the person with whom you want to be in relationship. Don't wait until you encounter the man or woman of your dreams before you begin that exercise program you've been wanting to start. Improve your eating habits. Clean up your finances. And because of your inner-directedness you'll feel better about yourself and become more attractive to others—remember: only half of beauty is in the eye of the beholder. Prepare yourself for the wealth of gifts the bank of life has in reserve for you.

Chapter 15

Intimate Lightning

Ron and Chris

I think you never
really stop trying to
change the other per-
son. At some point
you recognize that
you are beating your
head against the wall,
and that the peculiar-
ity—if it can be
called that—about
them that you may
dislike or with which
you are uncomfort-
able is as much a part
of them as all the
qualities to which you
are attracted. You
have to accept the
whole package or you
can't have any of it.

Ron

It helps to be a little crazy,
to be loose together. You
have to enjoy your partner's
company. You have to have
fun together. Our humor
and the way we do things fit
well together. Our craziness
kind of matches.

Chris

"I said to myself, 'This one's trouble!' " Chris told me when he described his initial im-
pression of Ron the evening they first met fifteen years ago.

"I won't say *what* I thought," Ron said, smiling slyly and taking a deep breath.

"The odd thing," Chris continued, "is that we were at a social, slightly political men's
gathering to explore the possibility of interacting with men on a nonsexual, nontraditional basis. Ron and I began interacting immediately. I remember, he had a great suntan
and a dark brown beard, and he was very warm and open. I felt an energy between us that
I'd never felt with anyone before."

Within twenty-four hours Ron had called Chris and invited him to a dinner party at his home. Ron is Italian on both sides, a phenomenal cook, an ebullient host, and an instinctively nurturing man. After a splendid meal on the deck of his San Francisco apartment and by the end of an unusually warm evening, Ron and Chris were looking forward to spending much more time together.

Ron, straightforward and candid to a fault, remembered that Chris brought "the *worst* wine you could possibly imagine. It was this awful sweet stuff. The only thing you could do with it was to put it in cakes."

"Or the gas tank of your car."

"You couldn't possibly drink it with Italian food," Ron exclaimed, pinching his nose in the air.

After a ten-month period of getting to know each other, Ron and Chris became partners, moved to Los Angeles, and began living together. They were working together as well. Chris, who had been teaching science and math at a private high school and was feeling a need to do something different, became an organizing partner in Ron's complex and somewhat unruly network of businesses, which were all related to film production and the distribution of imported films from Eastern Europe.

It has now been fifteen years and their five companies have evolved into a successful live-action and animation production company. They even have a "child"—a new animation character whose personality is a composite of theirs.

How do Ron and Chris manage to live, work, and travel together without making each other crazy?

"You have to enjoy somebody's company. You have to be compatible in order to handle that much time together." Chris admitted, "I was amazed at the amount of time we were able to spend with each other—right from the beginning. I'd never met anyone I could spend anywhere near *that* amount of time with."

Ron took the issue of compatibility a step further. "We've actually never had an argument."

"Oh, I don't know about that," Chris challenged.

"We've certainly disagreed on things, but we've never had an *argument.*"

"We've never been in a screaming match, that's true."

"Do you think that's healthy?" I wondered.

"If there's no reason to scream, why scream?" Ron reasoned. "Part of the reason we get along so well is that we talk to each other a lot. We don't let resentments or misunderstandings build up. We also do get time alone each day, which helps. I usually get up earlier than Chris does and he goes to bed later than me."

Ron showed me photographs of the "wild" rabbits that they feed by hand every morning at their mountain home atop Topanga Canyon in Los Angeles County, where they now live. They almost looked like members of the family, as they seemed to willingly pose for the camera. "I know it sounds crazy, but we spend a lot of time talking to them and to each other in the mornings. Making jokes and giving them names and dialogue."

"We play together. We're wacky in the same ways," said Chris.

"Talking, *really* talking to each other is so important," Ron continued. "Too many people spend too much time chattering without talking. They talk around the subject, or under and over the subject, but never get directly to the subject itself. If you can actually get past all that and say whatever is on your mind—without being afraid of the other person's reaction—that's really talking."

"Communication is so important," I agreed. I then raised the question about the effect of gender on the ability to communicate. Volumes have been written about the fact that men and women "just don't understand" each other, and that because "men are from Mars" (as a popular book asserts), they are often accused by women of being the bunglers in heterosexual relationships, and consequently the cause of much confusion between the sexes. "If that were the case, how on earth would *two* men living together ever be able to make sense out of anything?" I wondered aloud.

Because Ron had been married for eight years in a traditional marriage and has two grown children, he is in a unique position to speak from both sides of the fence. "For me, differences between men and women, in a number of areas, simply don't exist. We were given traditional frameworks before the liberation of the '60s and '70s. Basically, we're all the same animal in our emotional lives."

"Perhaps," I said, tentatively. "But the *expression* is very different," I specified.

"The expression is very, very different. Yes. Certainly in traditional role playing. But I'm not sure that we've had enough time to explore whether there are really differences in expression that are specific to gender."

"Your perspective is interesting," Chris said to me, "because I've always perceived Ron as having a beautiful balance between the male and the female components. He has both very masculine *and* very feminine aspects."

"But," Ron said, as he added the big qualifier, "you are attributing feminine qualities to things that have been traditionally done by women."

"Maybe that's it."

"I *may* be a good example of someone who has both traditional male and female qualities in one person."

"Did this ability to communicate so easily exist at the beginning of your relationship?" I asked.

"Instantaneously," Chris said without hesitation.

"It was like lightning. Boom! There it was," Ron agreed.

"I didn't have to make any psychological or emotional adjustments when you came into my life," Chris said, speaking directly to Ron. "It was very natural and easy."

"I describe this meeting of minds and emotions as 'intimate lightning,'" Ron revealed. "That's what happens when two people really click. If you think about how many people there are in the world, I don't think the chances of clicking with the right person are that great. I consider us very lucky."

"What are the chances of meeting someone on that level?" I asked. "Out of five billion?"

"I wouldn't even hazard a *guess*," said Ron.

"It depends on how you hook up intimately," reasoned Chris. "There's such a broad spectrum in the types of relationships. I don't think any relationship is 100 percent all-encompassing. *We* don't even have that."

"That would be like having a clone of yourself," Ron agreed.

"Exactly. But there are a lot of people you can get intimate with on varying levels. The uniqueness Ron and I have together can't necessarily be found with anyone else."

"There's another element here," said Ron. "I was thirty-five and Chris was twenty-nine when we met. I'm not sure either of us would have had the maturity to have a flourishing relationship if we had met ten years earlier. Eighteen or nineteen year olds won't have the same kind of relationship as thirty or forty or fifty year olds—or eighty-five year olds, for that matter. Maturity probably has a lot to do with what you can accept in people."

"And *expect* from them," I added. "Did you ever want to change each other, and if so, have you stopped?"

"I think you never really stop trying to change the other person," Ron said. "At some point you recognize that you are beating your head against the wall, and that the peculiarity—if it can be called that—about them that you may dislike or with which you are uncomfortable is as much a part of them as all the qualities to which you are attracted. Obviously you have to embrace the parts you love *and* the parts you don't particularly like. You have to accept the whole package or you can't have any of it."

"When I was younger," said Chris, "I probably had more desire to change Ron, to have us be a certain way, to force issues a bit more."

"What have you learned from each other?" I asked.

"We've actually picked up many of each other's good habits, which have improved each of us. It's kind of strange. I used to be terrible with money. I could never balance my checkbook and would spend more money than we had. Chris used to be pretty conservative—I could say tight, but I won't—with money. I've learned to be more prudent and responsible. He has learned to take risks."

"One of the things I've learned from Ron is to resolve conflicts or problems in a positive way. There's an art to that. If it isn't done right, people can become aggressive or abusive. He's taught me that there's a positive way to state the issue and work through it."

Next I asked them, "Do you consider your relationship a marriage?"

"I don't think I've ever tried to correlate it to a heterosexual institution. We are just two people who are together. But, yeah, I guess you could call it a marriage," Chris said.

"What is the definition of marriage?" asked Ron. "Until you define what marriage is, it's hard to answer that."

"Ron is my partner. He's not my husband, not my lover. The terms that are used in the so-called gay world don't fit. I don't necessarily consider myself gay. I don't feel like we are a 'gay couple.'

"Marriage is a bonding between two people. Another thing that can make a true marriage is the fact of children. Ron has two children, one of whom lived with us for a year. If I had to say we were ever married, it would have been during that time. It was a new dimension for the two of us to go through, having Ron's son live with us."

"We all suffer from labels: gay, straight, married, single. I don't know why people need labels," said Ron, mildly provoked. "People try to make frames around everything, and those frames create restrictions. There's no such thing as the perfect family. That concept was invented. We are surrounded by a mythology that wounds people constantly. That mythology says that if you formalize your relationship, lock yourself into a nuclear family with 1.2 children, then everything will be all right. In fact, half of marriages end in divorce. Half the people who come together grow apart. It's like one of those laws of physics: the moment it comes together, that same moment it begins to fall apart."

"The real question is how to *keep* it together," I said.

"For me," began Ron, "the answer is simple: you have to remain flexible, you have to be fair, you have to be honest with yourself and the other person, and *you have to want it!*"

"It also helps to be a little bit crazy," Chris said, laughing and shaking his head at Ron, "so you can be loose together. You *have to* have fun together."

"There's nothing more serious than comedy."

"Our humor and the way we do things fit well together. Our craziness kind of matches."

"If somebody followed us around with a video camera, we'd be in an institution tomorrow. Our families would have us committed," said Ron dryly. "We have conversations with rabbits. I'm almost convinced I communicate with them telepathically 'cause they always do what we want. And we do what *they* want. It's kind of strange. Maybe *that's* a marriage."

"Back to the general idea of marriage," said Chris. "We never considered going through any type of formal ceremony as some of our gay friends did. I find it a little bit silly. It's almost like taking the heterosexual institution and all its trappings and trying to apply it to your relationship."

"There is an unwritten contract in which both parties have agreed to do something, which is to be together," observed Ron. "Each of you has to uphold whatever end of the bargain you struck with the other person."

Bravely, Chris launched the subject of sex. "Another issue that is very important is that of monogamy. Each couple has to decide how they are going to deal with it. We made a commitment to be monogamous."

"Does the existence of AIDS affect that decision," I asked.

"AIDS is an issue, definitely," acknowledged Chris.

"No, no, not for me," Ron contradicted.

"Oh, really? But it is a consideration," Chris pressed.

"Not for me. The reason I'm here is because I *want* to be here."

"I have to say it is an issue for me."

"It's an issue only if you decide you want something other than what you have—which I don't," said Ron, almost reproachfully.

It was time for me to referee. "Life is life," I said, using the cliché. "Either of you could walk out of the house and see someone you were attracted to and think you want. It's a momentary attraction, something you don't necessarily act on."

"Absolutely," Chris said. He seemed relieved with the new direction. "It's what you decide to do with it."

"To stay alive is exactly what you decide to do with it *these* days!" Ron said with a certain finality.

"Have there been disappointments or disillusionments in your relationship? Things you've had to let go of?" I inquired.

"The sexual thing is something . . ." Chris began, openly.

"We'll do the famous scene from Woody Allen's film *Annie Hall*, where you see both Annie and Alvie in their psychiatrist's office," continued Ron. "The psychiatrist says, 'So, how often do you have sex?' and she says, 'Almost constantly' and he says, 'Hardly ever.' I'm not going to say anything more."

I ventured to guess, "Since Chris brought it up, I can imagine who thinks 'hardly ever.' "

"You're wrong," Ron corrected me.

"That's an issue I've had to deal with," Chris admitted. His candor in discussing this taboo subject was refreshing. "Our sexual natures are somewhat different. I find I have to work in my mind and emotions to keep sex between us interesting. It can easily become rote."

"So how *do* you keep the sexuality in your relationship alive and vital after fifteen years?" I asked.

Ron answered with an analogy. "I think there is a basic flaw in the expectation in most relationships: I can run a certain speed; another person can run a certain speed, but it's difficult to find two people who can always, or even most of the time, run at the same speed. It's not that one doesn't want to run at the same pace or is holding back; they're simply made differently. So each one has to accept that and work within that framework. Probably most couples have this problem."

"Especially with us," Chris continued, "because we spend so much time together and share on so many levels, the sexual part sometimes seems almost unnecessary. I don't have to have sex in order to fulfill my need for intimacy, because that need is met in many other ways."

"Once again," I said, "we are in need of a definition. What is sex? Is it a look across the breakfast table or driving somewhere together and laughing about an amusing situation? A multitude of experiences might qualify as *emotional* intercourse. A 'mind fuck' isn't always necessarily pejorative. Sex can be the by-product or climax—excuse the pun—of a variety of different stimuli or titillations; it's not solely the act of genital copulation in bed at night."

"I agree," Chris said. "There is a lot of intimacy we share all day long."

"This is very interesting." Ron seemed slightly perplexed. "This is the first time I've heard this perspective from you. My sex drive toward Chris is usually higher than Chris's toward me. And that's a frustration sometimes. That's a problem that always has to be worked on and there *isn't* a solution. It's something you have to accept."

"A balance has to be kept. And that can be done by asking each other, 'What else is happening between us in our relationship? Are we playing enough? Are we too worried about money? Are we focusing on an aspect that is trivial?' A relationship is multidimensional; it's not based only on one element."

"Just doing something like changing the house can be a certain stimulant. Our house seems to be as much a reflection of what we are doing in our lives as we are ourselves," Ron said.

"This week we moved our office away from our home, lock, stock, and barrel," Chris said, with enthusiasm. "So we will no longer be working at home."

"I think that's going to have a positive effect on the relationship," Ron said cheerfully. "We will have more privacy and more time for intimacy without the constant intrusion of the fax machine running in the middle of the night or someone calling from Europe and forgetting the time difference."

"Or just having stacks of papers and files in the other room. Even if you don't see them, you know they're there."

"It's really tough, especially in this age we live in. There is so much stimulation," Ron pointed out. "About the last thing you want at the end of the day is to have someone stimulate you sexually, because your brain is already on tilt from the speed of communication without communication."

"This is something we have discussed recently and we really agree on. I tend to get irritable when I'm overstimulated, and Ron is great at stepping in and saying, 'It's okay, Chris. It doesn't matter. Go home. You don't have to deal with it.' "

"Yeah, I mean, 'We're not doing brain surgery here,' I'll tell him. 'We're making cartoons, after all.' So if it waits until tomorrow, big deal."

"That's something that I really admire in Ron: he has the ability in his brain to do three or four diverse things simultaneously. I'm more the walking or chewing gum type of person. I like to do one thing at a time. I can get overstressed easily. Although I'm better than I was fifteen years ago. I'm learning from him."

The conversation turned to the components necessary, or at least important, in maintaining a long and healthy partnership.

"As we mentioned earlier," Chris began, "the ability to solve problems is something we've learned to do together. That's considerable."

"I think good food is very important," Ron said, seriously. "Spending time cooking together."

"You're right," Chris agreed.

"You get home, and you take that hot lasagna out of the oven; there's nothing like it."

"We've always eaten well," Chris elaborated. "There may have been times when we had thirty cents in the bank, but we would take our last money and buy good food. Also, having a clean house is important; we've always had someone to clean the house, even when we couldn't afford it."

"We've been broke, but we've never been poor."

"It's an attitude," Chris concurred.

"The physical pleasures that you give yourself are really important. Say you have a comfortable chair you like. If the pillow needs to be fixed, get it fixed instead of complaining about the spring that pokes you in the back. If the toaster drives you crazy—shall we talk about the toaster?" Ron asked Chris.

"We've suffered enough with it."

"For years we had what we called Chris's bachelor toaster."

"The toaster my parents gave me for Christmas when I was twenty-two."

"It drove me crazy. I couldn't make toast in it without burning it. For *years* this went on. Finally I said, 'I'm going to throw this goddamn toaster out the window.' Chris bought me a new one this past Christmas. It's a big fat one that you can toast bagels in! It's funny, you put up with a lot of stuff in relationships that you don't really have to put up with."

"Most things can be solved pretty simply," said Chris.

"You know, it's the little things that can drive you crazy about someone else. If they were big things, you wouldn't be together. That's something you have to watch out for. That, and those little things you can do *for* each other. Sharing those little pleasures. My advice for new and long-term couples alike is: 'Cook together!'"

Chapter 16

Always Filling the Bucket

Rosemary Jellison and Hannah Watkins

That's another thing Hannah has brought to me: she's helped me fine-tune the art of appreciation. It starts with paying attention. I've learned to pay attention to what Hannah does for our home, for our partnership, for our lives.

Rosemary Jellison

I do believe that the age Rosemary and I were when we came together and the work we'd already done on ourselves play a huge role in how well we live together.

Hannah Watkins

"I'm afraid you'll find us boring," Rosemary laughed, as we sat down to lunch on their sunny patio. "We're so happy, I can hardly stand it. There are so few problems. Every day of my life is wonderful!" I assured her that happiness and a sense of unity and contentment between partners were *exactly* what I was looking for (both in my research and in my own life), not their opposites, of which plenty are to be found.

I met Rosemary and Hannah through a friend, and, I'm pleased to say, I now consider them friends of my own. We had seen each other a few times at the homes of mutual friends, but when I was invited to their home to conduct our interview, I entered another world where I felt I was meeting them for the first time. Their love of European—in particular, Italian—culture, ambiance, and food displayed itself throughout their environment. The fabrics and textures, the eclectic collection of ceramic imports juxtaposed with thrift market finds, the volumes of poetry lying casually by an armchair or in the bathroom, the numerous vases of lush, fragrant flowers, the deep, subdued earth-tone colors on the walls and in artwork provide a warm and cozy backdrop for the joy and comfort of any visitor. Every space has been attended to with care. Everybody knows how good it feels to be around people who are in love. The only thing different between them and any other couple is that they are two women who are deeply in love— with each other—and, after ten years together, consider themselves married.

Rosemary, tall, slender, and equally elegant in a suit and tie or a dress, is a psychotherapist who works in an office in their home; Hannah, five years senior to Rosemary, is also tall and slender, although more casual in apparel. She is a nurse who works the graveyard shift on call four nights a week. When not working, they spend the majority of their time together. I wondered aloud if their luxurious lifestyle (a beautifully appointed home surrounded by well-tended gardens, frequent travel, many loving friends, shared cultural interests, the pleasure of preparing and eating meals together outside on a shaded deck) has grown from their compatible relationship or vice versa. Does the love between them swell from the lifestyle or is it their love that is a foundation for the lifestyle?

"It's both/and really," explained Rosemary. "For example, I love to prepare food and share it. So my love of cooking and eating provides a context for us to drop into a more intimate side of our relationship. The lifestyle and the love generate each other. Beauty and love beget peace." Hannah nodded her head in agreement.

In a sense, that's one of the contributions that a happy relationship makes. Primarily it displays the potential for, indeed, the actual existence of, this kind of happiness and compatibility. It represents possibility and suggests a similar eventual outcome for an observer, and, of course, it offers an aura of pure enjoyment in which to bask.

The stage of life at which two people meet can determine whether they have a harmonious, successful relationship or a contentious, disappointing one. People grow and change; at fifty-three, they are vastly different from who they were at twenty-three. By fifty-three, an adult's child-bearing and (in most instances) -rearing years are behind them. Many of those who experienced the freedom-loving and liberating '60s and '70s spent their early adulthoods in self-reflection and psychotherapy or analysis, unraveling a myriad of neurotic symptoms in their psyches. By midlife, they begin to live a more conscious, perhaps, more appreciative life. These two factors alone—the absence of children in one's romantic relationship and an acceptance of one's own psychological state—can greatly affect the workings of a midlife or late-life relationship.

"I do believe," stated Hannah, "that the age Rosemary and I were when we came together plays a huge role in how well we live together. In our forties and fifties we each had more sense of self; we were, and are, more able to claim our part of responsibility in our relationship, what part of the equation is ours. Rosemary might say something to me that hits me a little wrong, and instead of going off or being hurt I say, 'Oh, God, yes.' I'm more able to see *my* part in it without letting it wound me. That's *huge!* And I think both of us are able to do that in our relationship. From the very beginning we've been able to do that. And it has a lot to do with our age and the work we've done on ourselves. Rosemary has three children, but they were already grown when we met. Our finances were stabilized. We came together at a very healthy time in our lives."

I remarked on the fact that the qualities Rosemary attributed to Hannah—her athleticism and love of sports, her interest in politics and finances, her "handyman" abilities—are traditionally associated with men. In heterosexual marriages, the once distinctive roles and behaviors identified as either male or female have become increasingly blurred. "Is that also true in lesbian relationships?" I asked. "Or is there one person who typifies more of the behaviors traditionally associated with one gender than the other?"

"It's a societal bias," Hannah declared. "But in looking at our own relationship and those of other lesbian friends, I would say that's the case. There is one who is better at fixing things and one who can cook better. With regard to how they are in the world, you may have two very male-like women or two very female-like women, but, in general, I think people complement each other."

"Certainly I have seen this in my own relationships," I concurred, "the complementary aspect, that is. In some ways, it seems that we are drawn to the qualities in another that we lack in ourselves. We are drawn to the strengths in the other. That kind of projection, however, can be a blessing or a curse."

"Yes," agreed Hannah, "in my case, it is the feminine side of Rosemary that I so appreciate. More the emotional side, really, although that's changed for me in the last ten years—I have learned to integrate that into myself."

"Is that partly due to Rosemary's influence?" I asked.

"Sure. Absolutely," she agreed. "It was starting to change when we met, but being with her has played a major role. It's been wonderful."

At that moment Rosemary returned to the patio where we were dining alfresco. She brought the largest, reddest, and (I was soon to taste) sweetest strawberries imaginable. She clearly enjoyed serving both her partner and guest alike. As a couple they are tenderly affectionate in word and touch. "Honey" and "Sweetheart" are common forms of address. We caught Rosemary up on our conversation and she ardently insisted, "I *love* that we have these differences that balance us so we each don't have to be everything. I'm happy not having to focus on things that aren't as interesting to me, like balancing checkbooks, whereas Hannah finds that interesting. However, I also think if I didn't have a strong inner masculine, an inner strength or sense of identity, we couldn't play together. I have it in my spirit.

"I hate to say anything that will reinforce cultural stereotypes, but when I look at every couple we know, they either have their division of labor or have different strengths."

"That is also found in heterosexual relationships," I point out. "I know many couples in which the man is a better cook or the woman has greater earning power and the husband stays home with the children."

"But, in the beginning, I was attracted to Hannah's looks. I didn't yet know about her wonderful qualities."

"She married me for my looks," Hannah said, smiling. "It was pure sex for me!"

"How do you know when you can trust that feeling?" I asked.

"We just jumped in," Hannah answered, "and it got better and better. You take a risk because you can never really know in the beginning."

"You had no idea ten years ago that you'd be sitting here in this gorgeous environment," I said, taking my first bite of a luscious strawberry, "just back from three weeks in Italy . . ."

". . . feeling so peaceful," said Hannah, finishing my thought. "Unh-unh."

"We came together because we were really drawn to each other," Rosemary said, "and of course there was a strong sexual attraction. For the first year we lived together, we had a honeymoon period during which there was a tremendous focus on each other, and less on my children and our friends, who waited patiently for us to journey out to them. That all changed when we bought this house. It took us out of a tiny cottage and our life opened up again. Even though the house was a dump at first, we began fixing it up— Hannah worked on it eight hours a day with contractors and other workers. Friends began to visit us and we had a place to welcome them."

"That was another thing," added Hannah. "We worked so well together. We had no idea that our . . ."

". . . rhythm . . ."

". . . dance would be so like that."

"Do you still surprise each other?" I asked.

According to Hannah, "Yes. Rose has a sense of humor that, every once in a while, can make me just fall on the floor with laughter. And then at certain times when I look up and see her, I'm hit by my feelings for her. She means so many things to me. The intensity of the emotion is always a surprise."

Rosemary described their relationship as having an "ongoing element of surprise." She compared their most recent trip to Italy with the previous one made the year before as she addressed Hannah directly. "I was surprised it was so good. I knew we would have a nice time, but you changed, Hannah. You were not as uptight as the last time. You really did this trip differently than any other one we've been on together. You practiced flexibility, fluidity. That was surprising. It was profound. I knew you were working on yourself, but I couldn't have expected that you would get such good results. You know what I mean?"

"What happened?" I asked, curious.

"The trip we took last summer was helpful, but it was not an easy trip," said Hannah. "It was very meaningful but not easy. I came up against some of my own inner conflicts that I had to deal with. We went to school there to study Italian. The weather was extremely hot and we lived in a small house with a large family."

"It was an initiation rite, spiritually," Rosemary volunteered.

"That's true. I broke down in a way. I think this trip came out of that experience. From that time on, I had to let go of things at home, too, instead of being so controlling. I don't consider myself an especially uptight person, but I like things to be the way I like them. I let go of a lot. Also, as I age, I think my heart gets more open and that played a big role in my change. And this trip we stayed with some American friends, Trish and Gary, with whom we have a very special relationship as two couples. They were there with two of their children whom we adore, and it felt like we were all in this big balloon of love and appreciation."

"That's another thing Hannah has brought to me: she's helped me fine-tune the art of appreciation. It starts with paying attention. I've learned to pay attention to what Hannah does for our home, for our partnership, for our lives. One day I came upstairs and saw a bouquet of flowers she'd bought. I said, 'Oh, what beautiful flowers,' rather than 'Thanks for buying these flowers,' or 'You arranged them beautifully, Hannah.' She pointed out that I might remark on the object, but I didn't always include her part in it. I thought if I'm telling her, 'My God, the tulips are gorgeous' that I'm thanking her for buying and arranging them. So that was a nice piece of fine-tuning. She has helped me develop that awareness, so I'm very aware every day of what Hannah brings to me, and I talk about it. Right? Every day. Not any particular time of day, but every day. We're always filling the bucket."

"That's right," agreed Hannah. "Every day we talk about the couple. How lucky we are, what a wonderful life we have together.

"Another thing that's important to me about Rose is that, because she works at home, I see her at her work as a therapist—she comes and goes, we have lunch together or she comes upstairs for coffee—and I appreciate who she is as a therapist, how she is with the people she works with. It's remarkable. That's a unique situation to be in. Most people may never have the opportunity to see how their partner works, or who they are at work. Rose is very focused in her work. She has a fabulous heart. I feel her heart in her work. I love that about her."

"Something came up while Hannah was talking that I'd like to comment on. She has a sensitivity to see when I am in a particular state of concentration; she does not interrupt me, she never or rarely pulls me off my focus. She allows me room to move in different gears. We have created boundaries in which we can be in the same space together and, as close as we are, we don't have to be doing couple stuff all the time."

"You have successfully maintained your individuality," I presumed. "There hasn't been that total merging to the point of symbiosis that you find with some couples. Why do you think it's so difficult for two people to come together and find a balance of rest and stimulation, of contentment and excitement, of passion and compatibility?"

"I think part of the equation," began Rosemary, "is being unafraid to tell your own truth."

"I had no idea what to say, but as soon as you say that, I totally agree," said Hannah.

At that moment I referred to another couple I'd interviewed for *The Heart of Marriage*, Hal and Sidra Stone. "They talk about the importance of staying with the process. According to them, when you stay with the process, there is not a dull moment. I completely agree. I think that's another way of speaking your truth, of not being afraid to say, 'This is what I'm feeling and thinking right now about what you said or did; what do you think?' I've found that to be absolutely true under any circumstances, in any relationship, whether it be romantic, parental, friendship, or business. It never fails; definitely ups the ante! When you know what your own truth is and then tell it, when you stay in the process, interaction is vitalized—there's juice—you're alive. Fear and self-consciousness break down the vitality, and then the bridge of communication is broken."

"I think we shock our lesbian friends," Rosemary said, "but not the heterosexuals as much, by some of the pretty assertive things we say to each other. We encourage each other to have a different voice and to be honest."

"What has been the most difficult adjustment between you in your relationship?" I inquired.

"The one thing that comes up for me is the fact that you had children," Hannah said, speaking directly to Rosemary. "That was a real adjustment for me, more so in the beginning. Now it feels like such a blessing that she has children and that I, by association, have them in my life. When we first met, I had no children; I chose not to have them, and then I fall in love with a woman who has three kids! That was a challenge—I didn't know how it was going to look, and I like to know how things are going to look. If you were not the person you are, it would have been much more difficult. It has been helpful for me that Rose does not lead with 'I'm a mother.' She didn't need to see them every weekend or talk about them constantly. If she had, it might not have worked."

"What are the components for a long-lasting, loving relationship?" I finally asked them.

"Extreme good looks. A model's body. Nice feet. I'm being silly," laughed Hannah.

"Certainly there has to be an initial attraction of some kind—the pleasure in the company of the other. The delight in the sensuous presence—it doesn't have to be sexual necessarily. Respect for the other person is important, and an ability to listen to them."

Hannah summed up the components with: "Show up. Pay attention. Tell the truth."

"Yes, tell the truth," echoed Rosemary.

"And don't be attached to the outcome," added Hannah.

"We've had periods of time when the sexual dance has gone to the wings," Rosemary revealed without inhibition, "and we haven't had as much sexual connection."

"But our rhythm in that area is similar," explained Hannah, "so it's never been a big issue between us. I look at Rose every once in a while and go, 'God! I want to jump on her bones.' It's always there—whether or not we act on it."

"There are so many ways we can be together," Rosemary continued. "Because sexuality is *one* of the many ways we are able to share intimacy together, we might not go directly to sexuality for contact and closeness the way other people may. I feel there is a sensuous connection between us; is that sexual?"

"There is a lot of sensuousness between us on a daily basis. I think it's distinct from sexuality," said Hannah.

I agreed. "Perhaps sensuousness is more about that appreciation you mentioned, a curiosity, a way of being alive through one's senses. For me, swimming in the ocean has become a very sensuous experience. I love it. Whereas sexuality has to do with the act of having sex—something that is absent from my life right now. But both seem necessary in order to have a full relationship. Each is important. Each is a blessing."

Chapter 17

Intermission:
Two Years

Journal Entry: March 1995

It is now less than a week before the spring equinox. New life, rebirth, resurrection. Since June 1993 I have been caught in the spell known simply as "writer's block." But what is the information, material, or experience that this writer has felt a compulsion to block herself off from for nearly two years? If I knew *that* I wouldn't be wallowing in the romance of the block. My reticence and forced repression would break through the barricade, the obstruction of my own fear. But the fear, the paralysis of terror has become known and comfortable through its familiarity.

Since remeeting Angelo it has become clear to me what the block is about. In the summer of 1991 I began writing *The Heart of Marriage*. It seemed a simple task at the time: interview sixteen happily married couples, photograph them, and edit the material. Not much different from writing *Coming into Our Fullness: On Women Turning 40* except that I would be interviewing two people about their relationship rather than one woman about her life. It seemed straightforward initially. But when I began to interview couples I found myself asking questions that had no answers, at least no absolute answers; there were as many answers as there were people to whom I asked the questions. Quickly I became bewildered. Where were the absolutes I was seeking? It soon became clear that they did not exist; and like any important lesson, I would have to learn the answers on my own.

My intention had been to meet and marry (at least meet) the man of my dreams, my soul mate, by the time I finished *The Heart of Marriage*. No sweat, I told myself. I'll find him, marry him, and we'll live happily ever after. This time I'm older, wiser, more established in my career. What's the problem? I had it all planned out so pragmatically. Just as I'd "come into my fullness" with my first book and, eventually, began "celebrating my midlife discoveries" with the second, I'd enter "the country of marriage" with the third. How neat. How tidy—one life all summed up in a single word: "marriage."

Two years down that trail to "the country of marriage" I realized that, like Dorothy, on my way "home," I had skipped right into an Oz of my own making. The villages, the wayside stations, the *auberges* were named loneliness, projection, autonomy, divorce, romance, fantasy. My inability to continue writing the book stemmed from my recognized failure to meet and marry the promised man. I had set a nearly impossible task for myself and I had failed to satisfy my own expectation.

Now, after my two-year "intermission," I understand that there was a deeper, more important reason for journeying through the Country of Marriage: to break the myth once and for all for myself and any other woman or man who is willing to hear it, who can bear it: there is no "happily ever after," there is no sailing off into the sunset together. Though couples do find periods of ecstatic happiness together, the river doesn't stop there; it flows just as frequently through all the hideous times of betrayal and despair, the empty times of loneliness and death, and the placid times of boredom.

It is shocking to realize that, like Snow White and Cinderella, I have been waiting for my Prince Charming to come and set me free. All those years of feminism and therapy! I have internalized the fairy tales, the dream of *Pretty Woman*. I have been subconsciously asking myself, Where is *my* Richard Gere (or at least a more intellectually and socially conscious version)?

Somewhere during these past four years—I can't point my finger to any one moment or to any particular experience—I became my own Prince Charming. I know that finding love is an "inside job"; I must first love, honor, and appreciate myself. But why is it so difficult to accept this truth that everyone instinctively knows and every self-help book preaches? Once we become our own best friends, the search for the idealized Other is less dominant in our life's rhythm; it glides into the bass, say, from the lead guitar—it's presence is felt but, thankfully, less obtrusively.

By leaving *The Heart of Marriage* open-ended, i.e., by not setting myself up as a perpetuator of the myth, I relieve myself and every reader of the book, both female and male, of the desperate search for their prince or princess. I hope it is a step away from the insidious tyranny of this cultural fiction. And, as I write these words, the omnipresent child's voice in my mind says: But that doesn't mean you can't meet someone someday, does it? No, it simply means I have more time and energy for my curiosities and interests and that, after too many years of hiding my head in the sands of disastrous relationships, I've actually enjoyed discovering just *what* those interests are. My challenge here is to accept that, with or without a man, my life is of my own making and the mythic He is immaterial to or at least not responsible for my sense of happiness, well-being, and fulfillment.

Our innate desire and perpetual longing are for a redemptive union with the Other—the spiritual, the cosmic, the universal. We wish to belong somewhere, to someone, forever. Understandably we displace that yearning onto the singular rather than the infinite, which is, in it's very abstraction, difficult, if not impossible, to grasp. We are looking for the soul of *life*, but we try to embody that essence in a mate—one imperfect finite being who, we hope, will provide for and comprise everything to us, who will offer a passage into more promising, secure terrain. No one can meet that preposterous request, and, yet, we continue to demand it.

Chapter 18

A Marriage in the Country

I'm committed to being, to the best of my ability, a life partner for Janie. I'm committed to taking care of my own personal needs, but never losing sight of the fact that meeting the needs of the whole meets a greater need in myself.

Peter Eichorn

Janie Rommel and Peter Eichorn

I don't feel trapped or like I'm "giving myself up" in my relationship. I know if I didn't have Peter and the children, I'd have much more free time, but I had a lot of free time before I got married. I had fourteen years!

Janie Rommel

Janie went to the movie *Meetings with Remarkable Men* and met a remarkable man: her husband, Peter. She was dressed in the traditional costume of a Nepali woman, the beads, the boots, the dress, "the whole nine yards," because it thematically matched the film based on the psychological autobiography of the philosopher-mystic G. I. Gurdjieff. Janie had purchased her outfit two months earlier on her trip to Nepal, and it had become a trademark of sorts. One month later Peter took his own journey to Nepal, and within another month, back home, Peter and Janie, each with their own cultural ties to Nepal, met at a local movie house.

In Nepal Peter had "the sense of things coming together in unusual ways" on a regular basis. For the first time in his life, after experiencing the pain of his aloneness, he felt that he was "walking hand in hand with the divine." They didn't take that first meeting seriously. But after meeting again three days later—this time at a twelve-hour political party sponsored by the American Association of Humanistic Psychology, where, in a crowd of thirty-five hundred people, Peter sat one seat removed from Janie—Peter "followed her around from that moment on." They think this gathering was an important place to meet, as it established their shared planetary and ecological concerns.

Janie recalls that she had made a conscious decision after her previous relationship, saying, "No more challenges, and no more drama," because that's how it had been in most of her relationships. From the inception of her romance with Peter, they both experienced a solidarity between them. "There weren't bells ringing, but a more mature feeling" was undeniable.

They had both been single for over two years and had "done a lot of growing." The timing was right in terms of their own development. They came together as "fairly whole people who could go forward on a parallel path, but without leaning on each other, so if one stepped aside, the other wouldn't collapse."

Peter, who is dyslexic, has a natural ability to see the whole picture and has learned to work backward from the whole to the particulars, while Janie begins with the details and composes a completed unit. They think of their partnership as a rounding out.

The Eichorns have held the vision of building their own country home since their initial meeting. They presently live on forty acres of virgin land along the Big Sur coast of California in a 700-square-foot house with an outhouse several yards away. Peter joked about the enforced intimacy of their environment, but became more earnest when he described intimacy as "an unconditional positive regard for another person. Whenever I think about Janie, or mention her to a friend, the wonder of her is just *present* in me."

As a conscious maneuver to create a loving, intimate atmosphere at home, Peter and Janie have instituted a family meeting every Sunday morning during which they and their two children, Benjamin (twelve) and Elizabeth (six), share appreciations of themselves and for each other. Janie unexpectedly mentioned another aspect of intimacy. "We have some pretty good fights, and that's just fine, because I think fighting is part of intimacy, too. To have the safety to fight." She is amazed at the number of clients in her therapeutic practice, who, when asked about their parents' relationships, are convinced their parents had a good relationship because they never argued. Peter added a point of insight when he said, "When one partner is decidedly the dominant partner and wins every fight, the other person will eventually give up and retreat. It's the same dynamic in a global sense— there's little contest between a very weak country and a very powerful country. It seems obvious."

The desire to live an artist's life has always been Peter's dream, but with small children and a forty-acre farm, he decided that he would have to live his *life* as art, to "see art in my human relationships, in the way we care for and bring up the children" and care for the land. It's hard to keep that focus, "but when I do, it's really rewarding."

Janie agreed that Peter has generally come up with most of the creative ideas, and she has had the ability to help them "come into fruition." For example, when Peter writes a letter to the editor of the newspaper, because of his dyslexia he has Janie "clean it up" for him. They have developed this team effort more recently; earlier in their relationship Peter resisted his wife's help. Janie calls this example a metaphor for their learned ability to work together.

A dangerous setup for couples is when one expects the other to supply all of his or her intellectual, emotional, and psychological needs. Peter believes that it is imperative for each person to first discover and then describe particular needs, because "when you say in a vague way, 'fill my emotional needs,' that vagueness leaves your partner totally inept." They both agree that they have improved in their ability to fill their own needs, but "when we don't, we have problems and clashes," said Peter.

I mentioned that I often hear people complain about "giving themselves up" in a relationship. Janie made an interesting comment on this: "I don't feel trapped or that I'm 'giving myself up.' I know if I didn't have Peter and the children, I'd have much more free time, but I had a lot of free time before I got married," she said with a flair that matched her red hair. "I had fourteen years!"

Peter originally held the vision of the land, of the house and the property. But Janie admitted that she always wanted to live in the country and "do the organic thing." She had a sense of adventure and a willingness to "do something different," and welcomed the opportunity Peter offered to live in a house without plumbing—including a bathroom. She made a conscious choice to "step back in time while most of the world is hurtling forward. To forgo all the creature comforts we've become so used to in the twentieth century in order to see what's really important, what we can live with and what we can live without. Peter carried that vision and I came along to be a partner in it."

At the time of their meeting Janie had been a flight attendant with Pan Am for over ten years. Her personal vision began to evolve in the direction of planetary healing. "I realized if we are to ever get it together as a planet, we'd have to begin with our own families and learn new ways of being together, because that's what we take out into the world." When, as a couple, they visited the Findhorn community in Scotland, Janie first heard about marriage and family counseling from a California therapist. She made the decision to become a therapist and "help people to heal their families." Meanwhile, her own family was growing with the birth of her son, Benjamin, in 1983, and she began to learn firsthand ways of parenting that would encourage children to enter the world as "more whole, conscious people."

Being a certified organic farmer is significant to Peter as a symbol of his actual caring for the earth "in a physical sense—the dirt and hair of the earth and the plants that grow on it." He has taken this stewardship seriously, even to the extent of building their new home from rammed earth modules (a mixture of earth, water, and cement) "partly for ecological reasons"—it prevents deforestation and avoids the use of fossil fuels to heat and cool the house. "Going with rammed earth is a logical choice if we are going to survive as a planet," Peter reasoned. His larger vision is to proliferate the ancient concept of rammed earth throughout the world and, therefore, practice earth-saving theories on a very practical, physical level. As I listened to their story I understood how the Country of Marriage is a literal metaphor for their relationship as well as their lifestyle.

Following their "think globally, act locally" politics, the Eichorns founded, with other couples, a Waldorf School (based on the principles of the mystic-educator Rudolf Steiner). Establishing the school was a way of grounding their vision and they feel that it is their most important contribution so far.

Several months after a devastating loss in their lives, Peter and Janie realized that they had another contribution to make: one to bereft parents who, like themselves, had lost a child at, or soon after, birth. Janie's second pregnancy was full-term and healthy, until delivery. During the descent through the birth canal, the baby's air supply had been cut off by a knot in the umbilical cord. "I was like a mother animal who'd given birth to a nonviable child," recalled Janie. "Everybody was trying to get her to breathe, but I just held her foot and rubbed it. Later I thought, 'Why didn't I yell her name?' but on some level I must have known it was pointless."

I can imagine no greater loss to a parent than that of her or his child. According to Peter and Janie, the inevitable trauma is recorded in the exorbitant divorce statistics for couples who lose a child: 80–90 percent. The pain of that event placed enormous strain on Peter and Janie's relationship. Janie spoke of her need to "experience my grief. I used to say, 'I'm going to stay on this train until I get to the end of the line. I'm not getting off before I'm finished.'" She felt difficulty communicating the depth of her sorrow to her husband, who had chosen another path through his grief: that of work and activity. Soon after the tragic stillbirth, Janie became obsessed with getting pregnant again as soon as possible. She charted her fertile time and "would demand to Peter, 'We have to make love *now*,' and he would say, 'I can't feel loving and sexual toward you when you're acting like this. Isn't it supposed to be about love?'" Janie feels that "the hand of God" pushed her down until she "finally hollered 'uncle'."

After several years Janie views that passage as a teacher. "That process helped me get more in touch with the softer feminine and receptive side of myself. So, losing that daughter, I feel, gave me my womanhood. It took me to the very depths of my being. I think it's harder for the mother—especially of a child nobody knew—it's a private grief. It's different with a child who has been out in the world, one people knew."

Peter described the death of his daughter as "one of the most dramatic and intense spiritual experiences I've ever had. I felt as though I were in the presence of an angel—her spirit was so full and so strong and so loving—I was totally consumed by it. Although I felt sadness and loss, I also thought, 'My God, if this is loss, what a wonder.' It was a mystical experience carrying a beauty that transcends the earthly. I was dumbfounded by it all, but I still had the presence of mind to dress her up in her little outfit, so we'd send her away in style."

For six months the grieving parents honored their daughter's cremated remains at an alter they created for her, and then decided it was time to release them. They scattered Julia's ashes under a tangerine tree that has the bearing of a sentinel "up on the homesite where we buried the placenta. Eventually, we will look out our window toward the ocean and see the tree growing there. It gives me solace that her physical remains are there on the property," Janie confided.

One year after the death, they took a camping trip to their favorite spot in the Sierra Nevada. According to Janie, "I was told over and over again, 'A year, a year—wait a year until you get pregnant again.' I couldn't wait a year!" But as it turned out, after that traditional mourning period of a year, the couple recalls that "a veil lifted." During their camping trip they performed a simple ceremony of letting go. Janie reminisced, "The mountain azaleas were blooming, and I took two flowers down to the creek. I put one in the water and watched as it sailed out of sight and I put the second one in the water and watched it disappear also. It was my ritual of letting go. It was a simple ceremony, but it was very profound." That was July 4. Two days later, when Janie was forty-two years old, Elizabeth Lucia was conceived.

Peter and Janie had no idea how many people suffer from childbearing losses until they began sharing their story. They feel a certain responsibility to share their experience of loss with other "fellow journeyers." Said Janie, "I know hearing our story contributed to the healing of other people from past wounds. People who had repressed their memories or pushed them aside were now able to face them years later. Yes, it's been painful, but part of our healing was a result of this sharing."

During this most difficult of their years together, there was never a question of their mutual commitment. As Peter commented, "I'm committed to being, to the best of my ability, a life partner for Janie. I'm committed to taking care of my own personal needs, but never losing sight of the fact that meeting the needs of the whole meets a greater need in myself." Peter assented that his life would be totally different without the children, but he said his life is "so rich, so full, and so beautiful that it couldn't possibly exist without the children. Janie pushed for them, and I'm thankful that I have a partner who brings me a greater fullness. It's the *unseen* energy that is important. Not what I see, not what I ask for, not what I *think* I want, not what I *think* I need—I can take care of that. But it's the unseen that comes through a greater power. It sometimes comes through Janie, but my commitment is to honor the unseen energies, from *wherever* they may come." By "unseen energies" Peter meant the mysterious manner in which he and Janie were brought together; and how the death of Julia made a bridge between them and "every mother and father on the face of the earth who has experienced the loss of a child. I also had a tremendous connection with the earth and how we are poisoning her—all of this was going on at the same time that I was holding my dead daughter. I looked at her and felt such a deep connection with people I've never known or even seen before—that we were bonded and joined together."

Janie, in her characteristically brassy Texas accent, spoke about her and Peter's "different sexual rhythms. When we first came together, I used to think there was something wrong because we seldom had sex. In previous relationships I had measured my okayness by how much the man I was with wanted to have sex with me. But Peter went out and literally threw himself into the garden, sublimating his sexual desire. I used to say, 'What do you do when Mother Earth is your competition?' At least I always knew where he was!"

If a month or so went by before they had made love, Janie says she would gently (or not so gently) nudge Peter by bluntly stating, "It's been too long." After their lovemaking Janie would hope for a new resolve, but it seemed to dissipate like bubbles off champagne, leaving it flat. "I used to get mad about it, but I don't anymore. I've adjusted to it," she said.

In the company of two young children, one a precocious eight-year-old boy at the time, the couple came up with a witty euphemism for lovemaking: "marital activity." Peter, who coined the phrase, added, "It's not a question of keeping our sexual desire alive. If we just slow down and hang out together—allow spontaneous time—the natural attraction is there. But when your house becomes a pit stop for busy lives, your 'marital activity' tends to become—unless you're a sex addict—limited." He then referred to the Sunday morning affirmation and appreciation time, acknowledging that appreciating your partner can instantly change a mood. He's convinced that their regular Sunday practice is "a key to my well-being and my connection to the family matrix."

In her therapeutic practice, Janie works with people who, yearning for a relationship, find someone with whom they share excellent communication, but, alas, feel no physical attraction; or the opposite may be true. Janie observed, "I see so many people struggling with this. I believe that you can have a satisfying relationship if both people are committed to it, but it all has to be there: the physical and emotional attraction and the communication skills. It's all here for me in this relationship with Peter, even after fifteen years. There's always a sense of anticipation when I'm going to see him. I love being with him. Part of it is physical, but at this point, it's so much more than physical, because I know him, at his essence level, the truth of who he is. The more time we spend together—the more often the challenges come up—the more that diamond inside has a chance to glow. So, I need that physical connection, along with the spiritual, emotional, and psychological connections—we share on all those different levels. It just gets better. It's taken time and it's been a bumpy road, but there's no question in my mind that he's there for me and I'm here for him."

Chapter 19

Scenes from a Marriage

Molly Haskell and Andrew Sarris

I think you should look at relationship as a new job or career. You've got to work hard at it, put in a full day's work.

Andrew Sarris

There's no prescription that can be generalized for anybody else's marriage. I think a lot of it is luck and a meshing of fantasies. And those fantasies precede a marriage by a very, very long time.

Molly Haskell

W hile I was in New York doing research for *The Heart of Marriage*, a full-scale retrospective of the films of Swedish director Ingmar Bergman was being presented at several locations throughout Manhattan. Bergman is one of my favorite directors, and his movies are always worth multiple viewings. I already had the film festival schedule before I left for New York and in fact arranged my trip to coincide with it. The film I most wanted to see was the 1973 *Scenes from a Marriage*. This masterpiece was originally made as six one-hour weekly segments for Swedish television, and I had seen it in its entirety on PBS shortly after the separation from my own husband in 1973.

Scenes from a Marriage is undoubtedly the most penetrating and shattering film ever made about a marriage, its dissolution, and the ten-year relationship between the man and woman that continues long after the marriage has legally ended.

Twenty-two years later I sat watching *Scenes from a Marriage* again and felt once more the searing effect and intensity of the story of Marianne (Liv Ullman) and Johan (Erland Josephson). Oddly, the film opens as Marianne and Johan are being interviewed for an article about long-term, successful marriages. (I'd forgotten this coincidence with my own work.) Although passion and excitement have visibly waned during their ten years of marriage, the couple speaks about how happy they are together.

A short while after the interview, Johan tells Marianne that he is actually in love with another woman and wishes to leave the marriage. Marianne tries to convince him to stay, but he confesses that he has been wanting to leave for some time. The viewer is privy to the gamut of emotions the couple experiences during the ten years that they try to unravel and make sense of their vulnerable and volatile emotions. The film is an eloquent statement and raises the question of the personal ambivalence inherent in the difficult and confusing evolution from marriage to a caring friendship after divorce.

In between screenings of Bergman films, I had my own "scenes from a marriage" interview to conduct—*sans* divorce. After reading the film reviews of Molly Haskell and Andrew Sarris for twenty-five years, I looked forward to meeting them at their East Side apartment in Manhattan around the corner from the Guggenheim Museum. I caught them together between film festivals: Molly had just returned from Cannes in France and Andrew was on his way to receive an award in Australia.

Andrew greeted me with the warmth and physicality intrinsic to his Greek American heritage. He laughs often and fully; it starts as a wheeze somewhere in his chest and changes to a contagious rumble in his belly. I was later to discover that, as befits a Southern blueblood from Virginia, Molly's humor is dryer, more subtle. She is wryly self-mocking and extremely funny, always quick to point out an inconsistency or irony in herself or another.

"You wouldn't look at us and say, 'These two people were meant for each other.' She's beautiful, but she's also smart," he crowed. And indeed when Molly entered the room her slender, long-legged, blond good looks were striking.

"He still sees me as I was twenty-seven years ago," Molly said in amusement when I shared Andrew's compliment with her.

Their "love miraculously dissolved the boundaries of class and geography," which is how, in her hilarious, often poignant memoir, *Love and Other Infectious Diseases*, Molly describes this unlikely partnership that was outside the expectations and orthodoxies of conventional marriage. Andrew, teaching at the School of Visual Arts (and later at Columbia University's School of the Visual Arts) and writing for *The Village Voice*, was thirty-eight and still living with his mother in Queens, when he met twenty-seven-year-old Molly Haskell, who was working at the French Film Office and starting to write reviews herself.

Long before they met, Molly had been drawn to Andrew's mind and sensibility as expressed through his reviews. It wasn't his looks, as Andrew is the first to point out: "I don't know how to be casual. I'm either overdressed or underdressed. Casual requires a little bit of grace and thought and a lot of effort. I don't know how to be casual; I'm just sloppy."

———————

As expected, film was threaded through our conversation. I had asked Andrew and Molly to choose a movie they felt epitomized their own marriage.

"I think so much of marriage has to do with the fantasies that you start out with before you ever get married," Molly repeated. "Suddenly you're living in this dream world, only you don't know it—you think it's reality, but it's something from long, long ago. So when I first saw screwball comedies in revival, I thought, 'This is what marriage is to me.' The equality of the male and female, the humor, the good times. Films like *Bringing Up Baby, His Girl Friday, It Happened One Night, The Philadelphia Story, The Awful Truth.* That kind of teasing and sparring, the mutuality, the equality. The idea that marriage would be that kind of game. In some way, I think I tried to make it be like that. I'd be interested to know what *your* fantasy movie is, Andrew."

Overlooking the movie aspect, Andrew replied, "The one model I had right in front of me was that of my father and mother's marriage. She never really wanted to marry my father, but he was her first good friend. She loved talking with him. The best thing they had in their marriage was getting up in the morning and over coffee talking about everything. So my idea of marriage was always to talk in the morning when you wake up. As it turned out, Molly doesn't like to talk in the morning," he laughed.

"Not first thing in the morning," Molly said in self-defense. "You never have a downtime as far as talking goes," Molly reminded him.

"Never. There's never a moment in the day that I can't talk," Andrew said, nodding his head, almost proudly. Molly may have wanted to marry the strong, silent type, but I'm the weak, noisy type," he said, laughing at his own expense.

"We both had an ideal of talking, and we enjoy talking with each other," Molly continued. "Whatever you have in a marriage, something is gained and something else is given up. There's no prescription that can be generalized for anybody else's marriage. I think a lot of it is luck. And marriage is a meshing of fantasies; that's really what it is."

This was an interesting idea to me. Not only do we each have fantasies about the relationship we want when we meet someone, but those fantasies don't vanish—they persist. And, depending on how adept we are at combining them, braiding the two together as it were, those fantasies influence the stability and longevity of the relationship.

"Those fantasies precede a marriage by a very, very long time," Molly pointed out. "I think having compatible neuroses is also very important," she said, without a hint of a smile.

"Either compatible or complementary eccentricities," Andrew agreed. "We have remarkably similar tastes despite our different backgrounds. Many people say, 'You like the same movies 'cause you're married' and I say, 'No, we got married because we like the same movies!'"

"Although we share many of the same aesthetic and political values, it's not such a great idea for two people to be in the same profession, especially writers, because writing is such a neurotic activity anyway," Molly revealed. "For every couple, it's part opposites attract and part similarities. You have to find the right combination of differences and similarities. Writers, of course, are all neurotic. There's all this self-loathing and self-doubt. One is bad enough, but when you have two miserable writers, I don't know quite how people survive."

"During a certain period when we were both reviewing the same movies, we found ourselves competing," said Andrew. "It was very difficult for both of us because it affected the very thing we love most to do together: go to movies and talk about them afterwards."

"Why does it seem so difficult for marriages to last," I asked them.

"I think it's the world we live in," Molly explained. "Before, the family unit was most important and you submerged yourself for the good of the family. Now, for better or worse, we have mobility, and families of origin are being torn apart. Then there is the whole issue of feminism, the fact that now women want to seek their own destinies, often *apart* from marriage. I think the more evolved we are, the more difficult it is. Women are much more educated than they used to be. Their tastes are more evolved, more refined, and we expect a lot out of life. It's very hard to do both a family and career, I think."

"There is too much mobility—like me going to Australia and Molly going to Cannes. Technology has a lot to do with it; it's tearing people apart," said Andrew.

"I think we do better when we have periods of separation though," Molly added. "It really *does* enhance the marriage. I miss him so much and I can't wait to see him again. The separation reintroduces some excitement. He tries to save up things to tell me and I save up things to tell him. You need some distance."

"Another crucial factor for us is that we don't have children," Andrew added. "That has an up side and a down side, as everything does. It's not a decision we made: we're not going to have children."

"Either way you give something up," Molly continued. It's very hard being a film critic because you have to go to screenings at odd hours, and it's very demanding and time-consuming. It's an irregular kind of life, although that's not why we didn't have children. About fifteen years ago I wrote an article about how wonderful it was not having children, but the issue is complicated and probably a little neurotic."

"Very often children create a big problem for a couple," said Andrew. "In the movies they're always talking about how children bring a couple together." He then went on to illustrate his point by reflecting on the scene from François Truffaut's classic film *Shoot the Piano Player*, with Charles Aznavour. Aznavour's character accidentally meets a man in the street who is taking flowers home to his wife. The man recounts the story of his marriage and how he originally had not loved his wife until she had a child. When he went to see her in the hospital, he made the decision to love her and has since brought her flowers daily.

"It's a lovely touch to a film that is full of murders and kidnappings," he laughed. "Having a child is like jumping off a cliff and hoping you land in soft water."

"But isn't getting married the same way?" I asked him.

"It is," both Molly and Andrew replied, in unison.

"How can you know what an experience is going to be like?" I asked.

"That's where the luck comes in. People can spend years together before they really know each other," said Andrew. "Luck not only in the sense that you haven't married an axe murderer, but also in the sense that both people keep growing and developing at the same pace."

"Some part of me didn't want to get married or have children," Molly admitted. "So when we did get married, I had nightmares. You can't really face it. If you thought about it rationally, nobody would ever do it! You have to be partly blind, partly deluded, and have all sorts of romantic notions or you wouldn't get married. The same is true of having children."

"So romance serves as an inducement," I suggested, "and perhaps we would never marry without it. Hurrah for Hollywood, after all!"

During the decade of the '80s, Molly and Andrew had eight operations between them. It seemed as if one of them was always in the hospital. Molly had collapsed on a tennis court in 1981 and had a total of five emergency surgeries for intestinal obstructions. Andrew was in the hospital for two months before he was even diagnosed with one of the opportunistic viruses that came along in the early '80s about the same time as AIDS.

Molly admits that was the toughest time of their relationship. In her book *Love and Other Infectious Diseases* she writes about her confusion and terror at seeing her husband suffer nerve damage and lapses in consciousness. It was during his illness that she realized how dependent she had become on Andrew, how symbiotic the relationship was.

"The '80s were a bad decade," Andrew agrees. "That was a really big test; we were under the gun. And we survived."

"They said he was the sickest man to ever walk out alive," said Molly. "It was one of the most expensive illnesses on record, because so many different specialists were brought in. His ailment was completely mysterious. I don't know how people carry on when a spouse is permanently impaired, mentally or physically. It must be the hardest thing in the world because it's not the same person you married.

"Andrew said a macabre, but funny thing: maybe the book would have taken off if he'd died. People were always writing books about spouses who had died. I said, 'Yeah, people are going to say "He's all right now, so what's the big deal?" ' But it was a very big deal at the time. You were slowed up for life by it, but luckily you didn't have brain damage—that's what we were terrified of, and that didn't happen. He's still a chatterbox.

"I think marriage is a very different proposition from our parents' time, whether you have children or not," Molly said. "We're having to reinvent it and figure out what works. And accept the things that don't work, like the travel thing. That was a *big* disappointment, that we couldn't travel together. I might have just kept forcing the issue."

"My reluctance to travel is a kind of addiction," said Andrew, "an addiction to standing still, to inertia. I *am* addicted; I admit it."

"You have to accept the things you can't change and work around them. We did that by my traveling and Andrew staying home."

The Sarris-Haskell union seems to be so much a life of the mind, a sharing of and talking about ideas. In fact, they both acknowledge that from the beginning Andrew delighted in Molly's career and was, in fact, her mentor. I asked them if they agreed with Timothy Leary's statement: "Intelligence is the greatest aphrodisiac."

"This is what turned me on about Andrew. He understands me. I wrote, 'Being understood is the most erotic thing of all for a woman.' Now I sort of disagree with that.

It's part of a rescue fantasy that we're in—the great big man is not only going to love us and be attracted to us, but also penetrate our mind. It's a mind-fuck kinda thing."

"I think I gave Molly a certain confidence in her intellectual ability and encouraged her to do what she wanted to do."

"I *always* want to hear what he's going to say about something. And I think he wants to hear me, too. That's why the mind is the seat of eroticism for me. Andrew has an original way of seeing things. He remembers things, knows history, and has a vast sort of encyclopedia of information. But it's not just information; it's insights.

"One time we were staying with friends in Providence and our friend said, 'I couldn't believe that you two were in there talking about *mise en scène* all night.' We love to discuss film in bed, and we do it a lot. When I'm away from Andrew, I keep thinking 'I've got to tell him about the movie I saw or that article I read in the newspaper.' There's always fresh material that it's fun to process together."

"What about fidelity?" I asked, rather bluntly. "After twenty-six years."

"Well, as far as we know, we've been faithful. We certainly wouldn't talk about it if we hadn't been," Molly said, equally direct.

"Is it a conscious decision that you made, that you continue to make?" I pressed.

"It's not like there are a million people out there waiting to help you cheat," Andrew said, laughing. "You have to be predisposed. Where do people find the time?" he asked, incredulously. "We barely have time for each other; how are we going to set up somebody else? There are a lot of logistics involved. Here I am, I can't meet my deadline, and I'm going to set up somebody else? The whole idea of it becomes so unworkable. I think part of the solution is keeping busy, and doing what you like—having work that you like. And when the two of you write, as Molly and I do, and you are each other's best friends, the odds become much more logical *not* to do it than to do it. Paul Newman once said something very sweet: 'I could only have an affair with someone who had as much to lose as I do.'

"I've had no problem with women throwing themselves at me and weeping at my feet. Infidelity is not that easy. It's not like the world is full of women dying to have an affair with you."

"What advice would you have for someone like me—who is single—and interested in finding a compatible relationship?" I asked.

"I've often thought what would I do if Andrew had died or . . ."

". . . if I'd run off with Julia Roberts," Andrew joked.

"I wouldn't be too anxious to get involved with anybody," Molly said. "Of course, I don't know. I grew to love all those things like getting my back rubbed. That's the whole contradiction: I want to be independent and yet I really *love* being married. It's really a lot of fun. It would have to be somebody you can talk to; that to me is the main thing."

Andrew concurred, "The main thing is long dates and long conversations."

"Looking forward to seeing the person that night," said Molly. "Being soul mates, or being intellectually and spiritually on the same wavelength, is tremendously important to me, although I don't think it is for everyone. In fact, I almost envy people who don't need that kind of connection, because if they are artistic or creative, they probably get more into their work and their ideas. Whereas if you are very close, much of your mental energy goes into the relationship. It depends on what you want."

"I forgot to say earlier," said Andrew, "—maybe this is on the Oprah level—"

"So is everything about marriage—on the Oprah level," said Molly, under her breath.

"One mistake a lot of people make when they think about getting married," Andrew continued, "is to look for somebody to complete you, to give you the things you haven't been able to give yourself. We had already found ourselves, more or less, when we finally got together."

"The truth is I *did* want someone to complete me, and now I don't. That's what writing *Love and Other Infectious Diseases* and going through analysis was all about: becoming myself. That was really what it was about: seeing myself as a separate, free-standing agent, not someone symbiotically tied to Andrew. I don't expect you to take care of me emotionally and mentally the way I did before," Molly said, speaking directly to her husband.

"I guess if I were to give someone advice, I would tell them about several friends who had bad marriages, then went into therapy and made good ones. This is the one area where I think psychoanalysis or psychotherapy can really work. It's crucial to figure out what our patterns are, what we sometimes conceal from ourselves. We have a vested interest in not acknowledging what we are doing. That would be the first step: as much as possible to unravel and figure out what your fantasies are."

"I think you should also look at relationship as a new job or a new career," Andrew offered. "You've got to work hard at it, put in a full day's work."

"And not expect too much," Molly concluded. "Which is another way of saying, 'Don't look to the other person to complete you.'"

Chapter 20

If Only Men Were Dogs or Why I'd Marry My Dog If He Asked

Her life was okay.

Sometimes she wished she

were sleeping with the right

man instead of with her dog,

but she never felt she was

sleeping with the wrong dog.

JUDITH COLLAS,
"CHANGE OF LIFE"

They're a kind of four-legged Bodhisattva—dogs, that is. Spiritually luminous beings who voluntarily return to an incarnation on earth in order to guide those souls who continue to struggle with the duality of good and evil and are less enlightened than they. Of course, some people think many men *are* dogs. But then they really don't know dogs. Very few men I've known come at all close to having the devotion, humor, and instinctive moral courage that I have experienced over and over again among my canine friends.

In fact, if I were to apply Judith Collas's poem to my own life, I might paraphrase it to read: I often thought I was sleeping with the wrong man, but I always *knew* I was sleeping with the right dog. Here's a case in point: men can say the darnedest things, you know. Like the first time a new lover saw me naked and asked: "What happened?" as he looked at my pendulous breasts. What happened? Indeed!

Burning my bras in 1966.

Pregnancy, which caused my breasts to steadily increase in size from my usual 34C to a 38EE.

Nursing my beautiful baby boy for a year.

Losing and regaining the same twenty pounds until, over a period of several decades of bingeing and purging, I must have lost and regained somewhere in the neighborhood of four hundred pounds.

And then there is the issue of my mother who refused to nurse me because she didn't want her breasts to sag. Am I carrying *her* karma, too?

I guess you could say those things happened, I thought, staring at him. But instead of asking what had happened to one side of his scrotum that was shorter than the other or why his penis was so small, I quickly jumped into bed in order to hide the source of my embarrassment. I didn't have enough self-assurance or, as we say today, self-esteem to flip him off and turn on my heels. No one had ever complained or questioned me before about my body. Eighteen years later those words still cut deeply into my raw flesh, like a continual ritual scarification of my psyche, and cause a piercing self-consciousness.

———————————

Every morning when I awaken, Sienna's right front paw is gently resting on my chest, directly over my heart, as if, even in his sleep, he assumes the role of my guardian. His head shares my pillow; our breathing is synchronous. Our comfort with each other dissolves any impediment a difference in sex *or* species might otherwise foster. We look lovingly into each other's brown eyes, as I tell him what a great big hairy chest he has and wipe the sleep from his eyes. Oddly, even his snoring is soothing to me. "Honey, you snore just like a man," I say, during the middle of the night.

I have often been accused of anthropormophizing, but can you think of a better comparison for animals than people? When I meet someone new I usually conjure a celebrity figure to compare them to: Sean Connery, W. S. Merwin, Barbara Hershey. I have a friend who can't control her impulse to compare everyone she meets with an animal: a fox, raccoon, goat, lion, etc. The curious part is that she is unfailingly accurate in her bestial similes. Currently there is a spectrum of books in popular culture that discuss the theory that animals have (choose one) emotions, intelligence, soul. This is *new* information? Share your life with an animal and you will learn firsthand what these books are saying.

Love comes in so many forms. The Eskimos have many different words for snow based on its temperature, texture, hue, and the use it is put to. In the English language we have but one word to describe the most complex, varied human emotion between a child and parent, between friends, between humans and the divine, between humans and Nature, between sexual partners, and between humans and their pets.

From an early age I associated dogs with heroic deeds of courage and kindness and devotion. When I was but three years old, the house in which my mother and I lived burned to the ground, very nearly with us in it. The only reason we survived is that our loyal companion, Major, alerted the neighbors through his barking, and thereby saved our lives from this 3:00 AM inferno. My mother and I were in oxygen tents for ten days, but Major lost his life. Like the widow of a valiant fallen soldier, my mother was given a medal to honor his bravery.

Throughout my life dogs have continued to provide steadfast friendship and companionship. When I was lonely as an only child (which was often), with a working single mom, our dogs were my friends, baby-sitters, teachers, and family. As an adult I lived with my golden retriever, Sierra, for thirteen years—longer than anyone (even my mother) except my son. We were inseparable, and when I would receive an invitation for dinner at a friend's house, I assumed it included Sierra. If my host or hostess asked me to leave Sierra at home, I would stay home, too. My motto was: Love me, love my dog. And I lived it.

So the pertinent question remains: Is there a man somewhere in the world who is magnanimous enough to share me with my dog? Whose heart is expanded enough to *include* my dog? Whose bed is capacious enough for all three of us? I hope so. I know it's unfair to expect someone else to accommodate all my needs—even a dog. And, as much as Sienna and I love each other, he can't dispense the two things I miss most about a man: sex and conversation.

Chapter 21

Committed to the Process

Hal and Sidra Stone

My surrender and commitment are to the process between us, not to Sidra and the marriage. And there is no guarantee where that will take us. There is no insurance policy for marriage.

Hal Stone

A good marriage does not come cheaply, there is so much work to do— and both people must be committed to that process. We've had some very rocky times and we have earned our love and this relationship over and over and over again.

Sidra Stone

It wasn't until we sat down at the oriental carpet–covered dining table that I first noticed them—the hats, Hal and Sidra Stone's hats, perhaps a dozen—covering the wall next to the kitchen door. Hats for many occasions—twelve distinct expressions of one couple's countless facets. They hung without any particular order, but orderly. Each was weathered and worn, some battered, yet, if only by the prominence of their display, each seemed appreciated for its uniqueness. A perfect metaphor for an entire psychological theory, Voice Dialogue, which was collaboratively developed by Drs. Hal and Sidra Stone during the 1970s.

Having known Hal for nearly ten years, I was invited to conduct our interview at Thera, the Stones' country property in Mendocino County in northern California. Thera is named in honor of the volcanic island sixty-three miles north of Crete in the Aegean Sea. It would be difficult to find the character, topography, and weather patterns between two regions more dissimilar: one, ripe from and satiated with sun, its natives psychologically sculpted by the whims of multiple mythical gods and goddesses; the other, mysterious, pristine, reserved and wintry in its New England–like demeanor. Both are worlds away from Brooklyn, where Sidra was born, and Detroit, Hal's hometown.

In a cul-de-sac with towering eucalyptus trees, cypress, and white pines smelling of Christmas, Thera sits framed by the Pacific Ocean on the west while acres of spacious flowering meadows and wild berry brambles surround in the remaining directions. Their home, a restored farmhouse originally built about 1880, echoes the presence of the Stones themselves—unaffected and down-to-earth.

At lunchtime Sidra prepared omelettes while Hal toasted thick slices of hearty multigrain bread and we dined alfresco on a stunningly clear spring day. As we ate our goat-cheese omelettes and toast with jam, our actions were seemingly mimed by a mother swallow who brought food to her open-beaked triplets nested in the eaves of the farmhouse roof. Here at Thera Hal and Sidra have created space to be quiet and time to allow magic in their lives.

Despite their retreat from a metropolitan area, the couple remain deeply concerned about the world in which they live, and continue to establish centers worldwide for their work in Voice Dialogue.

Voice Dialogue, or the Psychology of Selves, postulates that operating within each of us are a myriad of subpersonalities or selves through which we experience life. Based on Jungian theory and using components from Gestalt therapy, psychosynthesis, transactional analysis, and psychodrama, the objective of Voice Dialogue is to develop an *aware ego*, a nonjudgmental vantage point from which to observe all our different selves and give expression to their unique experiences. During a Voice Dialogue session a literal vocal ensemble of characters is revealed—some with startling results. The client may "meet" for the first time an Aphrodite or Dionysian archetypal part of themselves they never dreamed existed. They may work on the Good or Bad Mother/Father–Daughter/Son syndrome that, unchecked, could destroy their marriage.

These selves are continually making contact with us in our dreams and fantasies, in our moods and maladies, and in a multitude of unpredictable and inexplicable reactions to the world around us. According to the principles of Voice Dialogue, the more sharply individuals become attuned to these inner voices, the more real choice they are able to exercise in the pursuit of their own destinies. My personal experience with Voice Dialogue has been that of a fluid, nonlinear approach to the human psyche—a method for tapping into and converging with my stream of consciousness.

During our two-day interview Hal and Sidra spoke with ease and assurance—using the jargon with which they are imbued (and, indeed, have coined)—and wove their shared psychological perspective like a subtext through the story of their work and lives. They used anecdote and metaphor freely to illustrate the multiple layers and dimensions of their relationship.

In early 1972, a friend of Sidra's suggested Sidra invest in a few sessions with a Dr. Stone, a Jungian analyst. The friend, a therapist and a teacher at UCLA, had recently attended a talk given by Hal at which he gave a demonstration of active imagination and orchestrated a guided imagery with a large audience. According to the friend "it was fabulous." And she encouraged Sidra (whose interest in active imagination had been piqued by reading an article by the psychologist Roberto Assagioli) to learn the techniques herself for her private practice as a psychotherapist.

Agreeing but insistent that she was *not* going into therapy or analysis, that she did *not* need any major psychological changes in her life, Sidra called for an appointment with Hal. A portentous dream shortly before their initial meeting had Sidra entering a salon for a haircut where she clearly told the hairdresser, "Just cut the front a bit. I want the rest of it left the way it is, nice and long." She ended up with a major haircut in the dream, and a radical life change in reality. There were no intimations of a shared future during that initial encounter, but by the end of the six-week series they knew they were in love, and since that time they have immersed themselves in the process of their relationship. Hal initiated our interview by describing what it felt like to experience "a deep and sensitive love" for the first time in his life.

"It's strange, when you haven't experienced a rather deep and sensitive love for another person, you don't know what you've been missing. I simply hadn't known it before Sidra, and it meant a great deal to me. *And* equally important, through enormous trial and tribulation I've always fought like a tiger to preserve that feeling." And there were many opportunities in those early months and years together to protect their newfound love. Sidra felt like a total outsider to his world and "he was a total outsider to mine." Hal was "a Jungian type," steeped in mythology and introverted. For him, Sidra was his Soror Mystica, or mystical sister; he felt that through this love they would transform themselves together. Hal claims he knew nothing about surrendering to a relationship and saw himself and Sidra as tools to help each other in their individual processes.

When they first met, their differences were glaring. To Sidra, who, by her own admission, was "a creature of the mind, totally rational and pragmatic, well read, well educated, well traveled," Hal opened up the world of magic and spirit. For Hal, Sidra was "a sophisticated Manhattan lady, a real dynamo; I was a laid-back California guy. She is an excellent money manager and a strong mother type; I'm much less of a parent type. She loved traveling in the outer world, I loved traveling in the inner world."

As Sidra recounts, "We joked about it. His idea of a big trip was going to Palm Springs, where he could write in his journal and analyze his dreams! We were opposites in so many ways it was unbelievable." In keeping with the early stages of most relationships, when they were first in love those differences had little effect, but eventually they began to come between them, and at critical times both have had to undergo some major changes. Compromises? "No!" Sidra is quick to distinguish between arbitrarily compromising and "actually seeing the value of change for *yourself.*"

When Hal "started catching hold of money," he insists it wasn't to please Sidra, but because he realized how "crazy" he was in relation to money. He remains grateful to Sidra, who had mirrored for him what he considers a lack or deficiency within himself.

And yet these differences are in keeping with the theory of Voice Dialogue: that we choose qualities in another that we disown or reject in ourselves in order to learn about them. They call this reaction the Theory of Disowned Selves. What became increasingly apparent to them after they began living together is that they carried the same patterns of interacting into this relationship they had struggled with in each of their previous marriages.

So in their relationship they learned that "across the board you always marry your disowned selves." How each couple handles that dynamic becomes the critical work in relationship. They disagree with therapists and counselors who encourage their clients to commit to the relationship in order to feel more secure, and instead maintain the rather existential stance that nothing is forever and that they "never assumed our marriage was forever. That notion is a real fantasyland." In their view it remains most important to commit yourself to the paradox of an evolving joint-process relationship, keeping the door open without having one foot out ready to leave.

"My surrender and commitment are to the process between us," declared Hal, "not to Sidra and the marriage. And there is no guarantee where that will take us. There is no insurance policy for marriage."

Sidra further developed this notion. "If you are totally committed to keeping your marriage in a preconceived form, then you start making those adjustments to fit into the marriage. It's like Cinderella's sisters cutting off their heels and toes to fit into the glass slipper. Each person becomes smaller in a sense, rather than holding their nose and jumping in to explore what's going on. And it's scary every time, because you never know whether you will resurface together."

"There's so much insecurity in living like that," Hal continued, " because you love each other and your lives are so completely intertwined. The idea of possible separation can feel and look very painful, but somewhere that has to remain an option. At this point in our relationship, it would be a big surprise for us to go separate ways, but, again, you never know what's going to happen and where the process of the relationship will lead you."

They have completed "thousands of hours of psychological work together." And certainly every couple who enjoys a deeply satisfying relationship would agree with Sidra when she said, "A good marriage does not come cheaply, there is so much work to do— and both people must be committed to that process. We've had some very rocky times and we have earned our love and this relationship over and over and over again. Our relationship has taught us much of what we are teaching others: about the psychology of selves and bonding patterns. Each time a problem or block arose, we'd have to learn a new way of handling it before we could break through."

The couple describes their relationship as "a kind of crucible." When they got married and began calling each other by their previous spouse's name, they realized they were experiencing the same learned responses they'd had before in each of their previous marriages, which both baffled and amazed them because they had been married to the exact opposite of each other.

"There have been a number of very central points in the course of our life where one of us felt a level of desperation, points where the vulnerability was so total. These usually were times of tears because the pain was so profound around some issue—it was so sincere," said Hal.

"There wasn't any manipulation, because it was always, 'I don't know where we're supposed to go from here,' " added Sidra.

"Whenever either of us got desperate enough about something, the other person heard it," Hal affirmed. "For example, when I couldn't tolerate the idea of being in Los Angeles anymore, when I couldn't continue in my private practice and continue that life, I felt desperate. When I shared those feelings with Sidra, there was no question that it was necessary to change our lives. That's always been the case with us; whenever one of us gets to that level of desperation, the other one hears. We've been very creative in dealing with our periods of disappointment or despondence."

They have "a process relationship," because they are constantly working on it. There is no goal; it's not fixed. "I want a relationship that's *alive*," Sidra explained. "I'm funny because I work hard to get life (situations) cubbyholed and static and then I can't stand it. The deepest part of me wants an ever changing, transforming relationship and another conflicting part tries to make it safer or more predictable." Her face glowed when she said, "I'm leading the life I want, the life I dreamed I would lead but didn't even realize was possible. That goes for the work and the man, and their quality of magic, intimacy, and spirituality."

An absolutely essential ingredient in their marriage has been monogamy. I was struck by their openness and honesty in discussing such difficult issues. Again, Hal used the paradigm of Voice Dialogue to explore perhaps the most fragile and sensitive aspect of any couple's relationship: fidelity.

As professional therapists they work both individually and as a team as transpersonal chaperones guiding other couples with their own hard-earned experience and expertise. Although they insist they "don't have any advice to give" on the subject, they are clear about the fact that only a monogamous relationship would work for them.

Hal obviously doesn't condone amorous errantry, although he asserts that often it is an extramarital affair that may help to break through a stultifying and energy-eroding marriage. But the partners must remain aware of the fact that an affair may eliminate from the relationship the presence of their most vulnerable part, which provides that deep level of intimacy and trust.

Continuing with his thought Hal said, "Now that means I have to carry a tension between the parts of me that would like to be intimate with other women and the part that says, 'I can't handle an affair.' Sidra also has to carry that tension. In order to be present in this relationship I have to sweat between those opposites. So I sweat. At this moment I'm not sweating very much, but next week I may be sweating a lot," he teased. "It goes in cycles."

In their personal and professional experience, Hal and Sidra have observed that an attraction outside the primary relationship or an eventual affair is inevitably provoked or preceded by the discovery that something is missing from the relationship. Sidra humorously illustrated the point with a situation from their life together. "Those years before Hal had a handle on earning and managing money would have been a logical time for me to have been attracted to a businessman. I might have thought to myself, 'What do I need this psychologist for? I want someone who has money in the bank!' In other words, I would have been drawn toward what was missing between Hal and myself."

Hal supported Sidra's statement, "I've also learned that when I am strongly attracted outside—I don't mean the natural male-female attraction (there are a lot of delicious men and women out there), that's present all the time—but when I'm *energetically* attracted outside my marriage, it's inevitably because something isn't working between Sidra and myself. I may have stopped reacting, or sharing my anger, irritability, annoyance—whatever the hell it is—I'm not dealing with the relationship where it is right now."

An affair prevents a couple from coming to each other and "kicking ass," as Hal put it. "She should come to me and say, 'Listen, you come home or this marriage is over! I don't care about your work, I don't care about making ten million dollars.' If she's having an affair, she never has to confront me. Or, I never have to confront her and say, 'Look, you need to realize that your connection to the children is too much, and I want more in this relationship.' I'm not saying this confrontation can't happen when you have affairs, but the affair can be a smokescreen."

Discussing the possibility of extramarital affairs naturally segued into the topic of jealousy. They both believe that each partner in a relationship must maintain a healthy sexuality and physicality. The trick is to be a sexual being in the world without succumbing to affairs outside the marriage, to "bring it on back home," as Bob Dylan put it. Sidra laughingly commented, "God willing, I'll never lose my flirt. Noticing a man and flirting with him is nice. It's natural. And when at times I do lose that, life seems dulled."

"This is where these issues are so complex," Hal added. "Trying to inhibit that natural libido in your partner is actually very damaging for your own relationship with them."

"But trying *not* to inhibit them is also damaging," Sidra continued in full force. "There's a lot of passion around this subject. I'm not sweet with Hal—I don't like it when he's attracted to other women or when they're attracted to him. I don't like it at all, *but* I like it. It's so complicated. If I become a Good Mother and say, 'Isn't that sweet, he's feeling his sexuality; it's so good for our relationship,' it's bullshit! That's the one place I protect my boundary."

Hal attested to Sidra's statement, "She's a killer. The primitive Earth Mother/ Priestess comes out. Sidra is very territorial; and I have always appreciated that about her. Now, you might think, doesn't that smother you? The answer is no, it doesn't smother me at all. In fact I'm enormously relieved. She smells the women who energetically try to wiggle in, even before I'm aware of them. She has a certain gutsy primitivity that I actually appreciate. So I have to be strong enough to stand up to that. If I'm not, if I give into my fear of her Tigress, then I become a Good Little Boy. I become Son to her Mother. I'm the same way, although I didn't used to be. Until I met Sidra I felt that jealousy was inappropriate."

"Helping to bring new consciousness through" is how Sidra described the common vision of a mission that she shares with her husband. The fact that their work is a core part of their lives is not necessarily a "recipe" for other couples. Individually and in unison, what they contribute to the world has always been enormously significant to them. Hal acknowledged that, "It is a gift to be able to share on the multitude of levels on which we share—a permeating interest in consciousness, the ability to share dreams on a personal level, the writing process on an objective level, cyclical co-teaching, international travel—we share our entire personal and professional lives."

However, working together as intensely and closely as this couple does means that they must make a continuous effort to remember the importance of their intimate romantic connection, because as Hal revealed, "You can very easily become good business partners. Because we are such fabulous workers, we can forget to look at each other. Then, of course, we pay a price, because both of us really get crazy when that happens—and that's happened a lot to us." The necessary process of renegotiating then takes place, in which a tight new working schedule is planned and to which they "religiously" adhere.

The importance of maintaining separate identities was raised at this point in our discussion. There are identifiable ways or patterns of being in relationship, and people may define these patterns by different names. The Stones have spent a lifetime creating a psychological theorem that calls them "bonding patterns." According to this theory, when a couple unsuspectingly locks into these bonding patterns, each individual loses his or her identity and boundaries, and that's the end of romance.

Hal elaborated on this thought: "I absolutely believe that you can be in a long-term marriage and sustain romance and sex—that it *can* work; and when it doesn't it's because of these bonding patterns. That's the crux: when a couple starts relating from these patterned responses with each other, it is absolute death. When we first began forming the idea of bonding patterns, we spent months on end analyzing literally every interaction we had, trying to figure out what in the hell was going on!" Hal observed that these bonding patterns are "going on all the time. They are present 99 percent of the time in *all* relationships." "All relationships" includes those between mothers, fathers, children, siblings, lovers, husbands, wives, employers, employees, friends, and even beloved animals.

"It's been years of hard work, and these are recipes tested in our own kitchen," Sidra added.

"Vulnerability is so central to relationship," I said. "It seems as if every interaction between two people perceptibly pivots around the individuals' vulnerability. Why?"

It seemed obvious as Hal explained, "If you look deeply enough into the bonding patterns, what you find is that *everyone's* inner child is afraid of abandonment."

The myriad selves or subpersonalities that compose every individual have been subconsciously developed in order to protect the inner child. In other words, "Our whole personality is based on this child!" Hal declared somewhat incredulously.

I wasn't entirely joking when I asked, "Do we ever outgrow this inner child business?"

Sidra laughed as she immediately answered, "Nope. But you become more sensitive. You learn to take care of your *own* inner child instead of projecting it onto the other to do it for you."

"You learn to be a better 'parent,' " added Hal. "And you learn to develop an aware ego so you can walk into your partner's study when she is overworking and say, 'Hey, I need some time with you,' and make sure that you get it."

Listening to them so meticulously describe the inner workings of their relationship, I asked what they do when they experience boring times or a sense of overfamiliarity with each other. Their response seemed obvious upon reflection, but at that moment I experienced it as new. Sidra led the discussion with an ironic allusion to Voice Dialogue. "You talk to another voice! I get bored when I'm not in touch with what's going on. If you think about it, there's always so much going on inside every individual: all the selves, and all the bonding patterns you're constantly dealing with, the dreams you have, everything's constantly changing and so fluid."

Hal concurred, "I think that's the big one, that's the key. Boredom is just bad press about relationship from people who don't know how to work on one. I'm much more reactive in our relationship than Sidra is. Most relationships are like that; one person tends to be more reactive."

Sidra expounded, "A good example of how this works, for instance, might be a time when things seem a little dull between Hal and me, so I'll ask him what's going on. He might reply, 'Well, I met Mary Jane at a party last week and I was really attracted to her.' *Now* I have something to react to. I might want to strangle him, but at least we are both present with each other again," she laughed.

They both explained that learning to react to their partner is the method that allows them to work through the bonding patterns. Hal insisted, "Working on relationship isn't just theoretical; both partners really have to deal with everything on the table."

As a couple, both privately and professionally, the Stones have given much thought to the meaning of love. In response to my question, Sidra, who had been contemplatively staring out the window through the lace curtains began, "I have a strong feeling about what love is at this point in my life. Each of us has a specific vibration—a psychic fingerprint—that's energetic. And when this energy matches in two people, we call it love. When it doesn't match you can make a sensible, comfortable, good partnership that may continue along very smoothly, very rationally, but you won't touch the depths that are possible when that energy is present."

Unfortunately, even with this opportunity for a meeting of souls, it doesn't necessarily mean that a relationship will last forever. "And," Sidra continued, "it certainly doesn't mean that your relationship will be free of difficulties. They will be present in either case, and both people must work very hard to clear out the debris in their own personality, and the cultural clutter, over and over again."

This question led to, for me, the most significant part of our discussion, for it coalesced in my mind many divergent pieces of information—a psychic ganglia, if you will—that I had been contemplating for several years. The idea of union—with ourselves, with a significant other, with our concept of God or a universal wisdom—has been central to my own esoteric study and spiritual quest.

In the initial meeting with another—that quickening of energy—we feel a sense of union, a deep sense of fullness and wholeness, a seeming recognition of our other missing half, or as Voice Dialogue describes it, the disowned selves. The act of seeking this union with another finite being can be seen as a grand metaphor for the greater union sought—a spiritual union. And if we continue to pursue the object of our desire with continuing commitment to the process of relationship and with enormous faith in this process, we may eventually integrate our own projected disowned selves and achieve our highest goal: that of becoming whole within oneself.

Picking up the thread of my thought, Hal embellished it. "That's a very profound idea, because it means that whenever you enter into a relationship, if you are aware that what you are attracted to in the other is what you have disowned in yourself, what becomes most important is the *process* of the relationship rather than the particular person with whom you are involved. That's not to say that it could be *anyone*; that initial energetic attraction remains crucial."

In their therapeutic practice, Sidra and Hal confirmed that there are numerous people who actually say that their relationship *feels* like a soul connection, but when it doesn't work out they are deeply disappointed. "We really haven't had the equipment to do this work," said Hal. "There's been no technology. You can have as deep a soul connection as you think is possible, but the fact is if you don't know about the principle of disowned selves and the bonding patterns, then there is very little chance of the relationship working out."

With distinct eloquence Hal explored the possibility of utilizing relationship as a spiritual path, "We have a very strong surrender to divinity. I don't know how any marriage can survive without that. There are so many instances in relationship where you cannot deal personally with the issues and with each other. It's often so overwhelming. When Sidra and I first got married, we had to solve enormous economic problems. Neither of us had a lot of money and we had to work very hard. We had five children between us and, of course, they always needed time and attention and money. So we had to work things out with them as well as to solve the problems between us in our own relationship.

"Life is so complex, relationship and families and family mixing are all so complex, without a clear surrender to some form of divinity, I can't imagine surviving it. There were times when we went to bed and simply prayed, 'Please, Dear God'. . . I feel that when you surrender, it gets heard.

"If I surrender to this process of relationship with Sidra, I don't know what divinity has in store for me. I don't know what the universe requires of us. So part of the spiritual path is exactly that: it's the commitment to the process itself, and you go where you are led to go. Part of the transformational process is tuning in to those lines of energy that belong to you, that take you where you need to go in your life."

Sidra also sees relationship as a spiritual path with its own agenda, "You may be with somebody in a wonderful relationship, and then suddenly reach a point where it just doesn't work in the same way anymore. I feel that if our relationship were to come to an end, it would mean that something better was out there waiting for both of us, that there was another step we couldn't take together. Either we needed to continue on separately or to be facilitated by another relationship. Ultimately it's having faith that if you take the next step on the path that appears before you, it will lead you where you need to go—if you do it as honestly as you can. The deepest lessons I have learned have been from my relationships. They have taught me about myself, stretched me, and challenged me to go further."

When I asked how honest they are with each other and how they developed trust, Sidra began, "We had nothing to lose. We were not expecting to be together, to get married, so there was nothing to lose by trusting each other, trusting the relationship and being perfectly honest."

Hal countered, "I don't think we are 100 percent honest. I mean sometimes we hold back our attractions to other people or our reactions. You can't be compulsive about it! It's easy to hold back negative reactions toward your partner, to lock up and then begin to stockpile negativity. The garbage dump begins to build until finally you break, but I think that's a natural part of every relationship; there's no way to avoid it. In a sense this process is cyclical: the harbored negativity or resentment builds and is released, builds again and is released again."

Sidra interjected that she thought the requirement to be totally honest exhausting. I proffered that perhaps it was possible to maintain a balance between an all-out honesty and a kindness or consideration to one's partner, realizing that it is unnecessary to burden him or her with every minor complaint, disagreement, or irritation.

Hal agreed, "Or you don't mention something to your partner because you feel blocked, or haven't had your coffee, or you're too angry, or you simply don't feel like it.

We're human! I hear a lot of people say, 'You must be 100 percent honest with each other all the time.' Of course you have to be fundamentally honest—you can't lie, you can't cheat—but people crucify themselves."

"We are dishonest with ourselves, let's face it," Sidra observed. "So how can we be totally honest with another human being? We try."

The couple openly examined how they keep sexual desire alive between them. Something as basic as simply remembering to make quality time for sexual expression with your partner and making sure it is counted as important between you were mentioned. Through traveling a great deal, Sidra and Hal have discovered that the bonding patterns "live at home"; that's where they have their roots. By constantly breaking form they prevent their sexual life from seeming ordinary and stale, and traveling contributes to a sense of romance.

In the nearly seventeen years Hal and Sidra have been married, Hal has experienced two major illnesses. In 1980 he underwent surgery for a rectal abscess, after which he felt totally vulnerable and dependent on Sidra to help clean his surgical wound. He describes this level of dependence as "an unbelievable thing for me to allow her to do, but I had no choice. After the wound had been cleaned, I then had to wear a pad to stop the bleeding. I later ended up needing a second surgery, because the first one hadn't done the job. So there was a period of at least three or four weeks after each surgery when I needed Sidra's assistance. I was completely vulnerable to her, and if I hadn't accepted the situation, I don't know what would have happened. It would have been terrible."

Several years later Hal had a bout with high-speed arrhythmia, an electrical condition of the heart in which his heartbeat was very irregular. He describes the condition as "not a big deal once you know about it and understand it, but when it first hit I really thought I was finished. I thought I would be crippled for the rest of my life. For three weeks it was out of control."

Although, Sidra says, she never thought Hal was close to death during the attacks of arrhythmia, she does feel that it produced a deeper sense of intimacy between them. "I became aware of the preciousness of our relationship and that something could happen at any time."

Continuing, Hal admitted, "Again, the core issue is being able to be 1 million percent vulnerable to another person. Strong people have a particularly hard time being vulnerable. Sidra and I are both strong individuals; vulnerability isn't one of our top pursuits. Of course, even before my illness we had learned to be quite vulnerable with each other, but you get busy and lose that awareness. Illness drops you back into it very fast. A heart arrhythmia absolutely cripples you. I would turn gray and couldn't move while it was operating."

An ever present sense of humor has helped them to deal with many difficult situations. "By definition, if you are without humor, you are without the ability to maintain a distance. Humor really is an indication that you have some distance from your own self-involvement," Sidra stated.

In answer to my question, "What is the saving grace in your relationship?" Hal surprised me by answering, "My unconscious likes Sidra, and her unconscious likes me. When the chips are down and we start to distance from each other or I become too judgmental, I may have a dream in which, for example, I'm going to lose her. When I wake up, I'm out of the bonding pattern so fucking fast you can't believe it. I have a very clear sense that the unconscious supports our relationship."

At those moments when they fear they have somehow lost their path, that they aren't moving along either as individuals or as a couple, they realize the possibility that they may have gone as far as they can together.

"Without a sense of journey—for myself alone or in the relationship—I can't stand it. Everything becomes dry straw," Hal revealed. At that point serious psychological discourse begins in conjunction with prayer and meditation. They use any means to break the form of their bonding patterns, "to get re-equilibrated."

Hal reflected, "Unfortunately, life brings you certain dry periods. It's not continually wet and juicy. And we also have an understanding of the fact that there are times when you inevitably lose the journey. But you hang in."

When to "hang in" and when to move on has invariably been one of the most trying decisions for me personally in relationship. Sidra reflected on the inherent paradox contained in the concept of commitment. "When you make a commitment to a relationship 'forever'—to a particular form with a particular person—you have no idea what that form or person will grow into. A stagnant image of what you expect from both that form and person crystallizes in your mind: 'My relationship will remain like this for the rest of my life.' When the inevitable difficulties arise, you try to fix the relationship so it will still fit that original form rather than allowing it to grow and seeing what new shape develops. It becomes a jail, a 'no exit' situation, a static form to which you are constantly trying to adjust. It's that 'no matter what,' that absolute that ignores the needs of the individual that is a setup for bonding patterns, or for disowning anything that doesn't fit into the small box you've built to house the relationship."

Further clarifying the distinction between commitments to either form or process, Hal reminded me in the context of Voice Dialogue that "there has to be some comprehension that you are with your partner for a reason, that you become involved with and marry people who *absolutely* mirror your disowned selves. And because of that *every* relationship is a teacher to you, and marriage is particularly a teacher. Marriage becomes a vessel to contain the craziness that develops between two people."

Their relationship remains a perpetual source of wisdom for them; and they both agreed they have learned about themselves and about life in ways that might have been impossible without their relationship. Sidra specified, "I have been able to reexamine myself, to think about why I'm alive, what I'm doing, where I'm going and why, in the context of our relationship, in a much more conscious way than I ever would have outside of the relationship. I'm constantly being forced to examine myself and my actions. When you look in a mirror you only see yourself from one angle. My relationship has put mirrors above, beside, behind, and underneath me. It's forced me to see myself differently and therefore to live differently."

"When you start making something more important than your relationship, you are fucked," Hal bluntly stated, pounding his fist on the table to make his point while cups and saucers jumped like frightened characters out of *Fantasia*. "You cannot live in the same house together. You can't ever stop dealing with the relationship because then everything in your life goes sour. Especially in our situation where we are together so much, we can't let any significant issue go for two seconds."

As the afternoon approached four o'clock it became time for Hal's weekly private class in martial arts. Closing our interview he delivered a final and fundamental advisement, "We live in a crazy culture when it comes to models of relationship. Everyone sees films and watches television in which every interaction between men and women is *spectacular*—that first look is spectacular, the first kiss is spectacular, the sex is multiorgasmic! Specialness is constantly flaunted in our faces. The women's bodies you see in magazines are ninety-six pounds with big breasts, the men are dark and swarthy and physically resemble James Bond or Arnold Schwarzenegger or are wearing gorgeous Italian suits. Even the ordinary people in movies are special—they're *all* gorgeous. I don't know how any of us live up to the promise of the spectacular sexuality we find in the movies."

"God, in the old days if you had an orgasm you were doing well," said Sidra.

"We must become aware of the barrage of specialness surrounding us," Hal continued. "That modeling is very damaging because life is ordinary—it's not always special. But there is a standard in our heads that makes it very difficult to be just an ordinary human being in relationship. Often what people call boredom is ordinariness. Each of us has to be in touch with our ordinariness, and to leave room for it in our relationships."

Chapter 22

Love and Marriage in Mexico—Los Compañeros

Lina Fernandez and Jorge Machorro

One important thing is that Lina pleases me. I'm convinced that we can see, enjoy, and talk about many things. In many aspects we are *compañeros*. We are companions. This is fundamental.

Jorge Machorro

We still love each other so much even after twelve years, because we think first of the other before we think of ourselves. We do things that we know will make the other happy. Very simple things. You don't need to buy diamonds.

Lina Fernandez

Lina and Jorge live in Oaxaca, Mexico, but we met in Carmel, California, when I attended the Oaxacan cooking class Lina offered. What first drew my attention to them as a couple was Jorge's solicitous and loving behavior toward Lina. He seemed to anticipate her every need during her cooking lecture/demonstration, and after our meal he was the first on his feet to clear the table and begin washing dishes. When I visited the couple in Oaxaca, Jorge's attentive behavior remained unchanged.

"Where is the stereotype of the macho Latino?" I asked him a few days later, when the three of us met for coffee on a cool and misty summer morning. Because Jorge spoke very little English (although he *understood* much of what was said), Lina did most of the talking and answered for him. "This way," she teased, "I can tell you anything I want about our marriage!"

"Jorge was the youngest in his family. And because his father did not live with them, Jorge's mother taught him to be *auto-sufficient*, independent. His mother died when he was fifteen and he went to Mexico City to study at the university. So he has always taken care of himself. In fact, sometimes he is *too* orderly, much more than me. He can be obsessive!" she laughed.

"He says that he enjoys doing things for me and it makes him feel closer to me. He washes dishes while I'm cooking, for example, or sets the table. We are talking during those moments and it's an opportunity to be together and talk about many things. Most couples have a special time during the day to talk, but we talk *all* the time.

"We try to be together most of the time, driving places or shopping or at the restaurant. Jorge is very good to go shopping with because he is patient. He never says, 'Oh, please, go fast.'"

If Jorge adores Lina, a look-alike for the sexy French actress Simone Signoret, her feelings for him are no less ardent. "In Oaxaca, Jorge is a very important person; everybody knows him. And he is a serious and good political journalist. You can talk with him about everything because he is very alive. He is always reading about all different subjects: culture, archaeology, literature, politics. He talks very well and for him it is easy to prepare speeches. He likes to speak to *thousands*. He is very friendly."

This is the second marriage for both Lina and Jorge, who each have two children. "There is a saying in Mexico," Lina smiled. "*El hombre es un unico animal que tropieza dos veces con la misma piedra*. Man is the only animal who stumbles twice over the same rock." They met twelve years ago in Mexico City at the university, where Jorge taught political science and Lina was an administrator.

"Was it love at first sight?" I asked, excited about their happiness.

"Si!" Jorge answered immediately.

"I think so," Lina said, more slowly. "He kept coming to my office and bringing me political writings to read. We recall very well having our first meeting, our first date on 24 November. We went to eat Japanese food."

"What do you think makes your marriage work?" I asked. "What makes you compatible?"

"The first thing is we love each other. And in many ways we are the same. We are both sensitive and have respect for others, even plants and animals as well as people. Because we both have very strong characters we might often get mad, but it is part of . . ."

As Lina struggled to find the right expression, I said, ". . . part of the passion?"

"Yes! We never fight, but we have a lot of disagreements, which I think is good because it means that we can think independently. But the truth is we think so much alike about everything! I am very direct and Jorge is much more diplomatic, but our friends know that they can trust us to tell them the truth about something. We just have different ways of expressing it."

"Do you think marriage is different in Mexico than in America? Is there much divorce in Mexico?" I asked.

They both shook their heads in unison. "A lot of divorce," Lina said. "The decision is usually the woman's. I think it's easier for men to be married, because the woman cooks, she washes, she irons, she takes care of the children. Many women now realize they can take care of themselves and they don't need the man only because he pays the accounts."

"So there is women's liberation?"

"They don't think of it like that. In Mexico City, yes. They have a big feminist movement. Not in Oaxaca. Sometimes the women are afraid of what people will say about them, because Oaxaca is a small city with many traditions and a strong religious atmosphere. Before, most Mexican women would say, 'I *can't* get divorced because of my children'; now they say, 'I *must* get divorced because of my children.' Men are funny, they are like bees with many flowers. They are looking for a servant, and women will no longer be their servants."

"You and Jorge have a deep level of appreciation for each other."

"Of course," Lina beamed. "I admire him and I know he admires me. We complement each other and have fun together. We are crazy about movies, for example, so we go to bed about one o'clock because we often watch a movie at night. And usually, if he's not too tired, Jorge reads to me before we go to sleep. I'll say, 'Please read to me, because I like to go to sleep listening to you read something nice.' The next day when we talk about what he read, I sometimes don't remember. 'You didn't listen?' he asks. 'No, I was sleeping,' I say shyly."

At this point, Jorge spoke on his own. "One important thing is that Lina pleases me. I'm convinced that we can see, enjoy, and talk about many things. In many aspects we are *compañeros*. We are companions. This is fundamental. Of course, it's extraordinary to know that our sexual relationship is also very good."

"Because we like each other very much, we have a lot of sexual attraction," Lina agreed. "It complements every part of our daily lives."

"So your sexuality sort of spills over into the various activities of your day," I said. "When you're setting the table or washing the dishes, cooking together. It's kind of the glue, in a sense. Your sexuality is not just the time you are in bed."

"Of course," said Lina. "It doesn't matter that we have twelve years of living together. I *like* him. So we might be washing the dishes, and I go, 'Oh, my Love. Hmmm. You are so cute!' We really like each other. It's not like we are doing things and then we have bedtime; all the time we are feeling love for each other."

"We don't have moments like other couples, for example, when he puts on the television and she is doing other things," Jorge said.

"That's true. In most of the couples we know, the woman is doing something or maybe nothing and the man is sitting watching sports and the only communication between them is, 'Bring me a beer. Have you something to eat? See this goal, this play in soccer.' And when she tries to talk to him he says, 'Please, I'm watching TV. It's my program. I'm too tired to talk.'

"That's not to say that our relationship is perfect, but we try to be because we think we deserve to be happy. And because I think Jorge must be happy with me." Here, Lina began to weep as Jorge kissed away her tears and cuddled her. "He knows that my life before him wasn't easy with my family and my first marriage. So we try to be together most of the time and we know that we deserve to be happy if only because we are good people."

"What advice would you give to other couples?"

"The same that we told you about why we still love each other so much even after twelve years, because we think first of the other before we think of ourselves. We do things that we know will make the other happy. Very simple things. You don't need to buy diamonds. We say in Mexico that when a husband buys a diamond for his wife, it is because he has been unfaithful and feels guilty. Maybe he spent a lot of money on another woman or at the races or on an expensive car. In Mexico, most of the jewelry is sold to guilty men. It's funny because simple things are not in the mind of most people. Sometimes friends will joke, 'Lina, what's happened that Jorge brings you flowers?' but for us is normal. When I cook and when I do things, I enjoy seeing his smiling face. I love his smile. We laugh many times because we are so fast to make jokes."

Lina and Jorge own and operate a popular restaurant in Oaxaca called *El Laurel*. Because Jorge does his freelance journalism at home, he spends most of his time with Lina. Their restaurant is open from 1:30 to 6:00 PM. "He helps out a lot at the restaurant. He buys me things. 'I forgot this; please go to the market for some parsley or basil,' I say. We have our evening meal at 6:00 with our son and the restaurant staff. We don't live to work, we work to live, to do the things we like. That's why we are not rich, but we tremendously enjoy our life.

"One of the characteristics of traditional Oaxacan restaurants is that the name of the restaurant was the name of the cook. People would say, 'Let's go to Lina's.' Many people have dishes they like and when I tell them I'm going to cook those dishes, they come to eat. We have an expression for our restaurant: 'All our customers become friends, and all our friends become customers.'"

Chapter 23

Solitude Crowded with Loneliness

Solitude is the profoundest fact of the human condition.

OCTAVIO PAZ,
The Labyrinth of Solitude

"Women are lonely in the '90s. It's our new phase," says Sarah, the pit-stop diner waitress and single mother of two teenage girls, in the film *Gas, Food, and Lodging* by Allison Anders. This morning I had an hour-long telephone interview with Jean Faroka from a Milwaukee, Wisconsin, NPR station centered around women and aging. The first half hour Jean and I were discussing women and midlife; the second half brought call-in responses and questions. While I tried to underscore the many positive aspects of aging, most of the women who called in were still stuck on the fantasy of meeting the right man to make their lives complete and worthwhile. Were they only acknowledging what I refuse to admit?

The Heart of Marriage is about love and relationship after all, and, God knows, I'm not immune to wanting a satisfying relationship with a man in my life too, but I'm not postponing living right now. That's the problem: we become so obsessed with the exclusive, heterosexual, genital mode of romantic love that we can't recognize or appreciate other possibilities that exist right in front of us. When will we ever trust that only by developing our own lives—inner and outer—will we then have something to offer another, a life to cultivate with them? I do believe that only by learning to be content alone will I have a chance at being happy with someone else.

Why is it that we tend to think of happiness as inextricably wound (interesting that this word, meaning "to encircle," "to wrap," "to twine about," is the same as one meaning "to injure," "to grieve," "to burden") to exclusive, heterosexual, genital "love"? If our life doesn't have this specific form of expression, we are miserable. Still, if I don't meet someone soon with whom to do the wresting and jousting of life, I don't know *what* I'll do. "There's nothing *to* do but feel it, sit with it, go through it, surrender to it," says a barely audible voice buried somewhere inside me. Loneliness has become my spiritual practice, a kind of purification of the soul. Birthdays and Christmas are the hardest. I'm forty-five years old. So many years, so much fear. Ironically, I still feel sixteen—I embarrass myself. This is my fourth year as a single woman. How many more will there be? Five, six, eight, ten? I know of a woman in her fifties who waited ten years after a divorce before she met her new husband, her soul mate. It was bliss, until he died of a heart attack only one year after they were married. The one permanent truth in life is there are no guarantees.

Basically we are talking about contact. Everyone wants to feel passionate, ecstatic, engaged, connected. It's so easy to misinterpret the fear of being alone for feelings of love. I have never been so lonely as when I was unhappily living with a partner. I would rather be in a bed by myself any night than be in a bed with someone with whom I could no longer (if ever) communicate—even if we did have sex. My primary commitment is to my life and my work, with or without a man.

It's true, as the women said this morning, there is nothing to take the place of the loving intimacy of a sexual union, but when life hasn't offered you that particular piece of the pie, what do you do? I don't believe you can *look* for that kind of love. When it happens, you welcome it gratefully and hope you have done enough work on yourself to warrant and sustain it.

In *Letters to a Young Poet*, Rainer Maria Rilke asks the reader whether he is "willing to stand guardian over someone else's solitude." Is he willing to encourage the beloved to do what is good for her—what nourishes her—to do those things that make her more of herself, more of an individual? The concept of solitude, aloneness, autonomy is a pivotal one in relationship. The shadow side of solitude, of course, is loneliness. Solitude brings internal peace and quiet; loneliness brings vulnerability and fear. Perhaps a marital or romantic relationship should never be undertaken until a certain familiarity and comfort with solitude is reached in one's life. The mastery of solitude brings the ability to be content on one's own and then to be even better with someone else. As Stephen Mitchell writes in *Into the Garden*: "The deepest intimacy with the beloved becomes possible when we have experienced intimacy with the self."

Chapter 24

New Love at Fifty

I add my breath to your breath

That we may be one person

That our days may be long on the earth

That we may finish our roads together

May our life paths be fulfilled.

NAVAHO PRAYER

Anna Keck and Anthony Tomasso

What I know to be
true is that—almost
on a cellular level—
there is such a deep
level of relaxation
that occurs in the re-
lationship, a harmony
and a rest that is hap-
pening to my cells. It's
so health giving, so
life giving. I've never
had that before.

Anna Keck

I think if you want to be with someone, you realize
you have to change. If you stay rigid in yourself, you
just end up being alone. You have to be adaptable.

Anthony Tomasso

It's never too late to fall in love, to be in love, to *love*. In fact, if love was the religion of one's youth, it deepens to become the spirituality of one's later years. But when two individuals who have spent perhaps many independent years living alone as singles or divorced adults—or living unhappily with a partner in an unsatisfying marriage—find the one person who becomes "home" to them, what do they do? How do they make the many adjustments—personal, social, familial, financial, psychological, sexual—that are required of them? Who moves into whose home? What furniture goes or stays? Does one of them rise before dawn, while the other is a night owl? Are there still children living at home in a "yours, mine, our" situation? Who pays for what? How do you still make time for the solitude that became an integral part of your life as a solitary person?

These were some of the questions Anna and Anthony were willing to discuss with me. I had met Anna, a holistic nurse practitioner whose area of expertise is women's health, only one month before her marriage to Anthony, a builder (and look-alike for the Merry Prankster, Ken Kesey), and was privileged to attend their very moving wedding ceremony in their community. "Our marriage is more than us," read the announcement. "We join our two families and our two worlds. Your presence honors and supports our new beginning as husband and wife." Eight months after the wedding I had dinner at the couple's country home, where we spent an evening of lively conversation and laughter.

"It was the worst scenario," Anna recalled, shaking her head at the memory of their first meeting thirteen years ago when they were both in their late thirties. She was "literally purple" (recovering from a life-threatening reaction to an antimalarial drug she was given in Africa), wearing a baggy old housecoat because her skin was so bloated and "those little slippers, you know, that you shuffle around in." Anthony was recovering from open-heart surgery, "so he was looking pretty gaunt himself." Ironically, it was Anthony's wife who orchestrated their introduction. Even in their weakened state, they both remember that meeting as very powerful and "electric."

Although the two felt a strong connection, they would have only two brief encounters during the following ten years. "He was married. I was getting well," Anna succinctly explained. They once met at a twelve-step meeting in the basement of a local church. "It kind of says it all, that you're there," Anna laughed, referring to the low point they were each experiencing in their lives. "Nothing's left to the imagination!"

Some years passed before they again ran into each other at a Safeway market. By now Anthony was divorced and Anna had married and divorced another man herself. The time was ripe to develop a new friendship. "We were friends for nearly a year," said Anna. "We talked on the phone and took walks together. We were not thick as thieves at all. It was a very respectful friendship." Then, on her fiftieth birthday, her children hosted a birthday bash in her honor—and Anthony came. Only a few days after the party, they became lovers. Within two months Anna was diagnosed with breast cancer, "and that put a whole other spin on the ball," she said, describing that time. "Everything was amplified."

"How exactly did the diagnosis affect your relationship with Anthony?" I asked.

"I'm a very passionate person," Anna said, intensely. "And my passion became my *healing*, not the relationship. I found that I had no tolerance for anything other than direct, very straight communication. I felt like I could handle any truth, but I couldn't handle a dysfunction." It was the crucible of the relationship. "I wasn't emotionally demanding, but *exacting*—I asked you to be really clear with me," she said, speaking directly to Anthony.

How was the experience for Anthony? "It was a *big* wave," he said. "Anna's illness was too much pressure for me. Life and death were too big, coming from my own reality of life and death." A twenty-five-year veteran of surfing, Anthony uses metaphors drawn from surfing terminology to describe life's events. Two heart attacks led to his open-heart surgery and, as Anthony described it, "That was the end of the program. It's important to grow beyond surfing. There are other things to do when you grow up. I realized that it's as exciting and important to be present in whatever you are doing, whether it's building or working in the garden or working with the bees or being with your family and friends."

"It was a bumpy year," agreed Anna. "I always felt there was something left unspoken. What I was learning in that process was how to really transform a part of me that always had a lot of fear around relationship. The cancer provided an opportunity for me to grow and let go more than I'd ever let go before, considering who I am and what my history is. I don't know that I would have made room for a relationship had I not experienced my health challenge. I had to stop my very full life. I had filled in all the dots—the picture was full. I was a full-on Me. The cancer kind of took me back to square one and made me start over. 'Sit and watch your flowers grow for a few months, Dear. See how you like that,' it seemed to say."

"All relationships can be bumpy," said Anthony, continuing on that thought. "Either you have a desire to explore those parts of an individual that you like, the part you can relate to—or you don't. I think we have an affinity toward certain individuals, and everybody wants to find a partner. Hopefully you get through the storms, 'cause there's constantly waves coming up."

"You're surfing relationship now," I laughed.

"Yeah, life is really surfing. There's a certain harmonic with the waves. But surfing can be an addiction, because you're hiding in the solitude of being alone; you aren't present with your family. The challenge with surfing is to take it to the next level of unity with family, occupation, and community. Anna continues to teach me about unity and trust—

those things that make relationship work. It's a building process. It's a continual process of dealing with past childhood realities and the traits that make you the person you are."

"Do you think a good, bonding relationship is a way of healing those childhood wounds?" I asked.

"Not that the relationship heals the wounds," Anna clarified, "because I think that's the individual's responsibility to do that work, and we both had done a lot of work on ourselves by the time we got together. What I know to be true is that—almost on a cellular level—there is such a deep level of relaxation that occurs in the relationship, a harmony and a rest that is happening to my cells. It's so health giving, so life giving. I can feel it in my body, and I've never had that before. Part of that sense is from my own peace of mind, but a big part comes from what we share together. Also, there is so much laughter between us, so much joy that, even with these bumpy places, that there is this other place we can find. Life is really theater for me."

"What does that mean?" I questioned.

"It means that at any moment we have a pretty large repertoire between us in terms of how we relate to each other. There are different places we can go where we really talk about the issues and feelings, but we're not doing this," she said, holding up her fists as if she were duking it out. "It's not that direct, head-on confrontation. Or the other option, which is: 'Honey, how do *you* feel about that?'" she said in a sweet, coquettish voice to denote subservience and obeisance. "That kind of response may be correct, but to me it's very lifeless. I appreciate that my relationship with Anthony is full of life. There's a life-giving quality to our days."

"We just keep building on our friendship," Anthony added. "Maybe relationship doesn't happen until you no longer need it. When you don't expect somebody to fill up your life. When you fill up your life totally with yourself, that's when you're finally able to have a real relationship. Because the minute you expect someone else to be the way you want them to be, or the way *you* want to be, you're in trouble. When you're full you just go about being yourself; that's what everybody wants to see anyway. They don't want to see you be a false person or be what somebody else wants you to be."

"I agree," I said. "The best we have to offer is who we genuinely are, our most authentic self. Is this the first time you have each felt that you could be your true selves in relationship?"

"Absolutely for me!" Anna answered. "The first time I've ever felt teamed."

"If it had happened before," reasoned Anthony, "I wouldn't be here. Marriage at fifty is totally different. Marriage to Anna is totally different."

"Clearly there is, or can be, a process of maturation and inner work that begins to pay off in our middle and later years," I pointed out.

"That's right," concurred Anthony. "There's tremendous learning in your twenties, thirties, and forties. All these different parts of yourself are coming out and you're trying to find your identity. Ozzie and Harriet were not good role models; that never worked. The Catholic church didn't work either. By and large, most everybody's lost in their younger years—some people stay lost forever."

"It also helps to have matching eccentricities," Anna laughed. "We have the same bizarre sense of humor, the same iconoclastic approach to life; we've both been highly independent."

"How was it actually moving into Anthony's house?" I asked.

"What do you mean, how was it? How *is* it?" Anthony corrected me, his slightly contentious side showing itself. "Put it in the right tense, please; it still *is*. We're still dealing with it. You have to keep wanting it and working at it. The surf's up most every day. I try to jump in every day. We each have our own rhythm, but we have this commitment to hang in there."

For Anna (whose children already had moved out on their own), leaving the privacy of her own home into the family situation at Anthony's was an important challenge. "I scaled down my expectations in a pretty big way. I realized I'd had my own home and my own life—I knew how to do that. What I *didn't* know how to do was what I'd been given the opportunity to do now: to have a really harmonious relationship with someone who I felt was my partner. To do that in *his* setting, for me, meant that it was just a matter of going slowly and not doing my usual fiery, has-to-happen-yesterday bit."

"You hit every nook and cranny," Anthony reminded her, in the teasing persona that they call "Little Anthony, the Tor-men-*tor*."

"Well, I'm a big colonizer. I had lived *alone*, kid! I had every room filled with my stuff," Anna defended herself.

"What are the differences between your first marriages and this one?" I asked them.

Anthony answered by saying, "You have to have common ground. I didn't have that before. And you have to like to do the same things together."

"And since your children are all grown, you don't have to deal with them," I pointed out.

"Oh, no," Anthony replied, forcefully. "It's still ongoing. There is just a different set of problems. All the families are still there, the ex-husbands, ex-wives, the kids, the grandkids, the relationships. It sounds good. I mean, I don't have to change diapers, but every week there's something new to deal with."

"Now there's more time for companionship, right?"

"Well, you *make* more time for companionship," Anthony modified. "If it's important you make time."

"So it's more important to you now in your fifties?"

"Yeah, if you go through the pain of divorce. The pain of seeing your kids wander. I mean, divorce is painful. Living with somebody you're not compatible with is painful."

"There's a little embellishment coming here," Anna said, with a gleam in her eye.

"I can imagine there would be," said the Tor-men-*tor*. "Give it a little embellishment!"

"It's harder to know what you want in companionship when you are younger, because you don't know who you are. Without that self-knowledge, you're constantly outer-referencing: Maybe what that person likes or dislikes is what I should be or shouldn't be. By the time you reach our age, you have some experience in your own right with what you like and what you don't like. How things feel to you. What you can let go of and what you want to hang onto.

"It's remarkable that we have as much harmony as we do. I see many people our age who get so territorial about who they are, and maybe even a little brittle about who they are. Something in the heart gets frozen, closed down. And that seems dangerous; it's a dangerous place to be when you're living with a human being. So to have the sense of something going back and forth like a figure eight feels really remarkable to me. Maybe our companionship comes from the fact that we have worked on ourselves and *been* with ourselves, been *alone* with ourselves, been with our emptiness as well as our fullness."

"I think if you want to be with someone," continued Anthony, "you realize you have to change. If you stay rigid in yourself, you just end up being alone. You have to be adaptable."

"There's another little piece of this that has to do with why you can tolerate things in your partner that otherwise might annoy you; it helps you to understand and go beyond. There's a bonding that happens through sexuality and spirituality, a complete downtime of letting go. That doesn't necessarily exist in a nonsexual friendship—unless it's very special and unique. It's not particularly about making love; it's that the lovership is part of the friendship and, if it is a healthy and vital part, *can* make one more forgiving.

"What that means for me is that I could not live with you," Anna said, speaking directly to Anthony, "if you did not touch me like you do—not sexual—just touch. You are a touching person and that's really important to me because I'm very kinesthetic.

"After menopause, a woman's sexuality is more like a man's: their hormone levels of testosterone and estrogen are becoming more alike. Having that place to just sink into is very bonding to the relationship. Bonding in the sense that it means there is this other dimension that occurs beyond companionship and beyond verbal communication.

"The extra spin on the ball for us is having had these remarkable health histories; it makes it such a spiritual walk because of that. Every moment feels like it has a preciousness. There is definitely an appreciation, a lot of gratitude. It helps smooth out the bumpy parts faster. So when the waves get really high, my appreciation for what we have helps smooth them out, because I know how precious life is. Each moment is one I'm grateful for, thankful for.

"And there's a lot to love. Being in relationship with Anthony has made it possible to be in my work life in a more effortless way. I think it's because of that little dance of our molecules. That part of me is fulfilled. I don't know that it was fulfilled before, even though I was very happy and really liked my life. I bring that experience of being fulfilled to my work place. It's a sense of belonging, of being matched in the masculine."

"So what's next?" I asked. "More of the same?"

"Yeah, keep having fun," replied the surfer in Anthony.

Chapter 25

For Better and for Worse

Pat and Gil Zimmerman

What is the secret to a happy marriage?
Stay loose, absolutely loose. Let nothing get
in the way of your looseness. That's it.

Gil Zimmerman

No matter how busy our lives were, when we came home we always sat down and talked. We looked forward to this, and it kept us together through thick and thin. That time provided a stability in our marriage that was very important.

Pat Zimmerman

Pat and Gil were married by a one-armed judge in the "City of Wedding Chapels," Reno, Nevada, in September 1970. After arriving late, only minutes before the appointed time for their ceremony, there was no time to change into her wedding dress and his black suit. Instead they stood before the one-armed judge like the tourists they were, hot and sweaty, in their traveling clothes—Bermuda shorts—and said, "I do!"

This was the unusually secular and almost farcical beginning of a second chapter for them, both of whom had previously been pillars of religious life. Gil, who had served as a Methodist minister for thirty-two years, had done missionary work with the humanitarian Dr. Albert Schweitzer in Gabon, Africa; raised four children and put them through college; and, at the time he met Pat, was recently divorced and relocated from Phoenix to San Francisco. He was fresh on the job market after leaving his ministry. Pat, an ex-nun, who had been in the Order of the Holy Cross for twenty years, had made her own way for two years as an independent, professional woman teaching high-school English across the bay from San Francisco.

After fourteen years together, in an instant their lives were irrevocably changed when Gil suffered a massive stroke from which he has never fully recovered. True to her nature, Pat continues to meet each day with genuine cheerfulness and resourcefulness, whether it is tending to the physical needs of Gil (who is now wheelchair-bound), overseeing the construction of an additional wing to their home near Sacramento, California, or responsibly attending to the couple's financial and property concerns.

With a frequent and infectious giggle, and more than a little nostalgia, Pat reflected on those "wonderful years with Gilbert" before the stroke affected him. She is slow to appreciate her own resilience, and she has an innocence of soul that is most rare. Remembering their wedding day with the thrill of a new bride and still nearly bursting with the infatuation of a woman who has proudly found her Knight in Shining Armor, Pat recounted the story of their wedding day, "When we went into the chapel, Gil asked the judge if he (Gil) could perform the service. He had the entire wedding ceremony completely memorized because he had done so many weddings in his life as a minister. I was so impressed! So Gil said the vows and the judge pronounced us 'man and wife.' It was so romantic."

"How did you and Gil first meet?" I asked.

"After I left the convent in 1968, I moved to the Bay Area and became part of a social organization called 'Next Step.' It was a great place for people, like me, who had left the convent, priesthood, or ministry. There must have been two or three thousand members. The group met on Friday nights for social gatherings.

"Gil saw me at one of the meetings, but we weren't introduced. He got my telephone number from a mutual friend. When he called me he said, 'My name is Gil Zimmerman. May I take you to Friday night's Next Step meeting?' He detected in my voice that I was a little afraid to go with someone I hadn't met before—he picked that up right away and said, 'You don't need to worry, because I'm a friend of Cele's and she gave me your number.' I especially liked the way he could read my voice—no one had ever been able to do that before.

"So he came to pick me up at my apartment on Friday night. He walked through the rooms—of course I had nothing—and said, 'Oh what a lovely apartment. Sort of early convent, isn't it?' I thought he had a nerve making fun of my apartment right off the bat, but it showed he was a man with a sense of humor who liked to tease, and I liked that.

"Then we went down to the car—he drove a green Mercury Cougar—and as we drove off, I mean he *really* took off, I thought, 'Boy, he's kind of an aggressive driver. I like that!' Then we started talking—I just went on and on, and he was the same way. I loved the way Gil phrased things (old English teacher that I am); he had such a gift for expressing himself that I found *really* attractive. We weren't paying attention and the next thing we knew we had missed our exit and were heading across the Golden Gate Bridge. I thought that was funny. I knew that night this was *definitely* a man I would be interested in.

"We finally made it to the party and stayed for a few hours, and then he said, 'How about going down to the Wolf Den by the waterfront?' It was a jazz club and we enjoyed that for a few hours. Then we started driving home and Gil drove right by my turnoff. I said, 'Hey, you just missed my exit.' He said he wanted me to come and see *his* place.

"The first thing I saw in his tiny apartment was a huge painting of an elephant by his son Dan, and he began telling me about his experiences in Africa with Schweitzer. I know this sounds terrible, but I didn't go home that night. Isn't that *incredible*? I just had no qualms about Gilbert, at all. I felt right at home with him and trusted him perfectly. That was the beginning of our relationship and we were married a year later.

"We've had a wonderful life together. He was a marvelous guy; such a complicated man with so many facets to his personality that I was continually learning something new about him. He was never, ever boring. Gil taught me a great deal. I began to become very dependent on his knowledge; he just seemed to know *everything*. I never had to look anything up in the encyclopedia. He knew history, philosophy, woodworking, manual repairs, automobile repair, real estate—whatever we had to deal with, he already knew. So consequently, when he had the stroke, in an instant all that knowledge was gone. I was devastated. It was a tremendous loss for him, of course, but a loss for me, too."

"Under what circumstances did the stroke occur?" I asked.

"We had been to a formal dance the night before the stroke happened. When we moved to the country from the Bay Area, we had left all that nightlife behind, so that particular night was the first time we'd been to a dance in four years. I was really excited and wore a pretty green gown with a purple and green sheer jacket. Gil was all dressed up, too. He was always charming wherever we went; he loved people. We knew a lot of the people there, and that evening the international dance club asked him to be the chairman for the Christmas dance. He spent much of the time talking to people and eliciting their cooperation for the future event. We'd had a fabulous evening and came home.

"Gil was always a bundle of high energy and never required much sleep; he could get by on four or five hours of sleep easily—he was a dynamo. That night I went right to bed when we got home, and Gil stayed up reading in his chair. Finally, he came to bed. The next morning about seven o'clock I woke up and he was thrashing around in the bed. I thought he was having a nightmare, and I said, 'Gil, what's the matter? Wake up.' He didn't hear me at all, and rolled right off the bed onto the floor.

"I knew something terrible was happening when I couldn't wake him, although I'd had no experience with a stroke before and knew nothing about it whatsoever. He continued to thrash around on the floor, so I dashed out and called 911. I'd hardly gotten my clothes on before the firemen arrived. They knew immediately it was a stroke and rushed Gil off to the nearest hospital, where they tried to stabilize him; he was having difficulty breathing and he couldn't move.

"Later they took him in an ambulance to Kaiser Hospital in Sacramento. Like a fool, I drove by myself to Kaiser. I should never have done that. I was crying and very upset, I felt so alone. I'd become so dependent, I'd never even driven the hundred miles to Sacramento by myself during the four years we lived near Placerville. When I reached the hospital, they were taking Gil through the CAT scan and giving him different tests. It was six o'clock in the evening before he was stabilized and the doctor told me what had happened to him and what to expect. I was devastated. It was the worst thing that had ever happened to me.

"Ten days later he was moved to a rest home. For three months Gil was in a coma and unable to speak. That year, 1984, we had one of the hottest summers on record, with fifteen days over 100 degrees. Every day I drove the two hundred miles, round trip, to the rest home in that blistering heat because I didn't trust them to take care of him properly. So I sat there from ten o'clock in the morning until four o'clock in the afternoon, and then I would drive home before the evening traffic started.

"Gradually he was coming out of it, and then he said his first word and could turn himself over in bed. He was in physical therapy and speech therapy. Gil was terrible to his speech therapist; he hated doing what she made him do—to move things and name things he couldn't name. It was a very traumatic experience.

"Finally, he was well enough to be moved to intensive rehabilitation at Kaiser Hospital in Vallejo—that was even farther for me to drive! The staff didn't want me to come during the week, but said I could bring Gil home on the weekends if I wanted to. Well, the first time I brought him home he looked around and said, 'This is a nice room.' He did not remember having lived there. He didn't remember anything that had happened before the stroke. I think he didn't even remember me. Things come back to him now sporadically and intermittently.

"There were so many things I had to take care of at home. For one thing, I was taking care of a stroke victim, which I'd never done before. Gil had a garage full of power tools. He had loved working with wood and had made our china cabinet and our mantlepiece—but he didn't remember any of that. He would never be able to do that work again, so I had to sell his tools and his truck. I didn't even know the names of the tools, let alone how much they cost. Then I had to oversee the construction of the new wing on the house for Gil's spa.

"More importantly, I had to deal with all the financial responsibilities that the rest of our lives would depend on. I was used to doing the monthly bills, but Gil had always done the investments and the real estate. What a nightmare! We had a large rental building in the Bay Area, and a few years after Gil's stroke, our tenant, which was General Electric, said they would be moving their operation to another location. I knew that we would be stuck with those huge mortgages to pay every month.

"It was a scary time because I had to use up practically all our savings in order to get through that period. Thank God I was able to sell the building before the real estate slump happened. The final papers were in transit on the night of the 1989 Bay Area earthquake! Then, of course, I had three-quarters of a million dollars I had to decide what to do with—that was another nightmare of a different sort. I knew nothing about investing; that's how I got interested in the stock market.

"I love the stock market and belong to a stock club with fifteen women. This year I'm the president. When I sold our rental property, I had to learn about investing. So, I put up a sign that read, 'Anyone interested in an investment group?' Three women signed up and we started the group. The next week we had seven participants, and the week after that we had fourteen.

"We sent for information from the National Association of Investors, NAIC. Together we studied the manuals and kits they sent us. Of course, some of the women in the group were already very knowledgeable. Boy, have I learned a lot from them. We just dug it all out by ourselves; we decided we weren't going to depend on brokers. After that first year, I felt quite competent to be my own broker and buy my own stock. I have a whole drawer full now; it's really fun. I feel like I've been through the mill financially, but nothing bad has happened—so far. It's all gone very smoothly, exactly the way Gilbert planned it."

"I imagine you both started out with nothing," I commented.

"When we started out in 1970 we basically had zero money—I'd only been out of the convent for two years and Gilbert had just finished putting his kids through college, getting a divorce, relocating to California from Phoenix, and changing jobs. Because he made wise investments in real estate through the years, we had a nest egg to fall back on.

"Gilbert was so much more aware of the need to plan for retirement—it never even entered my head. 'Retirement? I'm only forty years old. I'm not going to retire for twenty-five years,' I used to think. But the time to plan for retirement, to plan for financial security is *when* you are forty years old. So he did that for us."

"Pat, how did your life change after Gil's stroke?"

"Our life changed a lot after Gil got sick. Before we moved to Placerville, Gilbert had been on the city council in Foster City. We had a huge social life—every weekend we were out with people, dining and dancing, going everywhere and meeting everybody. Our life is very different now. It's difficult for us to entertain or for me to take Gilbert out to places or people's homes that don't have ramps for his wheelchair.

"Although I do feel somewhat isolated at times, I'm perfectly happy with the life we lead here. It's a kind of survival. There are so many things to deal with all the time—not necessarily related to Gil's care, but just the upkeep of the property—that I'm completely occupied. It's not a pressure like going to work. Every morning I get up and there are at least eight things to choose from—maybe the wood needs stacking, or the garden needs watering, or the plum tree is loaded with fruit and something has to be done with it—it's all interesting and challenging. I've learned a lot that I never knew before, and I've become quite a repairman myself! As I get older, it's harder to do all the physical work that has to be done to keep the place up—I don't want it to get run down and look bad.

"Poor Gilbert, I know it's painful for him to be unable to move around, but to be unable to speak is the hardest thing and a *great* loss. But we have things we enjoy doing together everyday, and we just say, 'Thank God we have each other'—that's the main thing. I think it's important for a couple to have fun together, to enjoy being together. We play double solitaire every day. It makes a little competition between us. We used to enjoy playing chess often. We like listening to music and watching television together, and riding around the area sightseeing. So now we're going to walk into the sunset hand in hand. That's what we always said we wanted to do. That means we will stick together until we die, and it would be nice if we died together.

"It is difficult to define what love means to me. When Gil and I first met, ours was very definitely a romantic love with a lot of passion and excitement—it was a great feeling of security and connectedness. But our relationship has changed. For me, now, there is almost a maternal love in the way that you care for someone who is dependent on you. We still have the remnants of the old relationship—there is still some romance here and there. But all the passion and excitement that goes with a sexual relationship has changed into something more like a quiet companionship, a comforting feeling of being together. And we have a shared history, as much as Gilbert can remember.

"No matter how busy our lives were—and they were really hectic—when we came home we always sat down together and talked. We looked forward to this, and it kept us together through thick and thin. That time together provided a stability in our marriage that was very important.

"Certainly the worst thing that happened to us before Gil had the stroke was that his son committed suicide. Marc was diagnosed as a paranoid schizophrenic and had been in and out of hospitals for many years. Gil had told me about Marc's condition when we were first acquainted. The suicide occurred after we had been married for about two years. I knew Marc, although we hadn't spent a great deal of time together. He also lived in the Bay Area and would come to see us for a weekend sometimes. It disappointed me that Gil never seemed to enjoy his visits with Marc. I thought it would be great to have a son come and visit, but Marc wasn't always coherent, and it was painful for Gil to spend time with him.

"Marc's suicide was a terrible, terrible shock. He followed a course common to paranoid schizophrenics: he was fine as long as he took his medication, but as soon as he felt 'better,' he'd stop the medication and quickly go downhill. Then he would commit a small crime like stealing a basket of strawberries—almost as if he wanted to get caught—and a lawyer would call Gil and say, 'Your son is in jail.' Gil would bail him out and help him get psychiatric care in a halfway house, but after he got back on his own, he would stop the medicine and the whole ritual would repeat again. It was very painful for Gil and, of course, for Marc. That was a sad, sad episode.

"One horribly stormy night Marc jumped off the Golden Gate Bridge. We had to go to the morgue and identify the body. It was awful. I could hardly talk about it, even with Gil; it just hurt so much. Gil was somehow more resilient; he had the inner resources to deal with it more than I did. Whenever anyone dies, I think there is always guilt for the ones who remain, but for a suicide, the guilt is overpowering.

"It was extremely hard for me to talk about Marc's death for months. It had deep repercussions on my relationship with Gil. We sort of drifted apart—it was like being in an emotional cocoon. Eventually we came out of it. Time has a marvelous healing capacity—I know this sounds like a cliché, but it's true. There is a real hurt when something like that happens. It's genuine; you can feel it—it's not just in your mind—the pain runs through your entire being. Then time slowly makes the pain go away, and it doesn't hurt as much. Pretty soon you can talk about it; then when you talk about it you can distance yourself from it more and more.

"Shared interests was another stability in our marriage. I learned how to play tennis the year Gil broke his leg and was recuperating. He had played tennis years ago, but we had never played together. After his leg healed, I taught him all I had learned in my lessons. We had some wonderful times playing tennis. Gil taught me all about camping—using the Coleman stove, lighting wood fires, pitching a tent. Camping was our main vacation for years because we were saving money. We loved it.

"He also taught me all about football. I used to hate it when he would watch football games on Saturday. I knew nothing about football—I thought the '49ers were the gold miners; I never knew there was actually a team called the '49ers. He taught me about the different teams and what was going on during a game—I can recognize Joe Montana's name as well as anyone else! Now I enjoy the football game as much as he does, because I know what's going on and I have the time to sit down and watch it with him."

"Do you ever think of your life alone?"

"If I have to go on alone at some point, if I will have a third piece of life after my twenty years in the convent and the more than twenty years with Gil, I think I will be very lonely. In September I'll be sixty-four. There are a lot of things I would like to do. I love doing the stock work, and I'd like to learn more about computers. I still want to help people; to teach adults how to read. I'm very interested in politics. I might like to get involved in politics in some way that could make a difference. I'm also interested in the organization WEAVE—it stands for Women Escaping a Violent Environment. I'd like to help those women in some way if I can. I guess that's a thread that goes through my life. I enjoy helping people, doing something for someone else. It makes my life happy."

Chapter 26

Love,
Marriage,
and Death

Journal Entry: June 1993

I've been seared by a revelation from this man with whom I've just made love. "I don't have AIDS," he said reluctantly, referring to our conversation earlier, "but I do have a life-threatening illness: I have diabetes, type I." And then, just in case I didn't fully understand the repercussions of diabetes, he began to list the agonizingly unpredictable breakdown of the body that can result from this disease. He needn't have bothered, however, because I'd already had a man in my life who had died from it.

***

The summer we met I wasn't quite sixteen. He seemed a wild man, so glamorous and dangerous shooting needles full of insulin into the veins of his upper arms or thighs, madly driving his ten-year-old, perfectly preserved Mercedes Benz (which would long outlast him) at dangerous speeds on stretches of deserted, moonlit country roads. At twenty-four he was an older man—a poet who wrote twenty-page, handwritten letters to me—and, although he terrified me, I was crazy about him. He terrified everyone because he was fearless in the face of death, having lived with it for over ten years, the way one hides from life, from happiness, in an intimate relationship that's gone off the deep end—you know it's ruinous, but you cannot leave it.

Now I can be thankful for my mother's ruthless intervention—she frightened me much more than he. She spared my experiencing firsthand his blindness, daily dialysis, eventual amputation of his left foot, the tortuous descent of a gifted soul that ended in suicide. She unwittingly "saved" me from his suffering and at the time I hated her for it.

"Everybody has to learn to die," observed Gertrude Stein. We all *know* death will come, but we're so careful to keep it in that abstract: the future. The paradox of life is to live so fully, so unequivocally in the present that it hushes our fear of the future and, consequently, of our compulsory death. That is the real death—being dead while we are alive.

Had I not known
that I was dead
already
I would have mourned
my loss of life.

OTA DOKAN, *Japanese Death Poems*

Death is the invisible component, the missing fragment, in the mosaic of life. Unfortunately, once it's in place, we can no longer make use of the stories it has to tell.

The mention of death, especially in connection with love and marriage, is almost taboo. But aren't religion—organized or otherwise—philosophy, art, even love just ways of coping with the miseries of the world, the uncertainties of life, the existential despair of recognizing our ultimate aloneness?

Within those first tantalizing moments of new love is also born the kernel of its demise. From the first lure of attraction, the end of the relationship is seeded. Yet, we still choose to love—"We taunt love / as the bullfighter taunts / death," Tess Gallagher demonstrates for us in her poem "Un Extrano." In relationship, as in life, we continually face change, transformation. Death completes the triangle of love and marriage: an ending of what has been up to this point; the loss of will and control in the solitary/independent self, which, like the phoenix, rises anew through an interdependent partnership; old patterns dying so that a new, creative relationship can be born; the slow, stumbling death of a once gloriously giddy romance; the surrendering of control; the whittling away by the *petits mals*, the small displeasing moments of daily disappointments and recriminations; the relinquishing of one's preconceptions and demands on the other, accepting them as they are; the predestined actual death or estrangement of a mate.

It is inevitable that the initial romantic phase of love eventually fades. Love may be reborn as a deeper knowing and commitment or simply dissolve altogether with one part-ner and seek heady renewal through another lover. Everyone fears abandonment—the dread that your partner could either die before you or leave at any time. "Is the risk of loving worth the price of loss?" we continue to question ourselves, plunging ahead one more time without hesitation, before we can even think about an answer. To say "no" would be in itself another form of death, because it is not only the joys of love that deepen our soul, but also its losses.

There is pleasure and comfort in paying attention. To be *alive* in *this* moment—that's what we all want. To know the ecstasy of being absorbed in the creative process, to be alert through the gift of our five senses, to be met in a pair of eyes. We are desperate for absorption, which can become a form of absolution, before the end.

Regrettably, "knowing" a truth doesn't necessarily make one capable of *living* it and, of late, my life is bringing me ample opportunities to witness how willingly I run from the pleasure, the discipline, of this moment straight into the time- and mind-altering throes of romantic promise. There are stretches when I feel nearly desperate to be in love. "To be in love with love," as Roland Barthes, putting words to my behavior, describes this peculiar physical and emotional urging.

Observing this about myself (and human nature), I am unable to trust my own judg-ment: What trap is my desire leading me into this time? I ask myself. What am I looking for? To be consumed, once more ("just once more," I swear to Eros and Aphrodite, god and goddess of love), by reckless abandon, by the twist and taste of sexual hunger. I vig-orously, flagrantly discard mindful thought and action. I become an addict who cares only about her next fix, a stalking jungle beast who cares only about the next kill.

The movie *Fatal Attraction* scared every American male, married or single, who saw it—and with good reason. The force beneath that primal, female sexual urge is scorching. But, on closer examination, rather than demonic (as it is often misconstrued), the root cause is simply a longing for contact, for connection with another human being, to feel the mammalian warmth of a body, an emotional intimacy of the heart, to be reflected back to oneself, to be able to pour one's soul unreservedly into another and have it be ap-preciated, to feel a sense of relatedness—to belong.

To some extent, this craving is an attempt to fill the part of the brain that is always thinking about sex and romance (albeit under the guise of "love"), that, in turn, reckons with the loom of the existential void. It becomes a distorted fixation on a certain image, a face, an idea. Gloria Steinem assured me this preoccupation will change after menopause, but will I survive the interim? I agreed when she said during our conversation, "I think I confused sex with friendship, love, affection, and aerobics all in one." In the meantime, I

remain an adolescent. My friend Linda Leonard jokes, "Once a puella, always a puella"—
an eternal girl. My new identity: "Hello, my name is Cathleen Rountree, and I'm a
puella." The socially accepted form of confession. Maybe I'll start a new twelve-step program called PA, Puellas Anonymous.

Aging has brought me confidence and a sense of purpose through my work in the
outside world, but within the context of the "man/woman thing," I lapse into a blither-
ing teenager or a dull, slow-witted child. I've had this conversation with too many women
friends: What happens to our brains when we are in the presence of a man to whom we
are attracted? "I'm really quite intelligent," one woman tried to assure a man by whom she
was spellbound. Thankfully, he was good-natured and handed her a pocket dictionary as
a gesture of humorous support.

The transfixed mind swells, becomes dizzy replaying over and over again monotonous,
one-dimensional images of the beloved object—the younger man, the *much* younger man:
now he stands over the bed stuffing his purple shirttail into seductively tight Levis as I
hold my breath; now I catch my first glimpse of him, after more than a year, slouched in
the plastic airport chair reading Plato, as he awaits my arrival, his soft leather jacket ro-
mantically reminiscent of Camus; now he sits at his desk, draped in an earth-tone cable-
knit sweater, hovering and intent, like a peering hawk, absorbed in the world he has
created through his novel, giving it reality.

"How was it?" he'd asked, right after the act, the sex act. (Curious. Is sex just an *act* we
perform for each other and for our own egos?) During copulation I'd been unusually dry,
due, I supposed, to fatigue, nervousness, my period, his softness, and a loss of emotional
contact with him and myself. It was disappointing. My acute need for sexual contact had
heightened a passionate aggression within me, which had, apparently, doused the fire between us. Suddenly, my gender evaporated. I knew what it must be like to be a man, as I
felt a maleness inside my female form: I was internally driven to fuck. At that point, we
were lost to love or even physical pleasure. Perhaps, as I'd been trained in Catholic school,
there is no physical pleasure without love. But I said nothing.

Later, confiding his diabetes to me was like a sting—not so much physical, although
that, too, but psychic, because it delivered me from my adolescent inebriation with him. It
infused our encounter with the sacred, fumigated the carnal, dry-cleaned the profane,
healed the disappointment, as sex never could. The seriousness with which he faces his
life is sobering and inspiring. "We are attracted not merely to the bodies of others but to

their psyches, the shimmering nonmaterial identities that used to be called soul," writes John Updike.

Last year when we first met, I was drawn to his intellectual breadth and, I suspected, his wide emotional range. It is what has remained with me, what matters most to me— the sacred, the sacred in life, in death, in the moment. And it seems to me *all* that really matters. A searing has taken place, a singeing of raw nerves. What I have been thinking and writing about has become three-dimensional, experiential, in my life. It has begun marauding my dreams with such unabashed accuracy that it unnerves me: death, the terminal nature of relationship, of life itself. When one covets depth in one's life, actively solicits it, invokes it, through life experiences, the conduits are not of one's choosing.

I'm convinced that one of the keys to sustaining interest and freshness in our own lives and, thus, in our relationships is by containing this awareness of our own and our beloved's mortality. Only then can we fully appreciate their vitality, their preciousness, their inimitable singularity. When we are able to stay cognizant of the finiteness of all life, we become grateful for what we've been given, and our experience becomes fruitful. Staying present in the moment of relationship is an extension of staying present in the moment of a spiritual practice. And, in fact, relationship *becomes* one's spiritual practice, just as it did for Tess Gallagher and Raymond Carver even when they knew his death was imminent: They "were *happy*. They had happiness." "Love *as if* you will be answered," Tess invites us, even in the face of death.

Chapter 27

A Poetic Love

Tess Gallagher and Raymond Carver

The heart begins its

savage journey

toward love and loss

of love.

TESS GALLAGHER,

"UN EXTRANO,"

Moon Crossing Bridge

I met with Tess Gallagher, poet, essayist, and fiction writer, on 9 June 1993, at the sophisticated Four Seasons Hotel in Seattle during the promotional tour for my book *On Women Turning 50*. As we had tea in the sunny grand solarium of the hotel on a spring day, the gypsy spirit in each of us promptly and exuberantly embraced. We spoke about her frequent and distant travels; her friends, writing, and poetry; my art and writing; poetry and her friend and husband, internationally acclaimed short-story writer Raymond Carver, who died from lung cancer in 1988; and, of course, love and its passing.

To know such a large love in one's life and then have to surrender it—how does one survive the figurative or actual death of a partner? Tess speaks and writes with great depth and eloquence of this. During our conversation that day, through a subsequent correspondence, and in a taped interview with the Canadian Broadcasting Company that she later sent to me, Tess vividly portrayed her life with Raymond Carver during his illness and his lingering "protecting generosity" after his death:

"We did valiant battle the ten months before Ray died, but by May 1988, we knew we weren't going to win. Ray died on August 2. So there was a period of time between May and August when we had to realize and deal with the fact that we weren't really going to get out of this. It was very, very hard. But it was also, strangely, a transcendent time. We were not as fully immersed in the agony of the ending as one might imagine. The closing down of our time seemed oddly to invigorate us and to make every moment more important than we'd ever believed it could be. It was as if, perhaps like hummingbirds, we'd suddenly discovered we could even fly upside down.

"It's hard to communicate what those days were like, *how* we could, in fact, be happy. And we *were happy;* we had happiness the way the sun has the earth in a continuous shining even when it's dark. Even now it probably sounds like a blasphemy to say so, because we're supposed to be paying attention: death is coming! But we didn't put our eye on death, we put our eye on *life.* So a lot got accomplished and deeply felt. Those were very important times and we lived them in a state of exhilaration, really. Which isn't to say that we didn't just weep together when we first received the news, the actual news that the cancer had returned. No, we staggered under it at first, and the shock of it even drove us to our corners as our hearts scraped bottom. I'm not saying dire moments weren't there, but they weren't the *controlling* energies."

"How did you carry on after Ray's death?"

"When the actual death and physical separation came, it made me numb at first. I went into a kind of spiritual torpor in order to preserve myself against the cold of it. I had been in such a state of fervent industry, trying to help Ray finish his book—the days were so full—and just to stay alive, of course, for as long as he could: our days were given over to those life-sustaining ministrations, hour by hour, moment to moment. But about a month after Ray died, I saw pictures of myself in the funeral group and only then I realized that my face is just blunted with the really immeasurable grief of losing him. That sudden bodily loneliness is immense, to be alone in the house with all the personal effects there—his shoes, toothbrushes, a stack of books he was meaning to read—all so plaintive and still. Yet, we had been together so *well* that it was hard to make the absence real to myself. I still felt his presence around me in quite a protecting, generous way, too. So it was beautiful and baffling at the same time."

"How did his death affect your writing?"

"For six months I couldn't write anything, and then the poems started to come like jolts of irresistible energy. They were very important in putting my eye back on life and, in acknowledging that Ray still had, *has*, a life within me—he still had ongoing, a generative essence from which I was taking nourishment. So I tried to make this palpable in the poems, to create a realm in which I could extend my knowing of Ray and my experience of the terms in which his presence is still active. I was trying to make a palpable body for the love in words and images in the book I came to call *Moon Crossing Bridge*."

Chapter 28

A Mythic Romance, an Artful Marriage

Jean Erdman and Joseph Campbell

He used to come to the studio and I would show him *everything* I was doing, and he would give me his comments; and Joe read every single word he wrote to me. So we had a very close working relationship without either one of us being in the other's field. It was miraculous how it worked. It worked because of the discipline that we *joyfully* took on.

Jean Erdman Campbell

The emotion of love, in spite of the romantics, is not self-sustaining; it endures only when the lovers love many things together, and not merely each other.

Joseph Campbell, "Metasophs"

Joseph Campbell, world-renowned mythologist and teacher, who died in 1987 at the age of eighty-three, was one-half of a great love story that spanned more than fifty years of the twentieth century. Jean Erdman Campbell, dancer, choreographer, and teacher, was the other half. Jean began her career as a soloist in Martha Graham's Dance Company, creating the role of The One Who Speaks in Ms. Graham's tribute to the poetry of Emily

Dickinson, entitled "Letter to the World." Knowing of this couple's enduring relationship, I was thrilled when Jean willingly agreed to meet with me to share some words and memories about her marriage with Joseph.

We met on an intensely hot and bright late summer day at the Marin County home of her friend Robert Walter, director of the Joseph Campbell Foundation. Even at seventy-nine, Jean's body still maintains the exquisite articulation of a dancer's. Experiencing first-hand her vitality, graciousness, and easy humor made it easy to see why Joseph Campbell, twelve years her senior and her professor at Sarah Lawrence, where they first met, was initially enraptured with her and what sustained this mutual fascination throughout their next fifty years together.

Although they both began their careers (Jean for three years as student and Joseph for thirty-seven years as professor) at Sarah Lawrence in the same year, 1934, they didn't come to know each other formally until three years later when Jean decided, despite her deliberate avoidance of the very popular and much sought after Campbell, that she wanted to study literature the way he taught it. Stephen and Robin Larsen, in their biography of Joseph Campbell, *A Fire in the Mind*, describe the potency of the Campbells' lasting attraction: "It was that most fatal of attractions, a passion of the body wedded to a passion of the mind."

From that preliminary meeting with Jean in Campbell's office, their life together embodied mythic dimensions. Jean remembered telling him that she wanted to study Pluto. Joseph had laughed and said, "You mean Plato?"

Jean's "Freudian slip" may not have been far off the mark. In Greek mythology, Pluto is the god of wealth, of the precious metals hidden in the earth; he abducts Persephone (the maiden of the spring) to the underworld. The "god of wealth"—not an unlikely title for a man who contained so many riches and talents of the mind, body, and soul; and it certainly could have been Jean (the maiden) he whisked into the great abyss of the unconscious and the kingdom of mythology.

She was shy with embarrassment but they agreed to a conference course. "So I had Joseph Campbell to myself once a week," Jean recalled, "and every girl on the campus knew it, because when the weather was good, we'd go outdoors for our tutorial."

At the end of that school year, Jean told him that she would not be returning to Sarah Lawrence the following year because she was making a trip around the world by boat and train with her parents and younger sister. During their final conference, Joseph presented Jean with a copy of German philosopher Oswald Spengler's *The Decline of the West*. It wasn't until many years later that Joseph admitted the motive behind this gift: "I knew that she wouldn't be able to understand it and would have to come back to me for interpretation."

That summer, Jean studied dance with Martha Graham at Bennington College in Vermont. Joseph came for several visits throughout the summer from his cottage in Woodstock, where he continued his research and reading, and their friendship bloomed. Before Jean left on her world tour, Martha Graham asked her to join her company. "I nearly dropped my teeth," said Jean. "I told her about my planned one-year journey, and she just said, 'Come back to me.'"

Jean's trip around the world gave her and Joseph an opportunity to reveal themselves to each other in a way that, by our accelerated contemporary standards, is sadly lost, that of the written correspondence. One of the great privileges of reading *A Fire in the Mind* is to eavesdrop on the dialogue found in the love letters between Jean and Joseph. Many of the passages that speak of his adoration of and longing for Jean are breathtaking. He calls her "the guide to my restless soul . . . identical with myself in destiny; your eyes the well in which I seek myself—and discover a forgotten dream." Jean insists that she was so intent on "keeping up with Joe's intellectual brilliance," that she didn't realize they had been love letters until she reread them for the Larsens' biography. "They were getting warmer and warmer and I didn't even realize it at the time I was receiving them."

One year later, on the afternoon of the Erdmans' return to New York from London via the Queen Mary, Joseph took Jean on a subway ride all the way to Coney Island. "We were glad to see one another," Jean recounted. "Of course, I wasn't aware of anything except that I was in Joe's company." Joseph then took her to dinner at the Hawaiian Room of the Lexington Hotel. "In the middle of dinner, Joe said, 'So when are we gonna get married?' He thought I would have known very well that was his intention from the letters he had written, but I didn't."

They had planned to marry the following year in Hawaii, where Jean was from and her family still lived. "In those days you didn't shack up with people you weren't married to," Jean explained. "So my dear father, who was a Protestant minister, a very openminded and lovely human being said, 'Jeannie, I'm here (in New York) now.' You know what that meant! That he would marry us right away. Joe said, 'Fine.' The blessing of the father-in-law was very important to him."

The wedding took place on Thursday, 5 May, at five o'clock in the afternoon. "Joe's mythological interest was very strong, of course, and things had to be done mythologically; otherwise it was not going to work," Jean said, smiling in her memories. "Thursday is named after the Norwegian thunder god, Thor, and according to James Joyce in *Ulysses*, the thunderclap denoted the *end* of an eon, the great awakening of the novel's main character, Stephen Dedalus. Also in the Hindu and Buddhist traditions, the thunderclap comes with the flash of *enlightenment*. Joseph knew it was the *end* of the Joseph Campbell he had always known. You see how *completely* he went into this belief in mythology?" Jean asked me, clearly still in awe of her husband's single-mindedness. "He knew he was going to be a different person. He had been so proud of his total independence. But he knew that now there would be *two* people together. So on the fifth hour of the fifth day of the week of the fifth month of the year we got married."

The newlyweds had a brief three-day honeymoon at Joseph's cottage in Woodstock, and, on Monday when Joseph returned to Sarah Lawrence, he found the flag at half-mast to denote the symbolic death of the faculty's most eligible and sought after bachelor.

Jean and Joseph made the decision not to have physical children early in their marriage. "I suppose he would have been *tolerant* of the idea of raising a family," said Jean, "but that wouldn't have been his first choice, so it was lucky for him that I was interested in a career rather than raising a family."

"The fact that there were always just the two of you must have made the bond between you all the more deep," I said.

"Oh, yes. Yes. Yes!" she replied expansively. "But he was an unusual person, because most people want to have a family; it's perfectly understandable, but Joe understood that the realm of the arts was his *métier*. Philosophy and art were absolutely his world; and the fact that I was in that world, too, on my own, made it very easy for us. He was *so* supportive of *everything* I wanted to do with my own art. He was *so wonderful!*" Jean stressed.

Just as art and creativity were the nourishment of their marriage, the love between Jean and Joseph Campbell was steeped in myth. Ever alternating between the roles of tutor and pupil for each other, theirs was a lifelong dialogue between artist and scholar and a perpetual refining of their aesthetic together.

"He didn't know anything about dance, but his aesthetic sense was so keen that it didn't take him any time at all to be able to make *very* helpful comments on my choreographic work. He used to come to the studio and I would show him *everything* I was doing, and he would give me his comments; and Joe read every single word he wrote to me when he started writing. What he wanted was to have his writing understandable by ear, not just by eye, because he had such a sense of music and rhythm in his language. I think that's one of the reasons his books are easy to read even though they are filled with difficult ideas. So we had a very close working relationship without either one of us being in the other's field.

"We were both so in love with our work that we didn't do much else. Joe was the kind of person who loved to be in the company of other people; he was very gregarious. So he had to discipline himself. He divided his day into four periods of four hours each with eight hours for sleep. Three sets of four would be for work with three of those hours for meals. The fourth period of four hours would be for socializing or going to the theater, whatever we wanted to do.

"Since I was with Martha Graham, I had rehearsals and classes. The difference between Joe and Martha was enormous—she never kept to her schedule. Joe always kept to his schedule, but he was so tolerant of my crazy time and would wait for me for dinner if he had to. He'd just go into the next four-hour period. How he managed that, I don't know. It sounds regimented but actually it made life so easy for two people who were doing totally different things to find a way to be together. It was miraculous how it worked. It worked because of the discipline that we *joyfully* took on.

"When I finished my touring days, Joe retired from teaching and started lecturing all over the world—that's when the world found out about him. I didn't travel with him until after we moved to Hawaii, and I realized how *much* it meant to him just by the way he introduced me to people, that he would have loved to have had me with him all the time, but it was too late. He'd never asked me to do it. He waited for me to be ready. That man was *incredible*. Not only was he the most wonderful man in the world, but he *was* incredible. So generous and understanding, with a wonderful sense of humor, and so willing to adjust to my requirements. I had to adjust to his, too, but I didn't have nearly as much to do as he did.

"Before we came out to Hawaii in 1982 and were still living in New York, Joe came out of his study one day and sat down in a chair. For the first time that I'd ever heard, this terrific sigh came out of him. 'Joe, what's the matter?' I asked. 'I don't think I can stand it any longer,' he replied. 'What?' 'New York.' 'Why didn't you tell me?' He said, 'I was waiting for you to get ready to go.' God, I never would have gotten ready to go because I was twelve years younger. I just never realized that he wasn't happy in New York."

Joseph and Jean had only five short years in Hawaii before Joseph died from cancer of the esophagus, and much of that time he had been traveling and lecturing. "He was so healthy all his life," Jean said, clearly still feeling her loss so deeply, even after eight years. I kept thinking he was going to get rid of the cancer because he had radiation treatments— I think that's what killed him—awful stuff. We had tried everything else first, all kinds of naturopathic remedies. But when they took X rays, we saw that it was an enormous cancer of the esophagus. He couldn't swallow and had to be fed intravenously. He was in the hospital and I'd spend whole days and evenings there with him. He was so wonderful. I just went home to sleep, but I'd come back for every minute with him. He was marvelous.

"Finally, I insisted that he come home. We were working with a naturopathic doctor and I was sure whatever he did would work, so the doctors let me bring him home. We got home and he sat down on a couch in our main room. The nurses were arranging everything—medicines, etc.—He was home! . . . In just a few minutes he quietly stopped breathing.

"I was a basket case at first, but Nancy Allison, who was arranging for the videos about my work in dance, needed me in New York. That's what pulled me out of it. There were so many friends who helped me during that terrible time; they saved me."

Consistent with the way he had lived his life—threading myth and meaning into his daily existence—in death Joseph Campbell was true to what he called "an instinctive vocabulary of experiencing." On the eve of Samhain, the Celtic New Year, Joseph Campbell passed into the world of the invisible. Samhain, or Halloween, is the midpoint between the autumn equinox and winter solstice, when, it is said, the veil is thinnest between the worlds of the living and the dead. In the hidden realms of magic and mystery, Joseph Campbell had lived. It was through his work that the world has come to better understand and appreciate the workings of myth in both its diurnal and nocturnal lives. It was his love for Jean and hers for him that supplied the electricity for their vitality, but it was their shared "love of many things together" that sustained their fifty-year union.

In one sentence (in those many letters written by Joseph to Jean during that year that turned out to be their year of courtship) that especially glistens in a manuscript illuminated with love, Joseph charmingly teases and poetically reveals his captivation with his young friend and soul mate: "The aggravating thing about you, Jean, is that you are simply the darling of my entire nervous system."

Chapter 29

Woven Destinies

Page and Eloise Smith

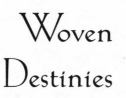

My friends Page and Eloise Smith died recently in August 1995. Theirs is a story of incredible devotion and warrants being told here. They met in 1942, when Page bought a painting he saw exhibited in a store window in North Carolina. He asked to meet the artist and, according to Page, the moment he laid eyes on Eloise, he knew he wanted to marry her. She accepted on their second date. Fifty-three years later they died within thirty-six hours of each other.

After their marriage, Page had gone on to graduate from Harvard, teach at the University of California at Los Angeles, and in 1972 teach at the newest UC campus in Santa Cruz, where they spent the last twenty-three years. Page was a nationally respected historian, who wrote more than twenty books. During these intensely full years, they raised four children and Eloise helped found the California Arts Council under the governorship of Jerry Brown.

Four months before their death, the last time I saw Page and Eloise, she shared with me her recent diagnosis of cancer of the kidneys. A month later Page was diagnosed with leukemia. Only a few weeks before their death, the couple left their art-filled home in the Santa Cruz mountains to stay with their daughter, who lived locally. It was said that Page, who was in great pain, had asked the doctors to keep him "alive until Eloise dies." His final desire was granted. On a Saturday at three o'clock in the afternoon, Eloise passed away quietly. Page then refused any further medication and within less than twenty-four hours had entered into a coma. Less than twelve hours after that he, too, was dead and on his way to see his Eloise again. It was their joint request that they be cremated together and their ashes be buried on their property. He had an extraordinary primal sense of pro-tectiveness—almost a stewardship—of the woman he loved. They were greatly beloved in our community, and, for as long as I live, I shall remember them.

Chapter 30

Marriage as a Spiritual Path

Deena Metzger and Michael Ortiz Hill

It's important to come together with someone because you share values and enjoy each other's minds and because you want to be in the world in the same way together— you want to do the work of *living*, together. That's what makes a marriage.

Deena Metzger

If you don't have a collaborator, you're not going to go anywhere in an intimate relationship. I mean someone who has a passion to collaborate, not someone whose arm you're twisting, but someone who cares as much as you do.

Michael Ortiz Hill

I t was the title that first engaged his imagination, *The Woman Who Slept With Men to Take the War Out of Them*, but Michael Ortiz Hill wouldn't meet the author, Deena Metzger, for more than two years. When he actually read her book, he explained, "I realized that she spoke the language that I was born into, the language I'd been speaking since before I was born. By virtue of that, in a very deep way, I entered into an intimacy with Deena through the language we share. That's been a core and grounding of our relationship."

In "Ruminations," a poem/prayer written in the alternating voices of Deena and Michael, Michael writes of a prescient dream:

> The night before we met
> I dreamt you were a giantess
> with two singing daughters
> Next morning, I found
> you would fit well under my arm
> [the proverbial dove]
> that your voice was from Brooklyn
> and very very soft.

Once or twice a year, they enact a ritual by retelling "the myth of origin" of their relationship. Each time the cosmology is different. These are two poetic minds at work and play, inventing and deciphering a married life.

Michael insists that for him there was no question that he and Deena would be together, would be lovers, even before they met. The beginning of their relationship has an air of mystery about it. He says that he was "passionately identified with the practice of trying to understand sexual/erotic energy. I don't mean to limit it to sexual—that gets so reductionistic in our culture—but where the spiritual and erotic and intimate come together. In Deena I saw a woman with whom I could wrestle—someone to contend with —whom I could learn something from and teach something to."

Their initial meeting and ensuing courtship came less naturally to Deena, who had to move through all her "preconceptions, prejudices, and fears, in order to see who was really there. I saw him as younger, a little awkward, very brilliant, but even that wasn't as interesting to me as the quality of his ethics or that his spiritual practice seemed authentic. Michael did not put on a persona, which he is very capable of doing! That was fortunate because I was so used to the kind of man who comes in and overwhelms you with how extraordinary and interesting he is. I felt that he was extraordinary and interesting, but in a quiet way." This was her test for their first year together: to be rigorous about seeing through appearances, to go for what was real and important.

Due to the fact that they are rooted in different places (Michael co-parents his daughter in another city—"Raising a kid is something you don't screw around with, you just do it as well as you can"—from where Deena, who has two grown sons, teaches writing and has a counseling practice), the couple spends about ten days a month living together, as well as two or three months spaced throughout the year. It's an unorthodox living arrangement, which many of their friends, "who are somewhat claustrophobic or smothered by their marriage," envy. Still they both believe that their marriage would thrive if they lived together all the time. In fact, they would prefer it.

Although Michael understands that "some relationships are so consumed by the domestic that they turn flat and mundane," and he agrees that their arrangement undoubtedly does bring advantages in terms of keeping things fresh, he misses the simple pleasures inherent in domesticity: "just cooking a meal together, not to mention taking for granted going to bed and sleeping next to each other night after night. There's some profound mammalian bonding in just sleeping next to the warm body of someone you love."

One of the dimensions that makes their marriage so expansive and that also prevents them from feeling smothered or overwhelmed by each other is that of shared and separate passions. According to Deena what they share is "a passion about passions. Sometimes our passions overlap, which is happening increasingly, but they always interest the other person, so there's a lot of cross-fertilization. From some very different areas, we are tiptoeing toward a common passion." For example, Deena works with people on a psychological level, while, as a nurse, Michael works primarily with physical healing, but their fields complement each other. And, of course, they share a common poetic and mythic language, to the extent that they edit each other's writing. They are delighted to admit that they each married the best editor they know. They share an interest in indigenous Navajo culture, which influenced the purchase of land near a Navajo reservation in Arizona. Michael studied the tribal language for over a year. Their connectedness to the land and a deep concern for the preservation of its ecology seem to blend naturally with their paradigm of myth.

For every couple during the first two or three years of a relationship there is an enormous amount of paring down of all the obstacles that stand between the lover and the beloved. Michael believes that for people in general, and for Deena and him in particular, the ability to *receive* love is more of an issue than to give it. "One puts up impediments to taking in the love of another person, and letting go of those impediments can be pretty terrifying." Eleven years ago, when they first met, they consciously and formally worked on the issues between them. Deena described the practice of *trespasso*, which Michael introduced to their relationship: "It is a kind of mnemonic for the fact that we needed to pay attention. It is a practice in which we meditate by looking into each other's eyes, go off and meditate by ourselves for a period, and then return until we have stripped away the impediments of self that keep us from communication. Now after many years our communication is almost instantaneous."

When asked if they "work" at their relationship, Michael replied, "The idea of *working* on a relationship is an odd metaphor—not that it's an inappropriate metaphor exactly—the metaphor I prefer is dharma. There's a dharma to intimacy just as there's a dharma or a 'work' to one's spiritual practice: the discipline of paying attention, staying awake, the dropping of one's ego, impediments, distrust—all those things."

Michael, from "Ruminations":

> *I never met someone*
> *I more enjoy giving gifts to.*
> *I've always wanted to love you well.*
> *This is the dharma I cannot betray.*

But it is necessary to know that you have a "collaborator" in your relationship. Michael said, "If you don't have a collaborator, you're not going to go anywhere in an intimate relationship. I mean someone who has a *passion* to collaborate, not someone whose arm you're twisting ('This is a priority in my life; it should be one in yours.'), but someone who cares as much as you do."

Deena added, "Sometimes we feel humiliated if we care more than our partner. It's not humiliating to care. It's essential."

After years of diligence, Michael says that if there is work on their relationship now, "it's very gentle. It's like tending a garden—you just go out and pull a few weeds—there's a tender quality to it."

Love for Deena has a very physical characteristic to it: "When I thought about love before I met Michael, I equated it with the word 'cherish.' It had a particular meaning to me because it had a physical quality to it. If you cherish something you want to touch it, protect it, because it is so precious. I wanted to cherish someone, and I wanted to be with someone who cherished me as well."

She also doesn't distinguish between love and beauty: "When you recognize beauty, you recognize the *nature* of somebody. They are completely naked in their presence. One of the things that I love about Michael is that there are so many parts to him, so many levels. And I get to know them all. He is a full human being who is not fixed, he's recreated in each moment."

For Michael, loving another is to be equally committed to their delight—at least to the extent that you can be committed to your own. It also has to do with the ability to see. "People don't want or thrive under a generic love. It's the specificity of who they are that's so important. There's a honing of one's *capacity* and commitment to see another person. It's a matter of beauty. It's odd, but it comes down to aesthetics; in this culture we reduce issues of beauty and aesthetics to very narrow margins, but in Navajo philosophy, the word for 'god' is 'beauty.' The 'beauty way' is fundamental. In an intimate relationship it is a matter of being able to see the specificity of who another person is and to let them know that you see it. Of course, there are impediments that one puts up to seeing and also to being seen."

An unexpected benefit to their marriage for Deena was loving Michael publicly and marrying him. As she put it, "It was blowing my cover. I knew that there were conventional places where I hid. As a consequence, being with Michael these eleven years means being more completely with myself. I stopped compartmentalizing and 'came out' with who I am in many areas. My life has become much easier; there's more flow between my private person and my public person."

This kind of generosity of loving can't help but carry over into other areas of a person's life, and Deena recognizes that, since she has been with Michael, she doesn't love her friends any differently. "Our marriage has not created an exclusivity at all. My ability to love others has increased, and I work, in the same way, at being present with them, at seeing and supporting them. That's very important to me. That's why I wanted to go on the path with Michael; I wanted marriage to be a ground from which I lived with others *and with myself* in a way that was more loving and caring and responsive."

"You can get into a shared narcissism with your partner, which really does encapsulate the relationship from the rest of the world," continued Michael. "I think there's a way to dissolve that dyadic narcissism in relationships so that it spills over, 'the cup overfloweth.'"

The inevitable presence of the "shadow" in a relationship was articulately commented on when Michael gave the best definition of that term that I'd ever heard: "The shadow is that aspect of one's humanness that one denies because one has an ideal of who one is supposed to be. When you marry someone, you *are* marrying their shadow. You're marrying their whole history and the turmoil of the nucleus in them that comes out of their childhood—you descend into all of that, and it's sometimes unbearable. Especially since virtually every relationship starts out on a romantic note.

"It begins in the realm of the gods and descends into the human realm. It's a hell of a process. The hardest thing is to live within human dimensions. How does one reconcile oneself with the fact that one is essentially not only imperfect but imperfectable—and then be generous about that fact? One cannot exclude the shadow from a relationship and expect deep intimacy. The shadow transforms. It is difficult but essential. On some level, you just have to be grateful for that kind of transformation, regardless of what was the catalyst: confusion, violation, or betrayal."

At that point in our conversation, Michael shared a Tibetan folk tale or myth about how the Buddha, sitting under the bodhi tree by himself, had reached a certain level of enlightenment, a place of emptiness and tranquility. "But there was something missing and so he took a consort, which in Tibetan Buddhist philosophy represents the dynamic aspect of the psyche, because if an individual is in the place of stasis, they are excluding the turmoil or the aliveness of the world. The beloved brings that confusion into your life, and the enlightened mind has to engage actively with the confusion; otherwise it becomes stupid in its odd way. It becomes self-complacent."

Deena, from "Ruminations":

When you touch me,
I cannot tell

> *if you are taking something*
> *or making an offering.*

Early in their relationship the couple made a trip to Santa Fe, New Mexico, where Michael had been raised as a child, a place about which he carries ambivalent feelings. "My confusion is about being a white boy who's half Mexican. Deena was penetrating into that realm from which, at some level, I had distanced myself. I felt she was infiltrating into my family, into my ancestry, into a whole world with which I wasn't sure I wanted to deal. It felt profoundly invasive." Michael had been "seen" by Deena in a way that was unbearable to him. However, it was only days later, after dropping his own barriers, that he proposed marriage to her, saying, "I felt that I had no defenses against that kind of loving. Intimacy involves the clarification of your entire life; it's not a separate little category—it can't be. You can't live a muddied existence outside of a marriage or intimate relationship without it affecting the relationship.

"In relationship you enter into the ecology of someone else's life or psyche, and just the entering itself is a profound act, but showing that you will respect the territory, and somehow conveying to the other person that you are trustworthy within that place, is also very profound. There's no reason (given what all of us have gone through in terms of intimate relationships, God knows) to presume that someone will act respectfully within the secret places."

He feels that one of the critical outcomes of marriage is that each person enters into a "kinship network of family and friends." People who choose to live together without getting married never quite enter into that network in the same way. "That's part of the sacramental container in which the whole process of intimacy transpires. There's the process of being included in the network of friends. This is especially important since community has broken down more and more as we approach the next century."

For Deena, intimacy is the place where they know each other together better than they know themselves separately. It is the place where all is revealed. "I know myself better with Michael than I know myself alone," she said.

"Intimacy isn't necessarily about Michael and I *knowing* everything about each other—I don't know if we do, but we sure know a great deal—it's about having developed a language and a way of being with each other so that we really do know what the other's experiences feel like. That is intimacy. To a great extent, how we treat each other in the daily life is a sign of who we are spiritually. Are you loving? Are you caring? Do you have compassion? Are you sensitive to someone else? Are you respectful of their divinity, of their person? It's either yes or no. It's right there in every moment."

Synthesizing the spiritual with the imaginative and the erotic is this couple's method of sustaining sexual aliveness between them—it permeates their life together. According to Michael, "For Deena and me the erotic has always been the core. There's a nucleus to it, and it radiates outward from there. It tends to permeate everything—just playing with our imaginations until two or three in the morning is very erotic. There's that meeting, the celebration of the other person, that is so replenishing. I was reading "Dear Abby" last month. They had a two-day series on women faking their orgasms. And Abby received letters from droves of women who stated that they usually faked orgasms as a gift to their husband because it affirmed his ego. There were women who for twenty, thirty, *fifty* years have been faking orgasms! I don't get it. From my point of view, that kind of dishonesty would contaminate the very core of the relationship. This is a way of looking at marriage that is utterly beyond me."

Deena added, "What I learned from Michael is that sexuality is simply loving. There are times when I put my hand on his face because I love him and I just want to *touch* him. It's not like a series of learned gestures that one goes through or moves toward, it's like trying to *get* to the beloved. That always feels fresh—to say the least!"

In both of their religious traditions, Catholicism and Judaism, sexuality in marriage is sacramentalized. "There's a private little garden that is maintained in the center of the relationship," Michael said, softly, reaching for Deena's hand. Undoubtedly it is the existence of this "little garden" that has given Deena the courage to extend herself so unconditionally to a man twenty years her junior.

Deena, from "Ruminations":

Because I belong to you,
I know you can never leave me,
if there isn't this life,
there's the next one

"I have actually come to believe as fact that twenty years from now, when I'm seventy-five, or in thirty years, when I'm eighty-five, Michael will still find me attractive and magnetic. He is someone I can talk with about my fears of aging and my body's changes without feeling like I'm jeopardizing the marriage or romance. Of course, our marriage was forged not only by my being twenty years older, but by the fact that I have one breast."

Michael, from "Ruminations":

The first summer I loved you,
I could not stop touching
the absence of your breast.
This pale body loved your dark skin,
this young boy liked to trace his fingers
along the wrinkles near your eyes.

Deena acknowledged that sometimes their language sounds so exalted, "but there is a real base of particulars with which we've been dealing. This last birthday I was fifty-five. It felt like a major transition. Part of that transition was coming to accept the likelihood that when I'm seventy or so I will not look like my friend Anaïs Nin, who was absolutely gorgeous at that age. I'm more likely to look like a little old Navajo lady. Michael once sent me a photograph of an old Guatemalan woman and wrote, 'You're going to look like this some day.' He saw the beauty of the old woman's life in her face. It took me until—if I'm going to be honest—this September to really see the beauty of my aging and to accept it. Now I complain to Michael about my hot flashes!"

For Michael there is no question that Deena grows continually more beautiful. "She comes into her own more. It's what we were saying earlier about the relationship between seeing and beauty and intimacy. When you are committed to seeing someone else and appreciating their beauty, that itself has its own erotic pull. The person becomes increasingly more radiant in your eyes." When Michael spoke of his appreciation for Deena's beauty, I remembered something that the mystery writer Agatha Christie had once written: "An archaeologist makes the best husband, for the older a woman gets the more fascinating she becomes to him."

Through our conversation I more fully understood that being committed to *seeing* another as he or she is, rather than through a projected image, is one of the factors that keeps a marriage from turning stale. Simply stated, the ability to actually appreciate the aliveness and uniqueness of another individual renders that person infinitely fascinating (assuming, of course, there is a willingness in the other partner to be authentic and with no need to project a certain image to the world).

As we rounded out our day together with a photo session, I noticed a playful, girlish quality in Deena that danced in and out through her body language. I saw that her youthful energy would emerge at twelve, twenty-three, fifty-five, or seventy-five, regardless of something as inevitable as aging, for that energy is archetypal and thus timeless. I asked Michael how he responds to that young girl in Deena, "I feel her presence and appreciate it very much. It's part of Deena's freshness. It's a quality that doesn't diminish. Unless one outright crushes it or circumstances go about crushing it, I think it's eternal. It's part of who people are."

At last when I asked Deena for any advice she might have for other couples, she said, "I would say that love really is possible, here, on planet earth, even in these times. But it is a practice. It's important to come together with someone because you share values and enjoy each other's minds and because you want to be in the world in the same way together—you want to do the work of *living*, together. That's what makes a marriage. Find a partner who helps you live your life more deeply, with more meaning, someone who supports you in taking more of the risks of being an authentic person."

Deena, from "Ruminations":

> I don't know
> how to reach you
> except through these bodies
> we must take off
> again and again.
> Rumi says,
> "I want to kiss you,
> the price of kissing is your life."

———————————

Since this interview was conducted, Deena has had two grandchildren, and Nicole, Michael's daughter, has started college. "These events have added new dimensions to our lives and enriched us," Deena recently wrote in a letter to me. "When Michael relocated from Santa Cruz to live with me in Los Angeles, he drove through the devastating Thousand Oaks fire. Some days later, he was evacuated from our Topanga Canyon house. I was on a writing retreat in Arizona during this time. The house was not damaged, but it was a dramatic and tense beginning. A few months later, we suffered the trauma of the Northridge earthquake together. Helping each other through that ordeal further transformed our marriage.

"After ten years together, we can say this: now that we are living together, we know we are married and marriage has no contingencies. It is absolute—this is its power and its possibility. This is its beauty."

Chapter 31

Discovering the Secrets of Enduring Love

Marriage is the practice of intimacy.

STEPHEN MITCHELL

The sign of a good marriage is that everything is debatable and challenged; nothing is turned into law or policy. The rules, if any, are known only to the two players, who seek no public trophies.

CAROLYN HEILBRUN,
Writing a Woman's Life

Love may be the answer, but marriage remains the big question: how to do it successfully. Like endorphins, love is contagious. To be in the company of a loving couple is a pleasure itself and a source of inspiration and hope for the observer, especially an unmarried observer. Meeting scores of couples during the writing of this book has given me a *direction* to pursue rather than a definite *plan* of action to follow. I have learned that love is not a state of mind or a standard of conduct, but an experience, a pursuit. In the *Pursuit of Love*, philosopher Irving Singer writes, "Love, as we experience it, is both thought and emotion, ideology and gut reaction, intellect and quasi instinct." Marriage can be a Promethean adventure or Sisyphean struggle. Usually it is a fluctuation of both that demands our unwavering attention, our ardent commitment, and our unfailing sense of humor.

The happier couples seem to view their relationship as a work in progress, a case of ongoing negotiations and compromises. They honor what is most alive between them: the process of their diurnal/nocturnal experience together. Rather than contempt, their familiarity breeds contentment; and yet they continue to be surprised by their partner, by the ever fascinating discoveries of the nuances, idiosyncrasies, eccentricities of that human being they know best but by whom they remain periodically baffled. They appreciate that their mate is an entire universe of likes and dislikes, of dreams and memories, of heartaches and passions, of vulnerabilities and inflations, of mysteries.

We are a "how-to" society that looks for easy answers to be spelled out for us. It was Zelda Fitzgerald who said that we are the only country in the world in which people think they can learn to play the piano in a correspondence course through the mail. We think we can read a book (or *write* one!) about marriage and we will know how to be happily married. Because every marriage is so unique and individual, there are no set rules or policies, but there are some guidelines, some major components that seem to be shared by most, if not all, the marriage partners I met and interviewed.

As Carolyn Heilbrun told me, because the two people are always changing, a marriage has to be continually remade, re-created.

This "re-creation" is best done with laughter. The couples cultivate a sense of humor knowing that an infusion of levity during the rough times is the adhesive of marriage.

They make a commitment to maintaining the integrity of the individual while surrendering to the requirements of the partnership. The marriage is seen as a teacher for both participants.

Both individuals are convinced that there is a purpose for their union—a kind of divine choreography, if you will—and that together they provide a stronger, more loving base from which to interact with the world than they would alone. The relationship takes on the aura of the sacred. My friends Maurine and Peter Doerken told me that the awareness of a divine purpose has "helped their couplehood, their marriage. I remember when we met," said Maurine, "that feeling of being divinely guided to one another."

When a relationship is open to a new honesty and freshness of expression, the couple finds unique and original solutions to common and not so common dilemmas.

Marriage is pervasive in a couple's life; it touches every aspect, personal, social, and professional.

In a true partnership, each takes pleasure in the company of the other—"they get a kick" out of each other. They luxuriate in the presence of each other. Joseph Campbell said most poetically when he told Jean Erdman, the woman he would eventually marry and remain married to for fifty years, that she was the "darling of [his] entire nervous system."

Good communication is paramount. Among the most bonding of activities shared in the marital relationship is that of conversation. The continuous sharing of ideas and feelings keeps a flow of interest and energy streaming between the individuals. Dr. William Masters defines good communication in a relationship as "the privilege of exchanging vulnerabilities."

They know that a current of contentiousness erodes away at a loving relationship. Acceptance of the other's foibles and actual *delight* in his or her eccentricities is essential. *Shared* eccentricities is a plus.

Sex helps reseed a life together. There is a mutual commitment to joy and pleasure in the marriage, but with the knowledge that sexual desire ebbs and flows like the tide and an understanding acceptance of their partner's personal rhythm.

In most good marriages, the partners are each other's best friends. There is a feeling of safety, a sense of belonging with and even to each other. Each partner is "home" to the other in a way they have never before experienced.

The components of an individual that exist within the context of a marriage are distinctive. There is a kind of merging quality that can't be duplicated with anyone else. This awareness helps curb unnecessary jealousy, because it confirms to each partner the uniqueness he or she brings to their union.

A good partner knows how to let the other partner love and comfort him or her. And companionship, although it sounds so unsexy, is a major ingredient.

Fighting and disagreement are part of intimacy, too. They are ways partners learn about each other. There has to be the safety to confront issues. However, reacting defensively intensifies a problem and leads to separation, while being vulnerable and communicating feelings, needs, and wants leads to closeness and resolution.

My friend Smoke Blanchard used to tell me: "We meet someone and fall in love with them because of who they are. Then the first thing we do is try to change them."

Successful couples work hard at trying to accept the whole package of each other, because they realize that otherwise they risk losing all of it.

Although it seems unanimously agreed upon that a successful marriage is equal parts of luck and hard work, it takes time to build the trust and feel the acceptance that allows for the sharing of the most personal revelations. Time is a major element in the intimacy of marriage. With time, couples build up a history of their own, chapter by chapter.

Finally, as Octavio Paz writes in *The Labyrinth of Solitude*, "Love is a choice . . . perhaps a free choosing of our destiny, a sudden discovery of the most secret and fateful part of our being." Marriage, too, is not just a feeling, but a choice. We may not have power over our feelings, but we do have power over the choices we make. Marriage must be consciously chosen daily and perhaps even several times throughout the day in order to discover its secrets.

We know there is no absolute truth, only the truth each couple must find together. What remains most memorable to me from my conversations about marriage is what Deena Metzger called "doing the work of *living,* together"; and, in my reading about relationship, what Gertrude Stein described as practicing together "the art of enjoyable living in unpretentious ways."

Chapter 32

Through the Labyrinth

Everything to do with love is a mystery.

It is more than a day's work

to investigate this science.

MARIANNE MOORE

The meeting of

two personalities

is like the contact

of two chemical

substances; if

there is any

reaction, both are

transformed.

C. G. JUNG

Journal Entry: 15 August 1995

A dream of marriage:

I am sitting in a car across from a store that is robbed and I go in to investigate the robbery. I realize that it has all been a hoax of the shopkeeper. When I'm about to leave, I meet a man to whom I am attracted. We both know instinctively and energetically that we are well suited for each other and fall in love. We have a brief whirlwind affair during which we grow to trust each other and recognize that we are soul mates and true companions. We get married. I notice that he is making frequent long-distance telephone calls, which turn out to be to his mother, who is gravely ill. I think to myself, "A loving son makes a good husband." Suddenly we are in the middle of a war in Eastern Europe. At some point we are separated. I am driving a bus to help the war effort and I don't know if I will ever see my husband again. From an omniscient perspective I can see that he is following the bus and trying to catch up with me, but just as he reaches it—without consciously knowing he is there—I pull away. It begins to rain. As if I'm watching a movie, an unconscious part of me can see that he is continuing to follow the bus. The streets begin to flood. He nearly drowns before I finally see him waving his arms in the rearview mirror and let him board the bus. We have an emotional re-union. I then wake up (in the dream) and realize that it was only a dream and I begin to interpret it. I think the message is that I will indeed meet someone, but I will have difficulty in balancing my creative work with my new husband. Or perhaps that it will be hard for me to relinquish control of my life and emotions.

Later in the dream, while driving, I meet a very young man who is confused and needs help. We are pass-ing through the town where my therapist, Hal Stone, lives. Although it is late at night, I call and ask if we can come for a visit and a session. "Of course," says Hal. "How about tonight?" [Only in my dreams!] I'm so happy to see Hal and Sidra, who are so welcoming to us. The boy begins to tell of his concern. (He says that he feels too close to his mother.) Suddenly I remember my dream and begin to tell Hal about it and ask for his in-sights. I think how convenient it is to have had the dream only the night before I see him. He says the dream demonstrates that a man will have to prove his love for me before I will stop the bus (my work, control?) and allow him to enter my life. I mention that the man, my husband, resembled Max von Sydow, the Swedish actor (someone I associate with depth, stability, creativity, and an interesting life. I remember that he played several roles in Ingmar Bergman films that dealt with marriage.) Hal mentions the dream of the three women with penises that I had when I first began writing The Heart of Marriage *four and a half years ago. "There has been a great transformation, an opening of your heart," he says. We discuss the relevance of this dream while I'm completing the book—especially since the conclusion is different from what I had anticipated at the book's inception (which is that I would be married in actual life). There is a resolution on the psychic level, but not yet on the physical plane. "It will come," says Hal. "The dream would be a good ending for your book." We say our good-byes and I leave.*

I wake up.

My friend Anna recently gave me some wonderful advice. She said, "Life is so myste-rious. It will bring you exactly what you need, when you need it." In other words, there is something irresistible, an irresistible force field. The more full and fulfilled you are, the more of a magnet you are to whatever it is you are supposed to have come into your life, what you truly have room for.

"It's important to live your life as if you are totally lovable and capable of loving greatly," she continued. "I mean, just live your life that way. Live your life as if you are loved, not like you're looking for love, but as if it's already happened. Make your decisions from that place. It takes the edge off, the anxiety off."

9 September 1995

"Love is a fever that comes and goes quite independently of the will," writes Stendahl. Or to put it in the words of Martha and the Vandellas, "Love is like a heat wave burnin' in my heart." At a writers' conference in San Francisco this weekend I met a man. Could my dream of marriage have been an uncanny premonition? I have reentered that universal vulnerability called love. Such a yearning comes with it. A desire for redemption through love—a passage into a more promising future. One woman's inner world meeting the inner world of a man. That moment when the circle is completed for eternity. Do two lovers recognize each other instantly because, as Rumi wrote, "they are in each other all along"? A synesthetic whirlwind fills my senses—the smell of him is indistinguishable from the texture of his skin, the tone of his flesh; I can taste the comforting timbre of his voice and arousing words; his salty, sweating pores speak to me of desire. I am in the throes of infatuation, an obsession that is a primitive animal attraction to another human being. And it feels divine. No, he is not Prince Charming (this is not a rescue fantasy), just a man. Will that be enough?

9 October 1995

Writing *The Heart of Marriage* has been a long, slow resurrection. Concerns about my ability to overcome the comfortable selfishness of single life and attachments to my eccentricities and idiosyncrasies have vanished. I work to relinquish my lifelong need to be right, to be in control. Of course, love doesn't necessarily mean marriage. At least not this love, but I now know that I stand ready to enter the country of marriage. That in itself is a gift and serves me well. Growth has become my context, more than any other, for marriage. I understand that marriage is a function of personal development—a lifelong process and a form of spiritual worship, or as Joni Mitchell has said, "Marriage is the new religion."

It becomes easier than I feared it would be to cast off the old, ineffectual, melodramatic, and hurtful ways of relating to a man. The deep grief buried in my fear of relationship is dissolving. Something new and unknown is taking its place. I am learning to choose peace over confusion and hysteria, harmony over the churning of an emotional tempest. There is no lag time. I have tremendous latitude and spontaneity, not only to *know* what I am feeling and thinking, but to be able to *express* it close to the moment of its occurrence. My emotions are a kaleidoscope.

"Life is brief and very fragile. Do that which makes you happy," writes Thich Nhat Hanh in *Being Peace*. I feel delivered from the stranglehold of the complex (even if temporarily or illusorily). Like a madwoman bound in a straitjacket, I have writhed and wrestled free to a new perception of who I am and what I want, to a new way of being human. The supreme desire to love and be loved inexplicably heals the fears of rejection. Love is a balm, medicinal in its effect. To be in love, to *love*, is to be in a state of grace. Trust brightly triumphs over the fear of abandonment. The palpable nature of emotional healing has been fostered by the process of making art, by writing this book. We always have a choice. Each time we implement that choice, we develop a little more inner authority, which makes it easier to exercise our choice next time. There is always free will—even in the context of predestination, as I was taught in Catholic school. And hard work and awareness are what allow us that choice. I am feeling great confidence in my intuition and instincts, in my intention, and in my process. "Love changes a woman completely," writes Octavio Paz in *The Labyrinth of Solitude.* "If she dares to love, if she dares to be herself, she has to destroy the image in which the world has imprisoned her."

I know what my parameters are, what I'm willing to concede and what I'm unwilling to compromise. I have learned to feel attractive again and that a man can find me attractive because ultimately he will be attracted to *me*, to all of me—my vitality and humor, my intelligence and substance, my authenticity. Aphrodite is reactivated. The juices are flowing once again. And I'm happy.

Those visceral emotions that are stirred up by and tied to sexual feelings and fear of abandonment can still be experienced and expressed, but I no longer feel tyrannized by them. In many ways I have been held hostage by those volatile eruptions, by a savagery of emotions. I can feel the intensity of my feelings without getting stuck in their sludge. There is some interior reconciliation. "Love is one of the clearest examples of that double instinct which causes us to dig deeper into our own selves and, at the same time, to emerge from ourselves and to realize ourselves in another," writes Octavio Paz.

It seems that our response to love gets more fervent as we grow older and become more ourselves. There's more at stake, we believe, as the sobering awareness of our mortality encroaches during midlife and the reality of death becomes a part of love. People's lives become so complex. We may find ourselves tethered to our past with responsibilities for and obligations to the emotional well-being and financial subsistence of loved ones. Graceful, anguish-free disengagement becomes an art all its own.

Though I have traveled known maps of the Country of Marriage through my own and many others' experiences, I still enter new, uncharted territory, a landscape with its own mysterious canyons and gullies, its magical meadows and ranges, its dark caverns and forests. Like an ancient cartographer I must continue to map out the path of my journey toward marriage as I am in the process of exploring it. I am once again willing to embrace the paradox of romantic love and personal neurotic needs. I feel hopeful that in the realm where real lives are lived there is a place somewhere between the fantasy of being married happily ever after and remaining single.

It is my theory that in relationships you pick up with the new one ahead (sometimes miles ahead) of where you left off with the last one. It saves so much time. And nothing ever gets wasted.

I entered the maddening, ruthless, nearly lethal maze of male/female relationships even before my adolescence. *The Heart of Marriage* has been my agent for the alchemical transformation of my soul that Linda Leonard introduced me to ten long years ago in her book *On the Way to the Wedding*. I embarked on a journey to find the pot of gold that lies under the rainbow of conscious relationship. The journey has been both literal and metaphysical. Just one month ago today, I met a man who seemed to hold up mirrors around the dark corners of this labyrinth. The meeting helped illuminate the passageway more clearly to me. The writing of this book has been an important guide through my labyrinth of tangled emotions. These past six years spent in the labyrinth of aloneness, the hours of loneliness, have been worth it, because I know that even if I remain single, I am whole. I'm free—for now. A *new* maze most assuredly has been entered, but at least I'm through the old one. Again, in the words of Linda Leonard, my "courage to be open to change [my] mind when faced with new phenomena and the persistence to transcribe and study for the sake of new consciousness" has been rewarded. My passions of the mind and heart have been steadfast.

Like Marianne Moore, I may have some amusing reservations about marriage. Still, when she was sixty years old and ordered the headstones for her own and her mother's graves, she requested that the stonecutter leave a space underneath her name for her possible future husband's—just in case she ever married. She never did, but hope continued to spring eternal.

So the question remains: Will I ever marry again? Perhaps only in my dreams.